What they are saying about this book:

"If you have decided that you are nothing but road kill on the information highway, take a look at *900 Know-How* by Robert Mastin. For those in the information-providing business, the 900 number could be an attractive source of revenue."

—The Wall Street Journal

".... a comprehensive guide to creating your own lucrative pit stop on the information highway."

—InformationWeek

".... a superb job of gathering and conveying the information....crammed full of information which is concise and accurate....I highly recommend it for anyone contemplating going into the 900-number business...."

—Ed Durham, Editor
Home Income Reporter

".... Solid advice to anyone wanting to start up the business....a good starting place for 'infopreneurs' who want to get in the game....presented in a factual, concise manner that can be easily understood and digested...."

—Mailer's Review

"It was only a matter of time until somebody wrote a frank, no-hype book on launching a 900 pay-per-call business. The author is experienced 900- number entrepreneur Robert Mastin and the title is '900 KNOW-HOW'...." —Joyce Lain Kennedy
syndicated careers columnist

".... a resource-filled paperback covering (service) bureau basics and much more."

*—Inc.*Magazine

".... 900 KNOW-HOW explores this explosive industry in-depth, including how to start and operate a 900 business, what pitfalls to avoid, the costs involved, and what kinds of 900 programs have been successful...."

—Business Opportunities Journal

"Medium-to-small businesses could profit from the acquisition of a 900 number, and this title is a good place to begin. It's a detailed examination of the 900 pay-per-call option which offers detailed advice on how to succeed with a 900 number — and what to avoid...."

—The Midwest Book Review

".... Really offers the readers non-biased information....This has to be one of the best, well written and informative books on the subject.... 900 KNOW-HOW is a must...."

—John Moreland
The Dream Merchant

"Everything one needs to know to start a 900-number phone service is surveyed ....Starting a 900-number service is relatively easy, but its success depends on the additional factors of marketing research, customer service, and costs which are also dealt with in this introductory guide."

—The Small Press Book Review

"Here's an exploration of one of America's growth industries. The author covers how to start and operate such a business, pitfalls, costs and marketing....a good primer on starting a business based on the 900 telephone numbers...."

—Orange County Register

"The book provides honest information about what it takes to be successful in this business, and clearly debunks some of the hype and blatant misinformation surrounding the 900 industry...."

—MAIL PROFITS Magazine

".... a good primer if you have ever dreamed of making your fortune with a 900 number.... This book will help focus your thoughts and give you the resources to study how to build a successful 900-number service...."

—Kathy Mathews
Stepping Stones

".... you'll get a nuts-and-bolts guide to starting and operating a 900 service....start-up and monthly operating costs....ways to effectively market a 900 service....details on types of services that are successful...."

—What's Working in DM and Fulfillment

"This is the bible of an industry that shot from $0 to nearly $1 billion in annual sales in only four years...."

—*SUCCESS* Magazine

"....explores the pay-per-call industry in depth....and what makes a successful 900 program...." —*FOLIO* Magazine

"... *900 KNOW-HOW* is a comprehensive guide that helps the start-up information provider..." —*The Newsletter on Newsletters*

".... the author shoots straight from the hip in his clearly understandable approach to the business, showing you what can and cannot be done, how and how not to do it... an extraordinary accomplishment... read it before you act..."

—*Entrepreneur's Digest*

"If you're interested in launching a 900 pay-per-call information or entertainment service, you will find this book helpful."

—*The DIRECT RESPONSE Specialist*

"This is a valuable book to have on your bookshelf."

—*Mail Order Entrepreneur*

"... provides in-depth coverage of the 900-number industry..."

—*Sales and Marketing Strategies & News*

"Well written and informative for new or experienced IPs (Information Providers). We even use it as part of our training for new salespersons."
—Robert Bentz, Director of Marketing
Advanced Telecom Services, Wayne, PA

"... A readable, informative introduction and guide to this new business idea..." —*COSMEP* Newsletter

"... this book will change your thinking and set you straight..."

—*Mail Order Messenger*

"... *900 KNOW-HOW* is one of the most factual books on that industry ever published..." —Dan Kennedy
The *No B.S. Marketing Letter*

Other Telecom Titles by Aegis Publishing Group:

Money-Making 900 Numbers:
How Entrepreneurs Use the Telephone to Sell Information
by Carol Morse Ginsburg and Robert Mastin
ISBN: 0-9632790-1-7
$19.95
Profiles of nearly 400 actual 900-number programs — the success stories as well as the failures. An idea book and a comprehensive overview of the industry.

Telecom Made Easy:
Money-Saving, Profit-Building Solutions for
Home Businesses, Telecommuters and Small Organizations
by June Langhoff
ISBN: 0-9632790-2-5
$19.95
Shows how to put all the latest telephone products and services to their best use — in plain English. Written for the exploding SOHO (small office/home office) market.

The Telecommuter's Advisor:
Working in the Fast Lane
by June Langhoff
ISBN: 0-9632790-5-X
$14.95
An easy-to-follow road map for telecommuters to navigate to work in cyberbia. Live at the seashore while working in the inner city, a one-minute telecommute away. A major work trend worth joining.

900 KNOW-HOW

How To Succeed With
Your Own 900 Number Business

Third Edition

Written by:
Robert Mastin

Aegis Publishing Group, Ltd.
796 Aquidneck Avenue
Newport, Rhode Island 02842
401-849-4200

Library of Congress Catalog Card Number: 95-83157

International Standard Book Number: 0-9632790-3-3

Printed in the United States of America.
First Edition, 1992
Second Edition, completely revised, 1994
Third Edition, completely revised, 1996
10 9 8 7 6 5 4 3 2 1

This publication is designed to provide accurate and authoritative information in regard to the subject matter covered. It is sold with the understanding that neither the author nor the publisher are engaged in rendering legal, accounting or other professional service. If legal advice or other expert assistance is required, the services of a competent professional should be sought.

Publisher's Cataloging In Publication Data
Mastin, Robert L.
900 KNOW-HOW: How To Succeed With Your Own 900 Number Business / by Robert Mastin. — third edition
Includes Index
1. Audiotex services industry.
HE8817.M3 1994   384.64   95-83157
ISBN 0-9632790-3-3

Acknowledgements

This book was a collaborative effort with the help of many people. Although it would be impossible to mention everyone who contributed materials, advice or assistance to this work, I would like to express special appreciation to all the participants in The 900 Roundtable, which, owing to their thoughtful contributions, is one of the most valuable sections in this book: Bob Bentz, Peter Brennan, Michael Cane, Gene Chamson, Bob Doyle, Carol Morse Ginsburg, Bruce Kennedy, Don Klug, Toni Moore, Phyllis Grant-Parker and Don Young. These industry leaders took the time to give invaluable advice to the readers of this book, despite some very busy schedules.

Thanks to all those information providers who took the time to describe their actual experience in this business, including Walt Zadanoff, George Marx, Dave Pilvelait, Mary Massengale, Greg Shemitz, Keith Mueller, Glen Chazak and Nancy Ava Miller. A very special thanks to Marc Robins for his huge contribution to the voice processing section in chapter 7.

Thanks to Betsy Walker for her capable editing help, and to John Robertson for an outstanding cover design. And none of this would have ever happened without the advice of my publishing consultants and gurus, Dan Poynter and John Kremer.

And finally, a special thanks to my lovely wife, Liz, whose patience and encouragement have sustained me, and to whom this book is dedicated.

Contents

Chapter 4 **Getting Started** **87**

Chapter 5 **Marketing** **115**

Contents

Foreword

When Bob Mastin asked if I'd be willing to write a foreword to this, his latest book, I jumped at the chance. When I read his previous edition, I found it to be the first writings on the 900 industry that wasn't simply a slanted sales pitch. Here was an unbiased look at 900 as well as a valuable guide to how to make money in the field.

Anyone who knows me or *Audiotex News,* the newsletter I publish and edit (now into its eighth year), is clearly aware of my belief in this industry as one with great substance and enormous possibilities. Although I'm acquainted with its dark side, the incredible potential as 900 matures allows me to recognize the positives. And now and again I catch glimpses of a pay-per-call application that pushes the envelope of technology — moving to deliver the next best innovation.

If you've been searching for a book that gives you a substantial view of 900 while showing you practical ways to make money in it, Bob Mastin's work within these covers is your best entry into the arena. The pay-per-call industry is an exciting, volatile business with twisted turns and sharp corners. Mastin has been able to illuminate the darkness — no small task!

Rapid technological changes and the individual creativity of each entrepreneurial spirit make the future profile of the industry difficult to predict. I do not doubt that at this very moment, someone reading my words has the concept for what will be a winning 900 number. Future uses for 900 exceed the imagination, possibly because we old-timers have our headsets filled with adult, weather, horoscopes, jokes and soaps. So it is you, the newly arrived reader, who will discover what the public will buy and how much they will pay for it.

Major corporations will continue to use 900 services wherever feasible. In this era of cost-cutting, 900 pay-per-call offers a simple way to conduct business with the added advantage of having the caller share the cost.

At a recent conference I attended, television executives reported that there was no way they could conduct an 800 campaign for a prize or game contest because they could not handle the calls. The 95 cents per 900 call made the difference — not so much in offsetting the costs, but in controlling the call volume.

Fax and phone give entrepreneurs the opportunity to provide a printed page of data delivered immediately for a small price, with both billing and collection taken care of through the 900 media.

There are opportunities to provide 900 programs through AT&T's 900-555 and 900-225 (dedicated business exchanges). With certain criteria to meet, businesses can unblock their phones for these services.

The promise of the information age is boundless. 900 pay-per-call is like Pandora's box — once opened, the contents can't be put back. Entrepreneurial interest will push businesses and individuals to offer new and creative programming that in turn will drive public use to higher and higher levels. Soon, when we ask for a show of hands for how many people have used 900, it will be the majority in the room.

It's ironic that some of the most creative uses of 900 have been by governments. So while on the one hand they have gone about almost dissolving the business (through over-regulation), with the other they have embraced it. This increased use of 900 by municipalities, Better Business Bureaus and companies like Microsoft will also lead to making 900 a household fixture.

If anyone needs further proof of 900's potential, they can look at how the TelCos put up with the industry's early problems — high chargebacks, low-value programs and scams. But still, the bad reputation of the early days is hard to shake. For some callers, years of positive reinforcement must occur before we can tempt them to pick up the phone.

But this will happen and 900 usage will become standard. I believe the entertainment category will still dominate the industry, in terms of call volume, repeat business and holding times, to a lesser extent than we now see it, but still a very major component.

The limitless potential of the 900 pay-per-call industry is humbling. Just think — now we can only deliver information, but what if we could accomplish product fulfillment? And what about screen phones? As they become widely used, how will they affect 900? What will be the impact on pay-per-call when almost every home will have a fax machine?

I don't know yet. What I do know is that only those of us who stay the course to learn and understand the action will be the winners!

Want to be in on the action? Then learn the basics and everything you need to know to create the thriving, lucrative 900 business of the future. This book contains the information you need to succeed.

Carol Morse Ginsburg
Editor/Publisher, *Audiotex News*
East Meadow, New York

Chapter 1
Introduction

When the first edition of this book was published in 1992, there was no question that *900 Know-How* was a good title. Nearly everyone knew what 900 numbers were, and at the time they were the dominant way to pay for information over the telephone. This is changing. Other methods for paying for telephone-based information have evolved, such as prepaid telecards, pre-subscription agreements and credit cards. The more generically correct term is now "pay-per-call." A 900 number is simply one pay-per-call method.

Nonetheless, most people know that 900 numbers are for paying for information, and *900 Know-How* has good alliteration. The term "pay-per-call" is a little awkward, and may not be readily understood by people who want to learn more about this business. Nothing worse than a vague book title.

It is not my intent, however, to ignore or to diminish the importance of the various alternative pay-per-call methods. Indeed, one of them may eventually eclipse 900 numbers as the preferred method of billing and paying for telephone information. This book does indeed encompass all types of pay-per-call services, and the title should not be interpreted as limiting the information to 900-number-delivered services only. Much of the information here will apply equally as well to any other pay-per-call service, particularly the information about the *business of selling information over the telephone*, which is the most important material in the book.

I simply haven't yet been able to come up with a better title. And unless 900 numbers cease to exist altogether, this is probably as good as any. Just remember that this book is really more about pay-per-call in general than 900 in particular.

Now that this book is up to its third edition, the obvious question is, how has the 900-number business changed over the years? Yes, it has changed, but not radically. The industry has matured and gained respectability. There are unambiguous laws and regulations in place which specify what can and cannot be done and which have driven away most of the unscrupulous players who plagued the industry in its infancy.

There are now many well-known companies and government entities using 900 lines to disseminate information — information they would not be able to offer if they couldn't recover at least some of their costs.

The Information Superhighway

Most people think of the information superhighway as some distant vision of the future, with sophisticated high-tech computer networks beyond the realm of their comprehension. Not so. The information superhighway is here today in the form of telephone networks, cable TV systems, satellite links, cellular networks and fiber-optic cable transmission systems.

Nobody really knows yet which transmission "pipe" will become the transcendent mode of communication (copper wire, coaxial cable, fiber optics), if indeed any one pipe ever completely replaces the others. It might not end up being a pipe at all. A friend of mine recounts a trip to China where he was amazed at the profusion of cellular phones. It seemed that everyone was walking around with cellphones in their ears. It's obviously easier, cheaper and quicker to build cellular (or other wireless) networks than their wired brethren. Necessity drives commerce down the path of least resistance.

We all travel the info highway whenever we pick up the telephone to get information. Telephone-based information services are but one lane — though admittedly one of the slower ones. The fast lanes are currently claimed by the Internet and by on-line computer services such as CompuServe, America Online, Microsoft Network and Prodigy, accessible only to those with fast cars and the ability to drive them.

Not everyone owns a Ferrari yet, and even fewer would know how to drive one. According to Link Resources, a market research firm based in New York City, only 30 percent of the 96.3 million U.S. households had a PC in 1995. And most of those were used for games and entertainment, not for sophisticated communications and data retrieval using the fast lane of the information superhighway. That leaves 67 million households without PCs of any kind — with no hope of access to the fast lane.

People with PCs and the skills to put them to good use aren't the only ones who need specialized information. We can all benefit from access to facts and figures that help make our lives more convenient, productive and enjoyable: stock and commodity prices, airline flight information, technical or professional assistance, movie reviews, sports scores, ski conditions, car pricing information and so on. The telephone gives everyone easy access to such data, even those suffering from terminal technophobia. The democratization of the info highway.

Will computers eventually replace the basic telephone? After all, many people are hanging their hats on computer-telephone integration (CTI) and computer telephony, new buzz terms you'll be hearing more and more about. Nobody really knows exactly where we're headed, and trying to predict the future is risky given the rapid pace of technological advancement.

Whatever happens, it won't happen overnight. A reasonably powerful computer, with the necessary peripherals and software, still costs around $2,000 — while the lowly telephone can be purchased for $20 or less. It is a pretty safe bet that this humble device will be around for many years to come.

What is 900?

What is the 900-number industry? First of all, calling it an industry is a bit of a stretch, but I'll keep doing it anyway in the interest of brevity, instead of calling it "The 900 pay-per-call information delivery service" or some other equally unwieldy title.

A 900 number is simply an alternative method of paying for information over the telephone. It is nothing more — or less — than a convenient information delivery medium, with a very efficient way of exchanging payment for information delivered. Whether the charge is by the minute or a flat rate for the call, the caller is charged for the telephone call on his or her monthly phone bill. Basically, the reverse of an 800 number. The person offering the information or entertainment, the information provider (IP), has the latitude of charging whatever the market will bear, within some fairly generous limits imposed by the long-distance telephone carrier.

As I mentioned earlier, the term "pay-per-call" is more generically accurate. You will also see the terms "976," "540" and "caller-paid" used interchangeably along with simply "900." They all mean the same thing: The caller is charged for the call, at a rate in excess of normal toll charges, in exchange for the information or entertainment services provided.

One reason for the rapid proliferation of telephone-based information services was the introduction of premium billing services in 1987. A 900 number allows the IP to charge a fee in excess of the basic telephone transport charge in order to cover the value of the information content offered by the program. The telephone company then bills the caller on behalf of the IP and sends the IP's share of the call revenue after holding back a percentage for its services and for future chargebacks. This is obviously a very convenient arrangement for all parties. The caller doesn't have to bother writing a separate check and needn't have a credit card handy; the IP doesn't have to prepare separate bills for potentially thousands of customers for a fairly small sum of money.

Interactive voice processing (using the telephone keypad to access programmed menu selections) has merged with 900-number information services to open up yet another lane on the information superhighway for people who do not have access to PCs. The telephone keypad becomes the equivalent of the computer keyboard, and any telephone owner has potential access to the same wide array of database information available to on-line computer service subscribers. Many more people have telephones than have computers, and virtually anyone knows how to operate a telephone with relative competence. The market is wide open to imaginative entrepreneurs who are responding to the challenge by providing an ever-expanding menu of information services. All it takes is a telephone.

History of 900

The 900 industry was launched in 1980 by AT&T as "DIAL-IT 900 Service," with the premier of DIAL-IT National Sports in September, followed shortly thereafter in October by ABC-TV's use of the service during the Reagan-Carter presidential debates to poll viewer opinion. On the final night of the debates, 500,000 viewers paid 50 cents each to register their opinions on who won the debate.

You may remember the *Saturday Night Live* episode in 1982 when viewers were asked to dial a 900 number to vote whether or not Eddie Murphy should boil Larry the lobster. A whopping 500,000 callers participated, voting to save poor Larry, but Eddie boiled him anyway.

The industry really didn't take off, however, until 1987 when AT&T began offering premium billing services. This allowed IPs to generate profits in addition to covering the program costs. During the same year, Telesphere (a now-defunct carrier) initiated the first interactive 900 service. By 1989, the three major long-distance carriers (AT&T, MCI and Sprint) were offering interactive 900 services, and industry revenues were growing very quickly. By 1990 revenues reached $1 billion, with more than 10,000 pay-per-call programs available.

Although the growth of the 900 industry was explosive in its formative years, it has experienced some growing pains along the way. Because the quick profit potential is so attractive, many less-than-reputable players jumped onto the bandwagon early with easily accessible (by minors) dial-a-porn programs or straight rip-off programs. Predictably, with virtually no rules or regulations in place, there were many abuses, and the 900 industry earned itself a bad reputation it is still trying to shake off to this day.

As you may already know, dial-a-porn programs haven't been the worst examples of sleaze in this industry. Indeed, most of the "adult" services delivered exactly what was promised — which was why they were so wildly successful. The real abuses have been with dishonest variations of the sweepstakes, credit-card and job-search lines. While a handful were legitimate, the vast majority were unequivocal ripoffs of the worst kind, preying upon unfortunate souls who can least afford to part with their hard-earned money.

There was little regulation in this emerging industry, and a lot of unscrupulous operators took advantage of this. Many people still equate 900 with sleaze. This is now changing, and the industry is working hard to improve its image. Federal laws and regulations are now in place, helping to clean up the industry by placing clear, unambiguous limits on what can and cannot be done over a 900 telephone line. A growing number of reputable companies are using 900, resulting in hundreds of legitimate, useful 900 information services. You will read about some of these later in this book.

In early 1994 AT&T commissioned a strategic study on consumer attitudes about 900 services, conducted by the Monitor Company of Cambridge, Massachusetts. Of the more than 1,100 consumers interviewed (who claimed to use 900 numbers at least four times a month), the two of the biggest barriers to calling 900 numbers were uncertainty about cost and lack of interesting programming, with cost uncertainty being the most serious barrier. This may indicate a flat-fee charge would be more acceptable than per-minute charges, which is certainly possible with programs of a predictable duration.

Other minuses: too expensive (40%), negative perception (40%), fear of ripoffs (36%), and blocked access (7%).

The study further determined that consumers were willing to use 900 numbers for specific program categories including such professional services as medical and financial information, auto repair and premium customer services like computer support. Also identified as desirable were such government services as tax assessment, professional licensing verification, background checks for firearm sales and motor vehicle applications.

The Business Opportunity

What's all the fuss about? Why are some people touting 900 numbers as the best entrepreneurial opportunity since the hula hoop or the pet rock? Why the proliferation of infomercials and seminars that promise easy riches and everlasting happiness?

Because most of these claims, however inflated, are based on truth. You can start a 900 business from home with a fairly small initial investment. You can get started pretty quickly. You can reach a national market that has 24-hour access to your service. And perhaps best of all, a huge, reputable *Fortune 500* company does all your billings and collections for you, sending you one check each month.

These are some pretty compelling reasons to get excited about the potential of 900 numbers, and would whet the appetite of any would-be entrepreneur. Nonetheless, being an easy business to get into doesn't necessarily translate to easy success. Far from it. To succeed in 900 is just as difficult as in any other industry, if not more so. Direct response selling, which is what 900 numbers are all about, is not the kind of marketing endeavor that should be undertaken by the meek of heart or slight of budget. It takes some real money and talent to make those direct sales. We'll talk a lot more about this later.

It all boils down to *what* you are selling, to *whom*. As with any business, you need a good product with demonstrated demand. And you need to know your market and how to reach it with your message. The 900-number part of the business is purely incidental

— simply one of several ways to deliver your service. In fact, with many successful entrepreneurs the 900 number is but one of several ways of communicating with customers.

The Future of 900

Is 900 a fad that will fade away after the novelty wears off? Will people continue to pick up the telephone, knowing that they are paying for the information? Will the industry still be around a few years from now?

First of all, we are already in the habit of using the telephone for getting information quickly. We call the airline for flight information, we call our stock broker for the latest price of Disney stock, we call the IRS help line for tax questions, or we call the weather service for local forecasts. We pull out the *Yellow Pages* and let our fingers do the walking. The telephone is the quickest and easiest way to get specific information right when we need it.

Why in the world would we pay for information when it can be had for free? Using the above examples, the airline may put us on hold for several minutes, we may play telephone tag with our broker, we might get inept tax advice from the IRS (not unusual!), or we may want more specialized weather information.

Not being able to get exactly the information you want when you need it can be very inconvenient in this hectic electronic age. Will we pay for accurate, timely information? Absolutely! As long as the cost of the information seems to be reasonable when balanced against the extra convenience of getting immediate results. We are in love with the telephone because it offers convenience, availability, accuracy and anonymity.

The telephone will remain a very efficient means for delivering information. Everyone has one. There may come a day when 900 numbers are no longer the dominant way of exchanging payment. Maybe prepaid calling cards or some mechanism that doesn't exist today will supplant 900 numbers as the pay-per-call method of choice. Make no mistake, however: Pay-per-call services are here to stay.

People have always been willing to pay for information they need. That's why we have so many bookstores. Sure, you can get free information at the library, but if you're looking for the very latest information on a topic you're more likely to find it in a bookstore. On the shelf, ready to be purchased and used. At the library, on the other hand, the same book might be checked out for the next three weeks. I get calls all the time from people who tried to get this book at the library only to be forced to wait for weeks until it comes back. They do not want to wait — particularly when it's needed to achieve important objectives (succeeding in business), so they order the book from me or buy it at the bookstore. They gladly pay for valuable information.

It costs money to package information in a form that is accessible to anyone, whether it be in a book or as part of a 900 audiotext program. And the old adage is true: You get what you pay for. Pay-per-call is no exception, and it will always be here in some form or another.

Definitions

Before reading any further, you need to understand several commonly used terms in the 900 industry. This is by no means a comprehensive glossary, which can be found at the end of this book.

Audiotext (also Audiotex). This term broadly describes various telecommunications equipment and services that enable users to send or receive information by interacting with a voice processing system via a telephone connection, using audio input. Voice mail, interactive 800 or 900 programs, and telephone banking transactions are examples of applications that fall under this generic category.

Information Provider (IP). A business or individual who delivers information or entertainment services to end users (callers) with the use of communications equipment and computer facilities. The call-handling equipment is often not owned by the IP, and a separate service bureau is hired for this purpose.

Interactive. An audiotext capability that allows the caller to select options from a menu of programmed choices in order to control the flow of information. As the term implies, the caller truly interacts with the computer, following the program instructions and selecting the information he or she wishes to receive.

Interexchange Carrier (IXC). This term technically applies to carriers that provide telephone service between LATAs (see below). Long-distance companies such as AT&T, Sprint, and MCI are also known as interexchange carriers.

Local Access Transport Area (LATA). This is a geographic service area that generally conforms to standard metropolitan and statistical areas (SMSAs), and some 200 were created with the 1984 breakup of AT&T. The local telephone companies provide service within each LATA (Intra-LATA), while a long-distance carrier (IXC) must be used for service between LATAs (Inter-LATA).

Local Exchange Carrier (LEC). This is the local telephone company that provides service within each LATA. Also included in this category are independent LECs such as General Telephone (GTE). The LEC handles all billing and collections within its LATA, often including long-distance charges (Inter-LATA), which are collected and forwarded to the appropriate interexchange carriers.

Pay-Per-Call. The caller pays a predetermined charge, in excess of the underlying transport fee, for accessing information services. 900 numbers are not the only type of pay-per-call service available. For local, intra-LATA applications, a seven-digit number is available with a 976 or 540 prefix. This service is usually quite a bit less expensive than long-distance 900 services, and should be seriously considered for any local pay-per-call applications that will not have the potential for expanding nationwide.

Pay-per-call services may also be offered over 800 or regular toll lines using credit card or other third-party billing mechanisms. When the caller pays a premium above the regular transport charges for the information content of the program, regardless of how payment is made, it is considered a pay-per-call service (the FCC's definition of pay-per-call, however, includes only 900 numbers).

Regional Bell Operating Company (RBOC). These are the seven holding companies created by the breakup of AT&T (also known as Baby Bells):

1. NYNEX
2. Bell Atlantic
3. AMERITECH
4. Bell South
5. Southwestern Bell Corp.
6. U.S. West
7. Pacific Telesis

These companies own many of the various LECs. For example, NYNEX owns both New England Telephone and New York Telephone. However, there are numerous independent LECs not owned by any RBOC. For example, Southern New England Telecommunications Corp. (SNET) is an independent LEC serving most of Connecticut's residential customers, and has nothing to do with NYNEX.

Although not an RBOC, a major telephone company that should be mentioned here is GTE. GTE is the largest U.S.-based local telephone utility providing voice, data and video products and services through more than 22 million access lines in portions of the United States, Canada, South America, the Caribbean and the Pacific. GTE's intra-LATA 900 service is currently available in California, Florida and Indiana, and should be investigated by anyone wishing to do business in those states.

Service Bureau. A company that provides voice processing and audiotext equipment and services and connection to telephone network facilities. For a fee, these companies allow the IP to offer a pay-per-call program using the service bureau's equipment, expertise and facilities.

The Joke Exchange

My first 900 program, launched back in 1991, was called The Joke Exchange. Basically, the premise was for callers to hear the latest jokes so they could be the life of the party, or leave their best joke for a shot at winning a $500 prize for the funniest joke of the month. The purpose of the contest, besides attracting more callers, was to encourage them to leave jokes, so there would be a constant supply of fresh material. My intent was to make it a true joke exchange, with callers both hearing and contributing the very latest jokes.

Why did I choose such a program? At the time it seemed like a pretty good idea, although it wasn't the first joke line. Foremost, I wanted to launch some kind of 900 program in order to learn about the business. I was just beginning to research the first edition of this book, and there is no better way to learn about something than by jumping right in and doing it. Firsthand experience.

The second reason, however, was even more self-serving. I have always had a hard time remembering jokes, and have never been known as the life of the party. My attempts at humor were often met with yawns — or even audible groans. Here was an opportunity to improve my social standing among my friends by being more amusing, while having some fun at the same time. And maybe I could make some money too!

It was a lot of fun setting up the program. The first step was selecting West Interactive in Omaha as my service bureau, because it had experience with similar programs, a solid reputation and the enormous call-handling capacity that I knew would be quite essential for the huge call volume that would be generated by my program (virtually all start-up IPs are afflicted with terminal optimism!). Then I dug up about 30 good jokes to start with, and

West Interactive forwarded them to AT&T, our long-distance carrier, for review and approval. AT&T gave the thumbs down to several on the basis of being borderline salacious or ethnically demeaning. The ethnically unacceptable jokes were easily fixed: I simply substituted lawyers or blonds for the ethnic minority in question (it's perfectly acceptable — indeed, even socially beneficial — to discriminate against and lambaste lawyers and blonds!).

Anyway, I figured the program needed a foundation of at least a dozen good jokes, which would be quickly replaced by those left by the callers in their own voices. It would be self-perpetuating, where the program callers, in this case those leaving the jokes, provide the basic program content. The menu was simple, consisting of three options:

1. Press One to hear all the latest jokes.
2. Press Two to record your joke and to enter the contest for a shot at winning the $500 prize. A slot was also provided for recording the caller's name and address.
3. Press Three to hear last month's winning joke, plus the name and hometown of the lucky winner.

Because my own voice is about as appealing a fingernails on a blackboard, and because I wanted callers to hear more than one voice, I decided to take advantage of the voice talent offered by West Interactive. The initial jokes were recorded in its sound studio by professionals with excellent DJ-like delivery.

AT&T at the time didn't have any NXXs (the first three numbers following the 900 number) that spelled anything relating to jokes or humor, so the best I could do was to spell "JOKE" with the last 4 digits of the phone number, which was 900-737-JOKE. The call charge was $1.95 the first minute, $1.00 each additional minute.

Of particular interest was how the program was updated with new jokes. A separate program editing line was designed and created by the programmers at West Interactive, which I could reach via an 800 number, with access using a private code (so a hacker – or anyone dialing a wrong number – couldn't get into the program and screw it up). The editing line allowed me to manage the program using the following options:

1. Press One to review the program. This allowed access to the exact same program as heard on the 900 line, so I could review the program without incurring a charge. Whenever appropriate, I used this option to input jokes of my own into the program, following the same procedure any other caller would follow.

2. Press Two to hear new jokes left by the latest callers. Because I had to screen every joke for appropriateness (i.e., not too salacious or ethnically demeaning) before transferring them to the program, this feature gave me the following options:

    a. Save the joke and go to the next one. This allowed me to give some thought to marginal jokes before making a final go or no-go decision.

    b. Transfer the joke to the program.

    c. Delete the joke from the system.

3. Press Three to edit the jokes. This feature allowed the following options:

    a. Delete a joke from the program.

    b. Transfer a joke to the winner's slot.

    c. Save the joke and continue to the next one.

4. Press Four to declare a new winner. This allowed me to record a new introduction for each new monthly contest winner, giving the name and hometown of the lucky jokester. This was followed by the joke itself, in the caller's own voice.

In reviewing the jokes, I had to be careful about violating AT&T's standards of propriety, so I had to kill quite a few good ones. Almost every day I would call the editing line and add new jokes to the program and delete those that had been on it for awhile. Occasionally, whenever I heard or came across a particularly good joke from another source, using the editing line, I would record it in my voice or get a friend to call it in. Because I was so attuned to getting good material for the program, one of my objectives was achieved very effectively: I was remembering good jokes and contributing to the general hilarity of my social gatherings, much to the delighted surprise and complete amazement of my friends. They couldn't figure out how I had become transformed from a social dullard into an exceedingly proficient humorist.

Except for the contest feature, this program was in fact easy to get launched. But I had no idea how difficult it was going to be to give away money. Because the legal issues are so complex, I had to hire a law firm specializing in promotion law, and ended up working with Hall, Dickler, Kent, Friedman and Wood in New York. The bottom line was that AT&T wouldn't allow a contest without a "conformance letter" from an attorney experienced in promotion law. By the way, don't even think about using your local hometown attorney for this work – you need the specific expertise offered by an attorney who specializes in promotion law.

The Joke Exchange was advertised in *Rolling Stone, National Lampoon,* some of the larger university newspapers, some alternative newsweeklies, and a local radio station. I even used matchbook covers to get the word out. All kinds of people called in leaving jokes, and I think the program went through every single blond joke ever in circulation. We even received a letter from a guy in Moscow, Eugene Vasiliev, who sent along a few Russian jokes, so I recorded them in my voice and gave him credit for the jokes in the program.

Was The Joke Exchange successful? Sort of. It was slowly gaining in popularity, and many people seemed to be enjoying themselves, myself included. What went wrong? I ran out of money long before I could possibly turn the corner toward profitability. I simply didn't have enough capital – and staying power – to properly market the program for a sufficient length of time to establish credibility, to gain a following and to adequately test the effectiveness of my marketing options. A classic mistake for many novice IPs, and you'll hear a lot more about this later in this book.

Granted, the purpose for launching the program wasn't so much to make tons of money, but that would have been nice! Nonetheless, I did learn the business fairly quickly. I pulled the plug on the program after about six months without losing too much money.

In retrospect, after having researched and written this book, I should have done several things differently. First, and most important, you don't go after a huge national, homogeneous market with a tiny advertising budget. It was simply much too ambitious an undertaking. Second, a lot more could have been done to promote the program and to generate free media coverage. I should have enlisted a reasonably well-known comic or comedy club to be affiliated with the program in some manner, lending name recognition and credibility to the program. And I could have been much more aggressive about sending out news releases for free publicity.

Third, the contest featuring a $500 prize was too complex and possibly unnecessary. On the direction of my attorneys, the contest had to be advertised as void in nine states, limiting the usefulness of the contest there — not to mention taking up valuable ad space in listing them.

One month the prize was awarded to a guy in Florida, whereupon we sent out our standard release letter, which had to be signed and returned to get the $500 cashier's check, giving us permission to mention his name and hometown on the program in the winner's slot. We never heard from him (and our letters weren't returned). We actually had trouble giving away $500! It seems likely that many people simply didn't believe we were giving away that much money, and perhaps such a large prize wasn't even necessary.

It would have been simpler to give away a promotional prize of nominal value, such as a joke book or tickets to a comedy club. I wouldn't have had to worry about all the complexities of running a full-blown contest, and more prizes could have been awarded more frequently.

As they say, hindsight is 20-20. The Joke Exchange was a valuable hands-on experience for me. Although I wasn't spectacularly successful, that doesn't mean such a program is a bad idea for someone who avoids my mistakes. That's one of the reasons for my writing this book. And a very good reason for you to read it and heed my advice — and of the other veterans who have contributed to this effort.

Had I been able to read this book *before* launching The Joke Exchange, it might still be on the air, contributing to the general hilarity of thousands of happy jokesters.

What Makes a Successful Program?

There is no mystery as to what it takes to be successful in this business. The elements that make up a successful 900-number information service are the same as those found in any other successful enterprise:

❐ A real demand or need for the service. This may sound a bit obvious, but many programs have been tried and failed simply because there was never any demonstrated need for the service. Like trying to sell ice to Eskimos in January. The most successful ones have invariably appealed to a fundamentally important human need, usually related to health, wealth, love and sex. It goes without saying that the market must not only exist, it must also be large enough to generate sufficient call volume.

❐ Sufficient capitalization. Most businesses – not just 900-number businesses – fail because they don't have enough money to hang in there long enough to turn the corner and succeed. This business in particular is characterized by a long lead time between getting the phone call and seeing the money for that call.

❐ Sufficient and appropriate marketing. Location (location, location) is to real estate what marketing is to 900: by far the most important criteria leading to financial success. This is a direct response advertising medium, which takes a lot of skill, savvy and money in order to succeed. Although most failures in this area result from lack of capital, few beginning entrepreneurs take full advantage of the free publicity and other guerrilla marketing strategies available out there. The marketing program needs to be carefully planned, highly imaginative, and relentlessly aggressive.

❏ Take full advantage of the medium; it is best suited to information that is time-sensitive or highly specialized. The most successful programs blend both types of information.

❏ Real value, delivered at a fair price. The result of delivering a quality service that meets or exceeds expectations for a fair price is CUSTOMER SATISFACTION. This reduces chargebacks, creates word-of-mouth advertising, and earns repeat callers.

As you can see, these elements apply to any successful business. There is no secret as to what makes a winning program. Remember, 900 is not a business in and of itself. It is nothing more than an information delivery medium. The IP must always remember that his business is selling information, and that the telephone is simply one of his options for reaching his customers.

The future belongs to those imaginative infopreneurs who first identify a specific information need for a well-defined target market, and then design a responsive program that delivers critically important information in a manner that is superior to all the alternative delivery methods, taking full advantage of the capabilities of interactive audiotex services.

900 Know-How is intended for individuals or businesses who wish to get started in the 900 pay-per-call information or entertainment industry. You will learn, step-by-step, how to launch a 900 information program. You will learn how to become an IP, or perhaps even more descriptive, an "Infopreneur." You will get ideas for possible 900 applications, how to market your service, how to choose a service bureau, how to project revenues, and how to measure and improve your advertising effectiveness. You will find a comprehensive Resource Guide at the end of this book, with useful nuts-and-bolts information to help you get started.

Chapter 2
Applications

There are two ways of classifying telephone-based information programs: by method of delivery or by information content. The actual method of delivery is clearly secondary in relation to the purpose and content of the program.

Nonetheless, before getting into the types of information programs out there, we must first understand the different telephone delivery options:

Passive. The caller simply listens to a recorded message of a specific nature and duration. Many of the early 900 programs were passive in nature, however few continue to be passive due to the limited information that can be offered. Many polling applications are passive — where the call is simply tallied as a vote by calling the telephone number that corresponds to the vote to be cast.

Interactive. This option is generally available only to callers with a touch-tone telephone, consisting of recorded information that is categorized in some logical fashion. The caller is given a menu of selections, to be chosen by pushing the appropriate number on the telephone keypad. There can be numerous sub-menus within the main menu, so that the caller can quickly zero in on specific recorded information. For a game application such as a trivia quiz, the keypad is used for answering multiple choice questions.

Live Operator. There are some applications where recorded information is inappropriate, such as legal, financial, medical, or customer service advice. Because it is expensive to hire such professionals as operators, the charges for these calls are typically higher than the recorded passive or interactive services.

Facsimile (FAX). This is an interactive application whereby a caller with a FAX machine can receive a hard copy of the desired information. This service is also known as fax-on-demand or fax-back. Any information with long-term value, or that is difficult to convey verbally — such as charts, graphs, or detailed financial reports — is a good candidate for an interactive fax program. Business-to-business services are the most logical fax applications because most businesses have fax machines, while fewer households are as yet equipped with such machines.

Computer/Data. There is no reason why 900 numbers cannot be used for access to specialized computer bulletin boards or on-line services which offer valuable, difficult-to-find information. Although few service providers, if any, are using 900 numbers for this purpose as of yet, this application is ready for some pioneers.

Hybrid. Many interactive programs have a "default" option for rotary telephone callers that results in a passive call where the caller hears the main message. Or, an interactive program may offer a live operator on the menu of choices should the caller be unable to get the information he or she needs on any of the recorded menu options.

Timely Information

What types of services and applications are suitable to the telephone delivery medium? Timely, or real-time, information is probably the most obvious. Any information that changes quickly or continuously falls into this category: Stock market quotations, foreign currency exchange rates, commodities prices, sporting results, and weather forecasts are some examples. All of this information will eventually become available in print or on television, but many people need this information quickly, and will gladly pay for instant access.

Specialized Information

Another type of information suitable for 900-number telephone applications relates to specialized information which, although available elsewhere in publications or from experts in the field, can be better delivered through the use of a pay-per-call service. The telephone may be more convenient, permitting the user to call at his or her convenience when he or she needs the information, instead of waiting for an appointment or driving to the library. A 900 number can be significantly less expensive, allowing the caller to get very specific legal advice, for example, without having to schedule a minimum one-hour appointment with a $200-per-hour attorney. A 900 number offers the caller complete confidentiality and anonymity, so the caller can avoid the embarrassment of talking about his or her substance abuse problem face-to-face with the counselor.

Other logical examples are medical advice, customer service assistance, income tax preparation, movie reviews, or even tarot card readings.

Customer service help is one specific application that is rapidly gaining consumer acceptance. We all hate to be put on hold indefinitely, play telephone tag, or get shunted around to various people before getting our question answered or our problem addressed. According to Kathryn Sullivan, AT&T's marketing vice president for business applications and information services, "Computer software companies have been among the pioneers in the innovative use of 900 service to improve customer support and satisfaction with pay-per-call technical support." Among the companies using AT&T's MultiQuest 900 service are industry heavyweights Microsoft Corporation and Lotus Development Corporation.

Information Content

It is helpful to categorize 900 programs in some coherent manner by information content. The purpose here is to give you a brief overview of the types of programs available. Many of these examples come from a book I co-authored with Carol Morse Ginsburg titled *Money-Making 900 Numbers*, which profiles some 400 different programs, providing a comprehensive overview of the hundreds of programs that are out there, past and present.

It wasn't easy coming up with categories that would cover most of the types of information programs. What follows, however, is a fairly logical division of information classifications.

Customer Service

As mentioned earlier, customer service is an area that is growing rapidly as consumer acceptance of 900 pay-per-call increases. People realize that the level of service improves when a reasonable fee is paid because the service provider can afford to staff the lines with competent personnel. Far preferable to being put on hold for an eternity, or playing telephone tag all day.

Microsoft

A leading example is Microsoft Corporation. Microsoft is the worldwide leader in software for personal computers, receiving some 23,000 calls a day for technical support. Before developing the Microsoft Support Network, the company listened to hundreds of customers about their preferences in how to access, utilize and pay for support. "We've incorporated customer feedback into all aspects of this support program," said Steve Ballmer, president at Microsoft. He added, "What have customers told us they want in technical support? The right answer is right now!"

The AT&T 900-555 prefix allows companies to unblock their phones for 900 calls with that specific prefix, which is reserved by AT&T for business uses only. The idea is that all 900 numbers except those that will help businesses can still remain blocked, preventing employees from running up charges for unauthorized access to 900-number entertainment programs.

Microsoft offers a wide range of electronic support services and information available to its customers in supporting some 170 different products. Options are available 24 hours a day, seven days a week, many at no cost. Before this program was initiated in October 1993, 800-number credit card calls and 900-number calls were about equal in number. Now, calls to the 900 numbers amount to an average of 1,000 per day, while 800-number calls average about 350 per day.

Perhaps the potential cost savings explains the difference. All 800-number calls cost the customer a flat fee of $25, charged to his credit card, regardless of how long the call lasts. On the other hand, 900-number calls are $2 per minute up to a maximum of $25 (Priority Desktop option), which is obviously advantageous for someone with only one or two quick questions.

On the 900 numbers, call charges do not begin until a support engineer comes on the line. The average hold time in queue has been less than 60 seconds, which is quite impressive by any standards. The hold time on the regular toll lines is longer, explains Mary Massengale, the marketing manager for product support, but the goal is to cut hold times below 60 seconds on 90% of all product support calls, not just the 900-number calls.

"Product Support is the fastest-growing group within Microsoft," says Massengale. When asked whether or not the 900-number side of the product support service was meeting expectations, Massengale was quite positive, indicating that its main advantage is in being a per-incident, pay-as-you-go service with the flexibility to fit the customer's specific needs 24 hours a day, seven days a week.

Government Services

The use of 900 numbers by government and non-profit organizations is one of the most exciting growth areas in this industry. These organizations are often constrained by tight budgets that prevent them from serving their constituents as well as they would like. A 900 number is often used in order to be able to continue giving out information that was often free in the past, before the days of lean budgets. Basically a telephonic user's fee.

In some instances non-taxpayers (or non-members and non-dues payers) are the ones requesting all the heretofore free information, consuming staff time in delivering a service to someone who hasn't paid for it. This is not fair to taxpayers — the people who must ultimately pay the salaries of the people providing this information. A 900 number solves this dilemma quite efficiently.

Tax Assessor

The Nashua, New Hampshire Tax Assessor's Office now uses a 900 line for information on property assessments. The line is designed for use by appraisers, developers, bankers, real estate agents, public utilities, attorneys and credit card agencies.

Calls to 900-448-8003 cost $3 for the first minute and $1 for each additional minute. The line is operational from 8 a.m. to 5 p.m. Monday through Friday. Nashua-based Innovative Telecom Corp. is the service bureau.

Property owners will still receive assessment information free of charge through a local phone number. Mayor Rob Wagner said he has supported the 900 line in order to reduce costs and increase local revenues.

California Department of Food and Agriculture

Because of budget cuts, the Market News Branch of the California Department of Food and Agriculture was faced with discontinuing its free information services for farmers and the agricultural community, until this service was converted into a self-funding pay-per-call program. Now farmers can call 900-555-0923 at $3 a minute for the latest farm commodity prices or specialized weather information for better crop management. When faced with either losing access to valuable information that was once free, or paying a reasonable fee, the farmers opted for paying.

Professional Services & Advice

This category is one of the more obvious applications for 900-number services, with professionals of all types using pay-per-call as an alternative method for delivering advice and for collecting payment from their clients. The efficiency of the 900-number payment mechanism now makes it feasible to offer even short, 5- or 10-minute consultations profitably — because all the cumbersome overhead associated with accounting for time and accounts receivable is eliminated.

Small companies and even individuals can now offer professional advice by the minute over the telephone. For example, AT&T offers a service called Express 900, which is designed specifically for live professional and technical services. For $75 per month (plus a $1000 one-time start-up fee, which is waived from time to time), incoming calls to your 900 number simply piggyback onto your existing telephone line (or any line you designate).

Lower cost options are also available. Resellers will pay all the costs for a dedicated 900 number through a service bureau, and then assign extensions to individual consultants and professionals. The start-up and monthly fees can be quite modes. Intermedia Resources in California is such a reseller (Appendix D).

Some people use such a 900 number not so much to make money but to screen callers or to prevent people from trying to take up a lot of their time without paying for it, saying in effect,"I'd like to discuss your situation in depth, but as you know I earn my living by consulting. Would you mind calling me back on my 900 number?" This will cut off those who pump you for free information, or those who can't seem to get to the point, rambling on interminably.

Tele-Lawyer

Tele-Lawyer is the oldest and longest-running live professional advice program in the country, according to founder Michael Cane, based in Huntington Beach, California. "This was certainly the first live professional consulting service (on 900)," he says, "and it may have been one of the first live programs of any kind." Cane is well known in the pay-per-call industry for his professional consulting and for his numerous articles in the audiotext trade publications. He is one of the pioneers in this industry, and has contributed significantly to its growth as a legitimate and respectable information-delivery medium.

Tele-Lawyer was established in October of 1989 on 900-446-4LAW at $2 per minute (now $3/min.). Shortly thereafter, in January 1990, Cane launched another line, 900-TELE-TAX.

Cane says that Tele-Lawyer is the only "attorney" many of its customers have. Because the program covers every major legal category, with a staff of 36 attorneys, many people really don't need to have another lawyer, and prefer the economy of being able to pay by the minute for instant advice. The service offers all the specialists found in big, expensive law firms. In many cases a personal relationship will develop between the client and a specific attorney and they will be on a first-name basis. One of Cane's clients, a real estate developer, has even discussed his marital problems on the line!

Tele-Lawyer will typically have three or four attorneys in the office answering the phone on an average day. Some of the specialists, however, such as the immigration and copyright attorneys, work off-site, from their own offices. The calls are simply forwarded to these attorneys.

A measure of how satisfied his callers are is the low rate of uncollectibles experienced on the Tele-Lawyer line. Cane says that AT&T is always remarking that his program ranks among the best in terms of low uncollectibles, usually measuring under 1%. This program is obviously filling a need by delivering top quality service.

Indeed, Tele-Lawyer has been so successful that Cane has decided to license the program to other attorneys throughout the country. Licensees will be assigned territories corresponding to telephone area codes, and a national marketing effort will be undertaken, including infomercials with TV personalities.

In 1995 Tele-Lawyer was awarded the American Bar Association's first Louis M. Brown award for providing low-cost access to legal services.

Investment, Finance & Business Information

Stock and commodity prices are the obvious applications of time-sensitive information that is well-suited to the 900-number delivery medium, and such programs are quite common. The interesting programs, however, are those that offer highly specialized information to a specific group of people.

Until recently, offering business information on 900 numbers was becoming increasingly infeasible, since most businesses blocked all access to 900 numbers as a matter of policy. Too many employees were running up huge bills calling their astrologers or their "fantasy dates."

AT&T met this problem head-on by instituting a dedicated business-to-business exchange for qualified programs that must meet fairly stringent criteria to be assigned the exchange, 900-555. AT&T also designated its 900-225 exchange for business-to-consumer applications, such as customer service. Similarly, MCI has designated its business exchange as 900-733. Businesses can now selectively unblock these exchanges in order to gain access to the wide variety of business information that is available — or that will be developed in the future.

The World Trade Center NETWORK

The World Trade Centers Association, headquartered at the World Trade Center in New York, has been offering a pay-per-call fax-on-demand service on 900 and 800 numbers since early 1990. The fax-on-demand service is but one component of its World Trade Center NETWORK, a subscriber computer network linking international traders with some 191 World Trade Centers in more than 140 countries.

One of the most popular features of the WTC NETWORK are the trade leads — offers to buy or sell goods and services covering virtually every industry imaginable. An importer in Istanbul might post (on the computer bulletin board) his desire to purchase 100,000 pairs of Jockey shorts, and a U.S. exporter can respond directly and close the sale. The fax-on-demand system offers the same information as the computer bulletin board. The only difference is that it is a one-way communication system — the caller has no way to post his own buy or sell messages. It is also available only to U.S. callers owing to coverage limitations inherent to 800 and 900 numbers.

The telephone numbers are 900-FAX-4WTC ($3 the first minute; $2 each additional minute) and 800-656-1234 ($5 per fax selection, with credit card payment). The reason for offering the 800 number option is to offer the service to those companies or individuals that have a block on all 900-number calls. An informational number describing the system is also available: 800-937-8886.

According to Manager George Marx, many subscribers first used the system via the 900 or 800 line, then decided to upgrade to the full computer network. The fax service is an easy way to introduce people to the WTC NETWORK without having to make any further up-front commitments. Indeed, this is one of the primary purposes for establishing the fax system. Once a caller discovers how useful the information can be, it's likely he will take the next step and go on-line, which would be more cost-effective for frequent users. Besides trade leads, the computer network offers access to more than 150 databases (such as Dun & Bradstreet, Moody's, S&P, TRW Credit Reports), a calendar of WTC events, a business news clipping service, and a currency exchange database.

When asked who were the callers to the fax service, Marx indicated that, "they are primarily small- to medium-sized traders of some kind — importers, exporters, agents." Further, they tend to be fairly savvy in international trade, as the purpose of the program is to facilitate it. Marx also knows that many of the callers are long-term customers because he gets telephone calls from users who tell him they have been using the service for years. And some of these callers have apparently never felt the need to upgrade to the computer network — perhaps they are only occasional users or they don't own computers.

It is easy to see how this system can help experienced international traders, or anyone else with something to buy or sell internationally. The fact that the program has a high percentage of loyal repeat callers is proof of its usefulness. And the idea of using a fax service to introduce people to a computer network service is both imaginative and promising for other applications as well.

Sports Information

Many major newspapers such as *USA Today* have their own 900-number sports lines, which are published in the sports section. Such programs are naturals for newspapers, complementing rather than competing with the printed information, which by its nature cannot be as timely. Newspapers are in the business of selling information, not paper, and a 900 number is simply one more tool to be used to deliver the information.

Lacrosse Scores With 900

The Lacrosse Scorline is the first 900 number to report on that sport. The Lacrosse Foundation's line, in conjunction with *Lacrosse Magazine* and Advanced Telecom Services, its service bureau based in Wayne, Pennsylvania, gives fans updated men's and women's Division 1 and Division 3 scores. Collegiate polls, major indoor Lacrosse League results and standings are available as well as feature news and interviews.

Updated twice weekly, the Lacrosse Scorline (900-454-SCOR) costs 99 cents per minute. Partial proceeds are donated to the Lacrosse Foundation. The interactive program uses ATS VoiceTone for the voice recognition of rotary dial phones.

This line was started to help relieve the small staff at the Lacrosse Foundation office from fielding phone calls all day from avid fans, who have nowhere else to turn for such information. There was no other choice but to turn to a 900 number to replace what could no longer be given away at no charge. The fans do not appear to mind paying for information they really want.

Big East Briefs

Greg Shemitz, based in Middle Village, New York, nearly doubled his income after launching his *Big East Briefs* Hotline (900-860-3400, 95¢ per minute) to complement his *Big East Briefs* newsletter. The newsletter, now in its eighth season, is published 16 times a year ($42 annual subscription) and covers Big East basketball, including in-depth recruiting reports, league news, behind-the-scenes recruiting analysis and interviews with Big East recruiters and high school coaches with promising prospects. Shemitz is serving a niche of nearly 2,000 subscribers, hard-core Big East fans who also appreciate getting the most up-to-date information possible via the 900-number hotline. Shemitz is using the hotline to augment the information in the newsletter with fast-breaking news about recruiting — providing better service to his appreciative customers.

The peak calling periods coincide with the spring and fall signing periods. The hotline will get an average of 150 to 200 calls per day, with the content updated daily. During non-peak periods the rest of the year, the hotline generates about 100 calls per update, which is twice a week.

Shemitz updates the line himself, reporting each update like a brief news item. The line has been operational since January 1994. Although he doesn't have any hard data to back it up, Shemitz believes that nearly all his callers are loyal subscribers, many of whom have memorized the 900 number. When asked whether there was a measurable spike in calls after mailing out the newsletter, Shemitz indicated that there was only a small increase. This is a good example of a line that generates substantial repeat calls despite the frequency of advertising.

Environmental Information

Environmental information is a category that has two of the most important components of a successful 900-number service: time-sensitive and specialized information. Different people need different kinds of environmental information for widely divergent reasons: travel, health, safety, economics or recreation. Whether it's air pollution levels or ski conditions, environmental information services will continue to be an important application for the pay-per-call industry.

BOAT/U.S.

The BOAT/U.S. Weather Watch 900 line was established in January 1992, targeted at recreational boaters who want instant access to the detailed marine weather information that is continually broadcast by the National Oceanographic and Atmospheric Administration (NOAA) and the National Weather Service. The telephone number is 900-933-BOAT, and the charge is 98 cents per minute.

The line is sponsored by the Alexandria, Virginia-based Boat Owners Association of the U.S., widely known as BOAT/U.S. According to Dave Pilvelait, director of media and community relations, it is the largest organization of recreational boat owners in the country with just over a half-million members.

This is a real-time weather program. After calling in to the main program, the caller selects, by telephone area code, the location of the NOAA weather station from which he or she wishes to hear the latest marine weather conditions. There are about 70 NOAA weather stations to choose from, and the caller must know the area code before calling. Most stations are along the seacoasts and the Great Lakes. After making the selection, the caller is connected to the live broadcast from that station, hearing the exact broadcast that is being transmitted by radio.

Why do boaters call? Because the information is not otherwise easily available, with tide, current, wind and other specialized information of interest only to boaters — for whom the weather conditions rank up there among the most important things to know, second only to knowing where you are located (otherwise known as navigation!).

Lifestyle, Travel & Leisure

This category, if indeed it can be called that, is admittedly fairly diverse, particularly with the inclusion of "Lifestyle." This category is an aggregation of subjects that deal with the personal lives of people, as distinct from the other subject categories outlined in this chapter.

Branson, Missouri

According to AT&T, the Branson Lakes Area Chamber of Commerce in Branson, Missouri has one of the most successful 900 travel lines in the country. People from all over flock to Branson to hear Mel Tillis, Bobby Vinton, Glen Campbell, Andy Williams and Boxcar Willie, among others, perform in their own theaters.

Callers to 900-884-2726, for $1.50 per minute, get an overview of what's happening in the Branson Lakes Area, and are given the option of leaving their address or fax number to receive show schedules, vacation packages, lodging information and area maps showing alternate routes for avoiding the traffic congestion Branson is becoming famous for.

During the season, from May to October, the 900 line gets up to 100 calls a day (versus a dozen or so during the off-season) over eight dedicated lines.

Education, Careers & Self-Improvement

In the early days of 900, when there was little regulation in place, some of the job search lines were the worst examples of sleaze, preying upon unfortunate people who were desperate to find work. Along with the phony sweepstakes and easy credit lines, these lines helped to give the 900-number industry a slimy reputation that it's still trying to shake off.

Fortunately, through federal legislation and self-regulation, the industry has been cleaned up considerably, and the majority of the programs offered today are perfectly legitimate.

Musicians Work Line

This application is the brainchild of two musicians. IP Anthony Steele, co-owner of Musicians Networking International Inc., the application's parent company, says, "We designed

Auditionline to be a one-stop shop for working musicians, both those looking for work and those looking for other musicians to work with." The convenience of a phone call and the ability for constant updating led Steele and fellow musician Tom Polifrone to think of 900.

Steele noted that the traditional print advertisement route of finding work or other musicians is subject to delays due to printing schedules. "We knew there had to be an easier way," he says.

"We feel that what it has to offer is unique," Steele adds. Auditionline uses two 900 numbers. Musicians looking for work call 900-77-2LIST, leave a 45-second ad and pay $4.99 a month. Bands or producers looking for musicians call 900-285-2JAM to listen to ads for $1.99 for the first minute and 99 cents for each additional minute. That line also features a Music Services category with ads from producers, recording studios, managers, publicists and photographers. Marketing has included print ads in publications such as *The Village Voice, Guitar World* and *Musician.*

Entertainment

This section covers one of the two major divisions of 900-number services: information and entertainment. Just like print or television, the telephone is simply another delivery medium that is suitable for a wide variety of entertainment applications.

Soap opera updates, crossword puzzle clues, telephone *Jeopardy*, movie reviews and music samplers are just a few of the types of entertainment lines that are out there. Not surprisingly, the entertainment applications tend to be among the most imaginative 900 programs. And they can be a lot of fun to plan and implement.

Adult

Adult lines, or the so-called dial-a-porn lines, are the most controversial of the entertainment programs. Adult programs were among the first 900 programs on the scene, and have historically been the most profitable.

Glen Chazak, owner and president of Paramount National Media, Inc. in Beverly Hills, California, has been an IP in the adult pay-per-call business since it began in the mid-1980s. He now spends his time and resources between both adult and psychic programs, and he has done quite well with both applications.

Adult pay-per-call started back in 1985 on local 976 numbers. In the beginning, according to Chazak, virtually all of the adult programs were recorded, with few live operators. In those early days, it was not unusual for the larger adult IPs to make a 20 to 1 return on the advertising investment for their programs — probably a result of the novelty of such programs and a pent-up demand for this type of entertainment. These pioneers, Chazak among them, were making huge sums of money. The most successful of these IPs were investing large sums in national advertising in expensive publications such as *Penthouse* and *Hustler*. At a 20 to 1 return, a $10,000 investment in one display ad would return $200,000 or more in revenue.

In 1989 long-distance 900 pay-per-call became available to adult IPs, and by then the advertising return ratio was still a very impressive 15 to 1 or so. Along with the advent of 900 came live adult programs, which resulted in longer call hold times and higher per-minute charges as compared to recorded programs. According to Chazak, "the vast majority of the money being made in 900 was from adult programs. . . and the bulk of the callers, maybe 95%, were male."

Nonetheless, the gravy train was relatively short-lived. After 1990, returns started dropping to more realistic levels as the novelty wore off, chargebacks became an increasingly serious problem, competition increased and people began blocking access to 900 numbers. "By 1992, returns were down to 5 to 1, and then maybe 3 to 1 by 1993," says Chazak.

When a phone-room operator gets a call, the computer screen tells her what type of call is coming in: an 800 credit card call with no restrictions, or a 900-number call to a "romance" or "chat" line, for example. This alerts her as to what can be talked about over the phone, and the operator is generally given detailed guidelines on what the boundaries are on the two different types of calls.

Iris Sanders runs a phone room in Vancouver that offers adult operators (as well as psychic). The company, Cybervoice, has been in business for several years serving both U.S. and Canadian IPs, and employs an average of 25 to 30 operators per shift, 24 hours a day. Many of her operators are university students who work there for an average of six months. But she does employ all kinds, from students to grandmothers.

Nancy Ava Miller of Edgewood, New Mexico runs a specialized S&M (Sadomasochism) telephone service that is surprisingly low tech. Her organization, People Exchanging Power (PEP), was founded in 1986 and consists of educational support groups around the country for people interested in dominance and submission in their love relationships. The phone service is actually an outgrowth of these support groups.

The PEP counsellors, as Miller likes to call them, work from their homes using a dedicated phone line for their counselling sessions. These counsellors live all over the country, and they are not simply hired hands who read from a script. Miller insists that they be genuinely interested in the S&M lifestyle. While most of the calls are actively sexual in nature, many are straight counselling inquiries about the S&M scene. Part of the counsellor's initial training is to read Dale Carnegie's book, *How to Win Friends and Influence People*, with emphasis on the following advice:

❐ Become genuinely interested in other people
❐ Be a good listener
❐ Make the other person feel important, and do it sincerely

Miller also encourages her counsellors to always go a couple of minutes *over* the stated time limit, and encourages them to invite the caller to phone back in a few days, *for free*, just to chat for a couple of minutes and to get feedback about the prior session. Here is a verbatim statement from the PEP Information Package for new counsellors: "It is important to utilize the caller's name throughout your conversation; it is also important to be loving and compassionate toward the caller, and accepting of his needs.

Remember, for whatever reason, the caller has chosen you to share these secret and intimate parts of himself — information he may never have told anyone before!"

Lady Tiffany, one of the PEP counsellors in California, encourages her callers: "Please don't ever feel embarrassed, humiliated, ashamed or apologetic about your fantasies. I'm not here to judge you. . . Don't feel guilty about any fantasies you wish to explore."

The counsellors are called directly at their homes on a regular phone line, and payment is made using a credit card. The counsellors are given detailed instructions on how to take all the required information and to get pre-authorization for the credit-card charge. With all first-time callers the card-issuing bank is called and the cardholder name and address are verified before the session goes forward. These procedures ensure minimal problems with bad debt and fraudulent credit card use.

PEP's rates, which compare favorably with the per-minute rates charged by other adult services, range from $89 for a half-hour to $119 for a full hour session. A recorded greeting by Mistress Allie is accessible by calling 908-284-8028, where the caller will hear a list of telephone numbers for numerous counsellors from coast to coast.

Miller also sponsors conventions of her PEP members and counsellors in different parts of the country, offering ongoing training and support. It is apparent that this is one of the most professionally operated adult phone services in this country. And because of this, it is very successful.

Product & Business Promotion & Marketing

The major purpose of these programs is to promote a product, service, event, company or organization. Many will typically include an element of entertainment to entice people to call.

Contests and sweepstakes are other ways to grab the attention of consumers in promoting a product or service, and they have been used extensively. Unfortunately, some past scams involved sweepstakes lines that never delivered anything of value. Recent legislation has improved this situation considerably, and most such programs that run today are quite legitimate. There are now in place strict standards imposed by the long-distance carriers for incorporating contests or sweepstakes into a 900-number promotion.

TBS Uses 900 for "Sweepstakes"

TBS Superstation used 900 in its "Win a Hog!" sweepstakes run in conjunction with the television special, *Harley-Davidson: The American Motorcycle*. The special featured one promotional ad letting viewers know that, through a 900 number or a postcard, they could enter the sweepstakes to win a motorcycle.

Each call to the 900 line cost 99 cents. The show aired twice, and its first airing drew 2,262,000 households as viewers. In total, 10.7 percent of the households viewing dialed the 900 number. Omaha-based West Interactive Corporation, the service bureau for the number, processed more than 400,000 calls during a five-day period.

A half-million postcard entries to the sweepstakes were received, for a combined response rate of 24 percent.

Fundraising & Charity

A growing trend in the pay-per-call industry has been the use of 900 numbers for fundraising purposes. These programs are often flat rate calls, and usually include a recorded message regarding the topic, often by a recognized celebrity who champions the particular cause. Some organizations that have already experimented with 900 fundraising include World Vision, Leukemia Society of America, March of Dimes, Amnesty International, and Mothers Against Drunk Driving.

What makes 900 fundraising so promising is the convenience, to both donor and fundraiser. It's much easier to dial a phone number than to write a check and address an envelope. The fundraisers' collection costs go way down, and the problem with generous pledges who never come through with the cash is completely eliminated.

High Seas 900

In what a famed sailor has termed "the highest and best use of 900," 900-820-BOAT provided daily progress reports of two Americans' attempt to break a 140-year-old sailing record. In *Ocean Challenge*, sailor Rich Wilson and co-skipper Bill Biewenga sailed from California to Boston, going around Cape Horn.

Calls cost 95 cents per minute. Information for the line was gathered from the sailors' daily radio calls to relay stations. High seas operators patched the calls through to service bureau West Interactive, which recorded the updates and put them on the 900 line.

"Our objective is to share the adventure taking place at sea with as many people on shore as possible," said Lyon Osborne, project manager for *Ocean Challenge*. "The only way *Ocean Challenge* can afford to make the daily reports available nationwide is through the use of 900."

News, Politics & Opinions

Opinion polling during the Reagan-Carter debates in 1980 was one of the first 900-number applications, and continues to be a popular method for getting instant readings on a wide range of topics.

Opinion polling need not be limited to simply casting a vote by calling the appropriate 900 number. *Newsweek* magazine has been using a 900 letter-to-the-editor service for those opinionated souls who are too busy to sit down and compose a letter.

Miss America Pageant

Miss America will continue to be chosen partly on the basis of how she looks in a bathing suit, thanks to the 900 polling conducted during the 1995 pageant in Atlantic City. By a margin of four to one, 79% of the nearly 900,000 callers voted in favor of keeping the swimsuit competition as part of the pageant.

Callers were given the choice of calling 900-268-2200 to cast a "yes" vote to keep the swimsuit competition, or 900-268-2300 to cast a "no" vote. The charge was a flat rate of 50 cents per call. A total of 11,000 incoming phone lines were dedicated to this program, which was handled by West Interactive in Omaha, using AT&T MultiQuest 900 services. This was the first time that the service bureau itself became part of the story. TV host Steve Kmetko in Omaha provided information on the call-handling capabilities of West Interactive (the service bureau) and updates on the call volume coming into the facility.

As I mentioned earlier, many applications will not fit neatly into only one of the preceding categories. Back in 1991 Playboy Enterprises introduced its Playboy Wake-Mate line, where you could schedule a wake-up call from a *Playboy* centerfold for $4, who greeted you in a silky voice with, "Good morning, sleepyhead. Did you have a good rest?" This application has elements of entertainment, customer service, product promotion and lifestyle all rolled into one. The preceding categories are not the only way to classify different types of 900 programs.

The Interactive Services Association (Appendix B) recently established application categories for pay-per-call programs in order to lend some uniformity to the industry, and to allow meaningful data comparisons across the categories. Hattrick Publishing Group, publisher of *Outside the Envelope* (Appendix A), used ISA's new categories and its own data collected from AT&T and MCI to come up with the following distribution of 900 numbers, from a total of 31,000 numbers assigned to AT&T and MCI in July 1995:

Category Distribution of 31,000 900 Numbers				
	Consumer & Business	Personals & Classifieds	Sports & Gaming	Entertainment
AT&T	10%	26%	17%	47%
MCI	10%	26%	64%	

Source: *Outside the Envelope*, December, 1995

Although the Consumer & Business category is the smallest, this is the fastest-growing category as of this writing. Many people close to this industry, myself included, expect this category to continue growing at a rapid pace as more businesses and governments adopt 900 as a legitimate means of serving their constituents.

Chapter 3
What Makes 900 Unique?

Launching a 900 program couldn't be much easier. That's not to say that every program will necessarily be successful. We'll talk a lot more about that later. But the fact remains that it is quite easy to get a program on-line, fairly quickly, with a minimal investment.

Start-up costs can be kept low – in the hundreds, not thousands, of dollars. By using a service bureau (Chapter 7), it is not necessary to purchase any special equipment. This is a good part-time business that can be operated easily from home. The working hours are quite flexible, and need not interfere with family, a full-time job, or playtime. With recorded interactive programs, because program updates can be accomplished from any remote location with a touch-tone telephone, business can still be conducted even in the middle of a prolonged vacation.

Assuming the program is successful, revenues can be generated 24 hours a day, seven days a week, while you are asleep or out fishing. If you're really successful, you can easily move yourself and your business to Florida, Hawaii or Aspen. Few other businesses are quite so easily portable, with no loss of revenue or business interruption when moving.

The 900-number arena is open to anyone with a good, workable idea. It doesn't require any special education, training, or an advanced degree. It does require knowledge, however, particularly in marketing. More about this later.

The industry is still new and growing, with plenty of potential for further growth. There are many ideas that haven't even been tried yet. Except for very specialized programs, the size of the market is potentially unlimited, and growing all the time as more and more people accept 900 programming as legitimate and useful.

These are some powerful advantages and characteristics that are extremely attractive to entrepreneurs who want to start out with a part-time, home-based business. The only other type of business that comes close to 900 with similar advantages is mail-order.

A good analogy is to compare a 900 business with operating a tavern — a business most of us are familiar with (hopefully, not too familiar!). Let's assume that your 900 program nets $2 per call after all long-distance carrier and service bureau charges — about the same you would net selling a mixed drink in your tavern. Let's further assume your 900 business is operated from home, with very low overhead, and the total fixed monthly costs, excluding advertising, are $400.

Now, using the tavern analogy, you need to sell 200 drinks a month to cover rent, insurance, utilities, payroll, and all other overhead. To break even on fixed costs, you must sell about seven drinks a day to your customers. To make a profit, you simply have to sell more than seven drinks a day.

Now this is a unique tavern with some magical characteristics. It's absolutely enormous in size, with no limit on its capacity. If you can get them to come, you can cram in hundreds or even thousands of people. And you don't have to rely on your local market. People from any part of the country can be inside your tavern instantly without actually leaving home, as if by some kind of magic teletransporter.

Finally, your tavern has a special license to stay open around the clock, and never needs to shut down for maintenance or cleaning. It operates automatically, completely by itself, with no employees or supervision, so you can be out on the golf course even when it's mobbed with merrymakers!

Sound too good to be true? Not necessarily. These are the very real advantages to the 900 industry. Getting people to come to your tavern, however, is the real challenge. To get people to come, and then come back again and again, you may have to offer a unique theme or ambiance that appeals to a specific market. Or unique entertainment that your customers cannot find elsewhere. Or an extremely good value on the drinks, such as oversized specialty drinks with those little umbrellas sticking out of them. Or a tasty buffet to induce more people to come. Or a daily door prize.

Just opening the tavern is by no means sufficient. Nobody will show up if they don't know about it. And once they find out about it, you must offer them a compelling reason to visit. And when they come, you want to treat them really well so that they will keep coming back again and again. A successful tavern has a following of loyal regulars.

So does a successful 900 line.

Premium Billing Services

Probably the most unique characteristic of the 900 pay-per-call industry is premium billing. The telephone company collects your money for you. In what other business do you automatically get the services of a large, reputable company for all your billings and collections? The fact that your charges are included on a monthly telephone bill almost guarantees that your customers will not dispute your charges or hold off paying for a long period of time. This is especially true for legitimate, reputable 900 programs. Most people do not question their phone bills, and they pay them promptly, along with other important utility bills.

This feature may not be very important if you're selling big-ticket items like cars or boats to a small number of customers. But what is the average price of your 900 service? Maybe $2, $3 or $5? And if the program is marketed nationally to a broad audience, customers could number in the thousands or tens of thousands. Imagine how costly it would be to collect small amounts of money from thousands of people. You would definitely need sophisticated computerized equipment to keep up with the volume. And a lot of people to run the equipment and handle the mail. And your collection rates would be much lower.

With a 900 line, the telephone company does all the work for you, and then sends out one check every month. One check for $50,000 instead of 10,000 checks averaging $5 each. You spend a lot less time chasing money you've already earned. You can concentrate on improving your program or marketing, earning even more money for the telephone company to collect for you in the future.

Obviously, you pay for premium billing services. The typical fee is 10% of the total retail call charge, which is split between the local and long-distance carriers.

Premium billing services are actually provided at two levels. First, the LEC collects the money from the customer as part of the total monthly phone bill, which aggregates all the local, long-distance and 900 charges. The 900 charges are listed separately as part of the long-distance IXC bill, and the LEC basically collects the IXC's money and forwards it to the IXC (getting paid for its efforts, of course, in its capacity as the IXC's collection agent). Second, the IXC forwards the appropriate funds to the client of record, which can be either the IP or the service bureau. If it's the service bureau, the process takes one more step before the money reaches the IP.

Premium billing services are currently available only for information or entertainment services. The telephone companies are reluctant to allow the sale of tangible merchandise in connection with their billing services. Some IPs are getting around this by offering a valuable recorded information program, while also "giving away" a related product to callers. Be careful. If you abuse the privilege, the telephone company might just shut you down.

Nonetheless, this situation may soon change. The telephone companies earn money for serving as collection agents for other companies, using their established billing and collection systems, which are already in place. The amount of money is quite impressive, and the telephone companies are not blind to the potential revenues that would result if products could be sold using

900 premium billing services. The main problem from the telephone company's perspective is what to do about chargebacks for defective or returned merchandise. If this issue can be resolved, product sales on 900 numbers will become a reality.

Alternative Billing Services

Premium billing services, as the term vaguely implies, is a voluntary service provided by the telephone companies. The telephone company, whether it be an LEC or an IXC, cannot be forced to collect money for other companies, or for categories of services it does not wish to handle. The telephone company may deny premium billing services simply because it doesn't wish to sully its corporate image by being associated with a certain type of service. This is often the case with adult services, where even the tame chat or romance lines are denied premium billing despite not being classified as "indecent" in content.

This gap in billing services is being filled by independent third-party companies that offer such services to IPs and service bureaus. These alternative billers get call data from the telephone company or the service bureau, including the caller's telephone number (through ANI) and billing address. In some cases, through agreements with the LECs, these company's bills are included with the regular telephone bill.

There are basically two types of alternative billing. The most effective is nearly identical to regular premium billing offered by the IXCs and LECs. The third-party billing company's bill is inserted into the same envelope as the LEC monthly bill, often designed and formatted to look like the regular phone bill, and the customer pays the entire bill with one check. Essentially, the third party biller is taking the place of the IXC, while the LEC is still performing premium billing. Like getting half of the regular premium billing service.

But not necessarily half of the benefits. According to the third-party billers, there are several advantages to using their services:

❏ Flexible reporting using report formats that can be

customized to the client's data needs.

- ❑ Fraud control measures.
- ❑ Flexible payment plans and factoring, allowing IPs to get their cash faster.
- ❑ Billing for adult (non-indecent) programs where allowed by LECs.
- ❑ Variable billing rate options that allow the IP some flexibility in structuring the call charges.
- ❑ In some cases, lower processing fees and lower holdbacks (reserves against chargebacks, or bad debt).
- ❑ These companies are specialists in one narrow field, and can do a better job because they are better focused on strictly billing and collections.

Alternative billing is gaining acceptance with both IPs and service bureaus. In some cases, IPs are requesting certain third-party billers in preference over the IXCs because of the level of services provided. Many service bureaus offer third-party billing as an additional option in their mix of services.

It should be emphasized that this type of billing, also known as LEC or Telco billing, must meet the standards set by the pertinent LECs. Except for adult programming, which most LECs are still willing to bill for, most of the other standards are quite similar to those promulgated by the IXCs.

The second type of alternative billing is known as private billing or private-party billing. The main difference here is that the private biller doesn't include its bill along with the LEC phone bill – it is sent separately to the customer. This means that no premium billing service is provided at any level, and the IP needn't be concerned with IXC and LEC policies as they relate to premium billing. The program content, however, must still conform to Federal law. For example, indecent programs can be offered on 900 numbers and billed by a private biller, but the FCC rules requiring written pre-subscription to such services must be followed in order to be legal (Appendix E). Also, product fulfillment using 900 numbers can be accomplished with private billing.

The problem with this alternative is obvious: Collection rates can be quite poor because the bill is not aggregated with the phone bill. It is much easier for the customer to ignore it when it arrives independent of the phone bill. Of course, this is actually how most bills, for virtually any other products or services, arrive at the customer's doorstep anyway, and the problem is only relative, because the alternative (LEC or premium billing) is so attractive. Like any other transaction, it will boil down to how satisfied the customer was with the service. The bill is usually paid if the customer's expectations were met.

The argument can be made that just the availability of private-party billing is a unique advantage of the 900 industry, despite its ranking at the bottom of the billing hierarchy. What other industries have third-party billers already in place who are ready, willing and able to perform such a valuable service? Unless the LECs change their policies and allow product sales, private-party billing may indeed become an important product fulfillment alternative for many direct marketers.

Although chargebacks certainly will not be an insurmountable problem for reputable companies offering good value and services to their customers, they have become one of the most serious problems in this industry, and will be discussed in more detail later in this chapter.

There are several companies that offer third-party billing, some of which are listed below. You will find others that advertise in the relevant trade publications listed in Appendix A, or in the *Audiotex News Resource Guide* (Appendix C).

ITA
340 Interstate North Parkway, Suite 200
Atlanta, GA 30339; 800-285-4263

VRS Billing Systems, Inc.
5883 Rue Ferrari
San Jose, CA 95138; 408-362-4040

Federal TransTel, Inc.

Two Chase Corporate Dr., Suite 170
Birmingham, AL 35244; 800-933-6600

Other Payment Methods

The billing and collection methods just discussed apply only to 900-number calls. There are several other ways to charge for pay-per-call information or entertainment services over the telephone. Some are legitimate, others are at best misleading, and a few are flatly illegal. The following are some of the legitimate billing and payment options:

Telecards (or Prepaid Calling Cards). Besides two-way long distance, telecards are increasingly being used for access to enhanced services. Stop at any Total Petroleum gas station and purchase its $10 telecard that gives you a total of 38 minutes of long-distance calling or enhanced information services. The information services include news, sports, stock prices, weather and travel information. It also includes an option for recharging the card (putting more money into the card to replace the spent minutes) using a credit card and an automated interactive program for capturing the credit card information, a feature common to many telecards.

IdealDial in Denver is one of the first service bureaus to install a telecard platform. The stand-alone system costs about $250,000 to install, and is completely independent from the other voice processing systems in the facility (it is linked, however, to the VRUs via T-1 connections). As a service bureau with numerous turnkey audiotex programs already in place, it can offer enhanced services as an option on telecards using its platform. Or a custom program could be designed to become one of the calling options on the telecard.

Ron Kubicki at IdealDial feels that the telecard market is ready to explode, and that enhanced information services will become a standard element in the mix, along with the usual long-distance access. For example, one of IdealDial's new products is Tell-a-Thought, and here's how it works: Hubby goes to the florist and buys a dozen roses for his wife, along with a Tell-a-Thought telecard, which the florist either gives away as part of the purchase or sells separately. Hubby dials the 800 number on the card and inputs a PIN number, leaving a private voice message for his wife. She gets the same telecard, along with the flowers, calls the 800 number and inputs the same PIN number, and hears hubby's romantic message (or his lame excuse for being a day late!). Other uses are for technical support and customer service, and there is really no limitation on what kinds of pay-per-call applications could be sold via a telecard.

Bob Bentz at Advanced Telecom Services, Wayne, Pennsylvania, uses an outside telecard platform service provider. He has provided enhanced telecard services for the popular country and western band Alabama and for celebrity wrestler Hulk Hogan. One of his biggest telecard customers is a cellular company that uses telecards with enhanced information services to get its customers to use their cellular phones more. The actual call is routed as follows: The caller dials an 800 number which comes into the telecard platform located in Florida. If the caller is making a simple long-distance call another outbound 800 call is placed to the destination, completely bypassing Advanced Telecom Services. On the other hand, if the caller selects one of the enhanced information services, such as weather, the call is forwarded to Advanced Telecom Service's voice processing system.

Gene Chamson of Gateway Communications (510-339-3646) recently introduced a telecard in honor of Pope John Paul II. The $10 card provides 20 minutes of long-distance calling or access to the Pope's weekly message from St. Peter's Square in Rome. The card features a color photo of the Pope in full regalia. The Pope's message is updated every week and lasts six to eight minutes, concluding with his solemn blessing in Latin.

The obvious advantage to a telecard for the IP is that he gets all his money up front. The challenge becomes distribution — how to get the telecards into the hands of the end-users and how to collect payment from them. Telecards are beginning to be sold in grocery stores and other point-of-sale retail outlets. Telecard vending machines are also popping up all over. For technical support and customer service applications, the telecard would be included with the product fulfillment as an introductory free service with an option to purchase more by recharging the card when it runs out.

In this way a telecard is being used as a loss-leader. According to IdealDial's Kubicki, one-third of their telecard minutes are from recharged cards, so a large percentage of customers are finding them convenient enough to continue using over and over. Plenty of people use telecards: students, travellers and mobile workers (from hotel rooms or cars), people with bad credit, foreigners, telecommuters or anyone without an unblocked residential phone in his or her name. Since few of these people have access to 900 numbers anyway, telecards become a natural alternative for giving them access to your program. You could even advertise a 900-number alternative on the telecard itself for when the card runs out. Indeed, this is a great way to promote any program, to prospects or to the media. Give them 5 or 10 free minutes with the telecard to get them into the program, then let them get further access by recharging it or by calling a 900 number. The customer will appreciate having some convenient options for payment.

As you can imagine, telecards are becoming quite popular for adult programs. There are no restrictions on content, and the card itself can feature an alluring advertisement for the service. According to Jim White at Worldwide Communications, a service bureau in Westlake Village, California, "The key with telecards is point of sale, getting them into the hands of the customer." His adult telecards are distributed through adult bookstores and men's clubs, and there is enough mark-up built into the $2.49 per-minute typical charge for live one-on-one conversation that the cards can go through a couple of levels of distribution (wholesaler and dealer) with everyone making some money.

As of this writing the use of telecards for pay-per-call services is still new. The trade publications listed in Appendix A will keep you up-to-date with developments. For specific details about the telecard industry itself, write for a sample issue of the leading industry trade magazine:

Intele-card News
Quality Publishing, Inc., 317 Sawdust Rd.
The Woodlands, TX 77380; 713-362-7141

According to Robert Lorsch, President of Smartalk, one of the largest distributors of prepaid calling cards, this industry is growing very fast, reaching $3 billion in 1996 after being in existence for only three years. Smartalk distributes to drug stores, 7-Eleven convenience stores and various other retail outlets.

Smartalk Teleservices, Inc.
2934½ Beverly Glen Circle, Suite 390
Los Angeles, CA 90077; 310-440-5051

800 Credit Card. This payment option is also a safe one for the IP, reducing the potential for chargebacks and fraud. The caller uses his or her credit card to pay for access to the program. The credit card information can be taken by an operator or captured with an automated voice response system. The IP gets his money almost instantly, usually deposited into his bank account within three days of the transaction. This payment option is popular with adult programming. One of the leading companies in this area is R.j. (sic) Gordon & Company, a consulting and financial services company that will set up an IP with a credit card merchant account and fraud control programs:

R.j. Gordon & Company
9200 Sunset Blvd., Suite 515
Los Angeles, CA 90069; 310-278-8080

Checks by Phone. This is a method of creating a check using special software designed for this purpose. The customer either faxes a voided copy of one of his checks or gives the necessary account and bank information to the service provider over the phone, who in turn uses the special software to print a check, which includes all the necessary banking information, using the required magnetic ink in his printer. In lieu of a signature, a statement such as this appears on the signature line: "No signature required. Depositor guarantees that check is authorized." The service provider simply deposits the check with his next deposit at his own bank.

AmeriNet, Inc., in Portland, Oregon (800-800-0467) is a company that specializes in processing checks by telephone, with service bureaus as its primary customers. A caller to an adult service, for example, is given "Telcash" check by phone as one of the payment options (instead of 900-number or credit card). If this option is selected the call is redirected to AmeriNet where a live operator takes all the required information. Besides the banking information, the operator gets the caller's name, date of birth, social security number, and the amount the caller wants to spend. This information is compared against a "deadbeat file," as a fraud control measure, and the caller's bank is called to verify the account information.

Say the caller elected to spend $100 with this method. AmeriNet gives the caller a new 800 number and a PIN number for access to the adult service, and the caller uses up the $100 in much the same manner as a prepaid telecard. AmeriNet's call-accounting equipment tracks the time remaining for the caller, with an automated voice stating how much money is remaining each time the caller dials the service. Like the prepaid telecard, the service is paid for in advance, which reduces the incidence of fraud and chargebacks.

It's likely that other payment options for pay-per-call will emerge over time. Debit cards, ATM cards and other electronic methods will become available for use with pay-per-call programs. It's important to keep in mind that the actual billing and payment mechanism is purely incidental, as long as it's effective.

International Programs

These calls terminate in foreign countries, but the IPs marketing the programs are usually based in the U.S. Such programs are attempts to use regular tariffed transport for pay-per-call purposes, which is at best misleading.

According to Brian O'Connor, chief of the Policy & Facilities Branch, Telecommunications Division, at the FCC International Bureau, the FCC has taken the position that using international dialing for audiotex or pay-per-call services is not legal. It is the FCC's position that common carriers engaged in such practices are not providing common carrier communications under both the letter and the spirit of the law.

The problem stems in part from a loophole in the Telephone Disclosure and Dispute Resolution Act (TDDRA), which defines pay-per-call service as "accessed through use of a 900 number," and exempts from the definition "any service the charge for which is tariffed." This narrow definition of pay-per-call has prevented TDDRA's consumer protection provisions from being applied to alternative non-900 dialing patterns, including international.

The passage of the Telecommunications Act of 1996 will help close this loophole. Section 701 allows federal regulatory agencies to extend the definition of pay-per-call services to include tariffed services providing audio information or entertainment.

10XXX. This signifies an access code, known as a carrier identification code (CIC), to a specific long-distance carrier. There is nothing inherently questionable with these numbers themselves – every long-distance carrier has one. All carriers are assigned such three-digit access codes, which allow a caller to use any long-distance carrier from any telephone by simply dialing the access code first. The three Xs can be any number between 1 and 9, and have nothing to do with a Triple X Adults-Only rating, as it might seem to imply. Nevertheless, some IPs use these numbers for access to adult services. Such services have terminated through a carrier located in Canada, or have been used to redirect a call to an 011 international destination. The IP makes his money as a commission on the call revenue collected by the foreign telephone company.

809 Area Code. This is the area code for several Caribbean countries, which are included in the North American Numbering Plan, and can be dialed like any U.S. or Canadian location. These calls usually terminate in the Dominican Republic, but they could go to any country in the Caribbean with an 809 area code. One reason IPs prefer this method over 900 is that 809 numbers are rarely blocked. The information provider gets his money as a commission on the call revenue from the telephone company in that country, usually between 15 and 40 cents a minute.

011 International. This is the access code for international calls (outside of the North American Numbering Plan, which includes the U.S., Canada and the Caribbean), which can terminate virtually anywhere in the world. These programs terminate in places such as Israel, Hong Kong, Holland, Sao Tome, Moldavia and others. Again, these are usually adult programs, and the country where the calls terminate typically does not have prohibitions or stringent laws about providing adult services, at least to callers from outside the country. Some of these countries' telephone companies artificially inflate the calling charges in order to attract heavy-hitting IPs who generate lots of minutes. Like 809 calling, the IP gets a commission on the call revenue.

Illegal Practices

Illegal methods are usually redirect schemes, where the caller dials one number, which is then typically forwarded onto an expensive international number. The advertised number can be any kind of number, including a regular POTS line or an 800 line. These schemes are all blatantly illegal.

A common redirect scheme uses a 500 number (used legitimately as a "follow-me-anywhere" number for people on the move) that is forwarded to an international adult line. The whole purpose here is to mislead the caller into thinking that he is calling a no-cost or low-cost service, with no price disclosure in the advertising, when in fact he will be charged for expensive international rates. It is harder to dispute these charges because they appear in the long-distance section of the phone bill, not as a separate pay-per-call charge, as 900 would be billed.

The Congress and the FCC are pushing hard to keep pay-per-call on 900 lines (calls that are billed on the phone bill, not 800 credit card or telecard calls) because the public already knows that they must pay extra for such calls. At an October 24, 1995 conference sponsored by the U.S. Department of Consumer Affairs, FTC and FCC staffers indicated that "there are relatively few problems associated with the use of 900-number services today." (ISA Public Policy Update, 10/26/95).

Given the uncertainty surrounding the legality of using international dialing for pay-per-call audiotex services, and the relative stability and acceptance of 900 numbers, some IPs are playing it safe by avoiding all international dialing schemes. It's too risky because the plug can be pulled at any time.

Instant Market Testing

Another unique advantage to 900 is instant market testing. Most service bureaus offer instant call-count information. Call at any time of the day to find out how many calls or call minutes have been generated by your program for the day. Many of these services are automated and menu-driven, so you can select specific information you want about call volume to your program — hourly counts, daily counts, or cumulative counts for the week.

Then, each month you receive a detailed report summarizing this information, including daily calls, billable minutes, peak call times, average hold time, and just about anything you need to know about the incoming calls. Many service bureaus can customize the monthly reports to suit your specific requirements.

The market testing ramifications of this are obvious: You can instantly measure the effectiveness of your advertising. You know what day your ad hits the streets, so call in for the next few days to see how many calls it has generated. If the results are good, you commit to the next issue or increase the size of the ad. If the results are way below expectations, cancel the next issue and stop wasting money immediately.

We'll talk more about market testing later. Suffice to say that the 900 industry offers the unique capability to instantly measure marketing effectiveness. And in an advertising-driven business, this is no small advantage. You will quickly learn how to most wisely spend your advertising dollars, achieving maximum efficiency quickly and cost-effectively.

Direct Response

How do customers actually purchase your 900-number service? It couldn't be any easier: They pick up the telephone and dial your number. No credit cards, no checks, no mailing. All they need is a telephone. If you offer information they need on a regular basis, they might just slip your phone number into their wallets and become regular customers.

Your customers have instant and easy access to your service from virtually every residential telephone in the country. You have a business with a national market that can be operated out of your home. Very low overhead, very high income potential.

It's called Direct Response. Someone sees your ad, which offers something they want, and they call your 900 number. The cost of your service is simply added to their telephone bill. And they didn't even need a credit card because their local telephone company automatically gives them credit for up to 30 days. They don't have to send away for anything, or talk to an operator to process an order. It couldn't be any easier to purchase your information or entertainment service.

Direct response has been around for quite awhile. You have probably used it many times with an 800 number. Records, cassettes and CDs have been big direct response sellers. Direct response is the only way you can order those melodious Slim Whitman albums! Or those incredible Ginzu knives!

With direct response, you usually have to advertise every time you want someone to call; this particular market is very impulse-driven. If customers don't call the first time they see, read or hear your ad, you have probably lost them. Advertising drives calls. Stop your advertising, and calls quickly dry up.

Yes, this is a really easy business to launch, but success is by no means guaranteed. Pay careful attention to the rest of this book, and avoid some of the pitfalls associated with the 900 industry. Be completely prepared before you jump headlong into launching a 900 program.

The Problems

To be completely fair, we must address some of the shortcomings and pitfalls surrounding the 900 industry. It is not without its special problems, just like any other business, particularly one that is still experiencing growing pains. Indeed, it's not even certain that the industry will be able to eventually shake off its lingering negative image, and radical measures could become necessary, like getting rid of the 900 prefix and starting fresh with a new number (which will also require a new title for this book!).

Public Perception

An August 1991 *Reader's Digest* article, titled "Dial '900' For Trouble," was typical of the media's early coverage. After citing several ripoff examples, author Remar Sutton stated, "Welcome to the Pandora's box of the 1990s: Let a too-good-to-be-true ad entice you to dial a 900 number and you'll likely find yourself ripped off, knee-deep in sleaze or hounded by bill collectors." This five-page article was completely devoted to the industry's seamy underbelly, including only one short paragraph about legitimate 900 programs.

In 1990 the Consumer Action Group out of San Francisco conducted a "spot check" survey of 144 pay-per-call programs, concluding during an interview on *Good Morning America* that, "many are unfair at any price" and that "they make outlandish promises." Of course, no mention was made how the 144 programs were selected, and it is very unlikely that this was a scientifically defensible random survey of the some 10,000 pay-per-call programs in existence at the time.

As we all know, the media has an unfortunate penchant for sensationalism — seeking the most titillating slant on the story. The 900 industry is particularly vulnerable to this kind of reporting as long as dial-a-porn or ripoff programs play even a small part.

The January 20, 1992 issue of *New York* featured a blatantly biased article, titled 900-DIAL-NOW, by Bernice Kanner, who admitted that her "warm-up was to chose from among 970 hot lines with DYKE, PERV, TOOL, and GENT in the suffix." Her inevitable conclusion was that "many lines are dial-a-porns that hook the caller for long periods while the meter runs." (We dare not ask whether she was one of the callers who was hooked!) From the overall tone of the article, and the selection of 900 numbers sampled, it appeared that her source for the 900 numbers came from the pages of Al Goldstein's *Screw* Magazine or some other equally erotically inclined periodical.

In January and February, 1991, Multi-Sponsor Surveys of Princeton, New Jersey, conducted a national survey (this one was conducted properly and scientifically) of 2,049 adults, titled "The Gallup Study of Consumer Attitudes and Response to 900 Numbers." The results, although not surprising, painted a fairly dim picture of the public's attitude toward pay-per-call services.

In the sample, nearly 70% of the respondents agreed with the statement, "I never considered calling a 900 line," and only 12% had ever used 900 services. Very few of the respondents agreed with the statements, "For the money you pay, 900 numbers offer useful and valuable information," or, "Most 900 numbers offer legitimate products and services."

Multi-Sponsor President Leonard Wood stated that, "a relatively large proportion were unable to either agree or disagree with each statement. This is likely due to the low level of familiarity with and usage of 900 numbers." He goes on to say, "those respondents most familiar with 900 numbers and those who have dialed 900 numbers are the groups most likely to have positive attitudes toward caller-paid services."

What all this means is that the 900 industry has an enormous credibility gap to overcome. When most of the population won't even consider using 900 services, the potential market size is slashed very dramatically.

Yes, things are changing, but very slowly. Some of the more responsible media, such as *U.S. News & World Report*, have featured positive, well-balanced articles about the industry. Many reputable companies and media sources have recently joined the 900 industry with useful, valuable information programs. This helps establish the legitimacy of the whole industry. *Money* Magazine ran a recent article titled, "When It Can Pay To Dial 900 For A Pro's Help," which profiled several helpful live 900 programs featuring legal, financial, and insurance information. *Newsweek* is now using a 900 number for callers to express their opinions in the letters-to-the-editor section.

The December 7, 1991 issue of the *New York Times* carried an excellent article by Leonard Stone about live professional services, titled "Pay-per-Minute Phone Advice Gets Personal and Professional." Similarly, the March 1993 issue of *Home Office Computing* featured an objective article by Alan Rider, titled 1-900-BUY-INFO, that discussed selling professional advice over a 900 line and profiled a Los Angeles attorney who was doing just that.

The July 28, 1993 issue of the *New York Times,* in discussing the new FTC regulations governing the 900 industry, stated, "Since their introduction about five years ago, '900' services have proliferated into a vast collection of offerings, from news headlines and sports scores to astrology advice, recorded messages from celebrities, 'adult' chat lines and contests offering money and prizes. Many newspapers use them to complement their published product, and some nonprofit organizations use them as a method for soliciting contributions."

The September 21, 1994 issue of *Newsday* carried an article titled, "Adventures in 900 Land," by Stephen Williams, which described numerous programs that Williams called. This was a fair representation of the variety of choices, and Williams was impartial in his evaluations.

The September 4, 1995 issue of *DM News* (Direct Marketing) featured a factual article by Dan Miller that described the positive direction the industry is taking, particularly in customer service and technical support.

It is apparent from the sequence of these articles that the coverage of the 900 industry is gradually getting fairer, if not downright positive. Honest commentators who do their homework can no longer accuse 900 numbers as being the sole purveyors of filth and sleaze. Public perception has no place to go but up.

And don't forget, the demographics of the adult population is continually changing as more and more teenagers reach adulthood. These young, electronically literate adults are much more likely to embrace all kinds of convenient 900 services, and their numbers increase daily.

Regulation and Oversight

The legal environment surrounding the 900 industry used to be a veritable quagmire. Prior to 1992, the FTC, the FCC, Congress, and many state attorneys-general all jumped onto the regulatory bandwagon with uncommon zeal. In some cases, conflicting regulations made it almost impossible to comply with everyone's rules at the same time. Particularly problematic were the efforts of individual states to regulate what is effectively an interstate industry.

Fortunately, this regulatory mess has been improved significantly by the enactment of Federal Law. On October 28, 1992, President Bush signed into law The Telephone Disclosure and Dispute Resolution Act (TDDRA), which was a compromise between the Senate's "900 Services Consumer Protection Act of 1991" (S. 1579) and the House bill, H.R. 3490, the "Telephone Disclosure and Dispute Resolution Act."

TDDRA required both the FCC and the FTC to promulgate rules for enforcement of its provisions, which both agencies completed by August of 1993. See Appendix E for a summary of the ensuing regulations promulgated by the FCC and the FTC.

Besides outlawing obvious illegal practices, the most important provisions of the regulations set standard preamble requirements, allow free one-time blocking of 900 services by residential subscribers, and prohibit disconnection of telephone services for non-payment of 900 charges.

The preamble is required on all programs costing more than $2 for a flat-rate call, or for all calls that are usage priced (per minute). The caller cannot be charged for the time it takes to listen to the preamble message, so the call charges must begin when it ends. The preamble must contain the following information:

- ❏ Name of the Information Provider.
- ❏ Brief description of the service.
- ❏ Price of the call, including average length of call for per-minute charged calls.
- ❏ Notice to the caller that billing will not start until three seconds after the preamble and that he or she may hang up before the program begins without charge.
- ❏ When a 900 program is marketed to or could be of interest to minors (under 18 years of age), they must be warned to hang up if they don't have parental permission.

A significant benefit with these new Federal rules is that states are now dissuaded from imposing preamble requirements or other restrictions on interstate calls that are inconsistent with those adopted by the FCC and FTC.

Although many in the 900 industry dreaded the prospect of federal regulation, reasonable federal regulation of interstate 900 services is surely preferable to the confusing tangle of state legislation that plagued the industry prior to TDDRA. One set of fair rules make life easier for everybody.

The regulatory environment for the 900 industry may remain fluid for a few more years. Despite TDDRA, several states have enacted their own 900 legislation that is more onerous than TDDRA. Some of the publications and organizations listed in the Resource Guide stay up-to-date on industry-related legislation and will be good sources for keeping current.

Chargebacks

Every business experiences bad debt of some sort. Any business that extends credit terms to its customers will run into people who don't pay their bills. Some don't pay because they are unhappy with the service. Others might be satisfied with the service but are either broke or dishonest. Most businesses will check out a prospective customer before extending credit by having the customer fill out a credit application and then checking references and credit history. Even with such safeguards in place bad debt will happen. This is a normal cost of doing business and must be accounted for when developing a budget.

Bad debts in the 900 business are known as chargebacks. While a return of merchandise, defective or otherwise, isn't the same as a bad debt, it is also somewhat analogous to a 900 chargeback. At least in a situation where the customer was legitimately unhappy with the service in question. The customer obviously cannot return the information received, but the IP can certainly refund the money charged.

Returns are also a customary business expense that should be anticipated by any business. The conventional wisdom is that returns below 10% indicates that you are offering a good product at a reasonable price. A rate higher than this either means that people are unhappy with the product, that it is not meeting expectations, or that the price is too high. This 10% rule of thumb works fine with merchandise, but it doesn't necessarily work for 900, as you'll see later.

Chargebacks invariably fall into one of the following categories:

- Fraud — no intention of paying.
- Dissatisfied with the service — unwilling to pay.
- Unauthorized access — minors, houseguests or workmen.
- Inability to pay — broke.
- Timeliness of bill — can't remember making the call.
- Lack of sufficient detail on the bill — can't recognize what charge is for.

Chargebacks are one of the most intractable problems associated with the 900-number industry. The legislation governing pay-per-call went overboard in its consumer protection provisions, in large measure a result of the early abuses by unscrupulous players. This is the only industry where the government mandates that you must tell your customers, in so many words, that they do not have to pay their bill!

Every time 900 charges appear on the phone bill a statement must appear that informs the consumer that his or her telephone service cannot be disconnected for non-payment of the 900 service bill. This is required by federal law. Here is a verbatim statement from my latest phone bill, appearing after some 900 charges I racked up recently:

Pay-per-call services - Local or long-distance services cannot be disconnected for non-payment of these non-communications services. Payment of disputed charges is not required while such charges are under investigation. Failure to pay legitimate charges may result in further collection actions by information providers and access to pay-per-call services may be denied. 900 number blocking is available upon request.

This statement is a tempting invitation to ignore the 900 charges with near impunity. What other business is required by law to tell its customers that they can effectively disregard the bill?

Walt Zadanoff, who operates a voice personals program and has published *Contemporary Singles Life* Magazine in Las Vegas for the past five years, calls this requirement "a license to steal granted by the federal government." Before the law went into effect requiring this statement on the bill, chargebacks to his voice personals program were zero. Everybody paid their bills, and were quite obviously happy with the service provided.

As soon as the statements started inviting people to ignore the bills, Zadanoff's chargeback rates soared to between 10 and 25 percent. There was no change in the service provided, and the market demographics were the same. The difference could be attributed to only one thing: His customers were now being told that they did not have to pay their 900 bill.

There is no question that this voice personals service is a good one, because Zadanoff works hard to achieve a 90% call-back rate to respondents, an impressive rate for any similar service. In fact, he used to *guarantee* call-backs until the chargeback issue arose. Now he loses too much money to uncollectibles to be able to offer such a guarantee any more. This is an example of how service was in fact diminished as a result of legislation that supposedly helps and protects consumers. In this case the opposite happened, and service had to be curtailed.

Zadanoff feels that government was "too overzealous in its effort to protect the consumer, and didn't think about the ramifications to the service provider, who has no protection and no recourse." The statement, "Failure to pay legitimate charges may result in further collection actions by information providers and access to pay-per-call services may be denied" is weak and doesn't really scare anyone. Many people have figured out that they can get away with not paying, and they abuse the opportunity at every chance.

In fact, Zadanoff's collection efforts were usually unsuccessful because the worst abusers intentionally ran up a big 900 bill during the course of one month, and then moved away from that address. By the time he received his chargeback documentation some two or three months after the fact, 60 to 70 percent of the phones were disconnected and no forwarding address was available. These people knew how the system worked and abused it intentionally.

Kevin Frace at International Telemedia Associates (ITA), a leading third-party billing company in this industry, reports similar chargeback rates. Four years ago, before the non-payment statement began appearing on the phone bills, chargebacks averaged between 20% and 22%. Now they average about 30%. It should be noted, however, that ITA's customers are heavily weighted towards the adult and entertainment side of the industry, which have historically had the worst chargeback rates. ITA's professional lines, on the other hand, average between 15% and 20%.

The IP must realize fully what is happening here. He is automatically extending credit terms to anyone who calls his program without ever checking into the caller's payment history. And he has little or no leverage to collect for legitimate charges when someone decides not to pay the bill. Few companies are willing to do business this way. It isn't the same as a return of merchandise in this respect, because payment has not yet been made. With a return, the customer has already paid for the merchandise, and must take action to return the product to get a refund or a credit. This requires some effort on the part of the customer, which generally precludes action unless the customer is truly unhappy with the purchase.

With a chargeback, all the customer has to do is ignore the bill, or at least dispute it by calling the phone company. Considerably less effort than returning a product. The caller already has the information or entertainment from the program, which once given can never be repossessed. This explains why chargebacks can be such a problem in this industry. Indeed, given the fact that blanket credit is being extended to essentially everyone, it could be argued that chargebacks are fairly reasonable under the circumstances. Perhaps the rates currently being experienced are about as good as we should reasonably expect. Chargebacks have become an ordinary business expense that must be included in the budget of any 900 service provider.

The phone company can disconnect service if that portion of the bill is not paid. The IP has no such leverage. The IP can block the telephone numbers of problem customers, but that happens only after getting burned at least once. Zadanoff's worst problems are with people who run up $200 and $300 bills in one month and then skip.

Not all information providers have the same experience as Zadanoff. Peter Brennan at Tele-Publishing in Boston, a major voice personals service bureau with some 300 newspapers using its voice personals service, reports average chargebacks of about five percent. With more than 300 newspapers and cable companies figuring into the calculation, this rate is a good representation of a broad, demographically diverse population. It should be noted, however, that these voice personals programs are advertised under the imprimatur of the host newspaper, lending solid credibility to the service. There are apparently some unexplained demographic quirks happening in Las Vegas (where Zadanoff's customers are located) for it to be so much worse than other areas. Too many transient gamblers with bad luck at the tables?

Earlier we discussed Tele-Lawyer, a live legal-advice service, which is getting chargebacks of less than one percent. There are programs out there with very low chargeback rates, so we must be careful about making broad generalizations. There is hope of achieving acceptable chargeback rates as long as the service is good. Perhaps the 900 industry must simply try harder than others in providing impeccable service that fully meets or exceeds the customer's expectations.

Canadian phone companies have learned from her neighbor to the south. A group of them, led by AGT in Alberta, have instituted a countrywide fraud control effort called the Risk Management System (RMS). This system imposes limits on the monthly 900 charges on any one telephone bill. According to George Harvie, the manager of service bureaus and audiotex services at AGT and the architect of RMS, experience has demonstrated that people who run up large 900 bills are either doing it intentionally because they have no intention of ever paying (like Zadanoff's customers) or they may not be able to afford to pay when the bill comes due. Either way a chargeback is the likely result.

One of the main functions of RMS is to keep the customers aware of the total charges that have been accumulated on their 900 bills for the month. This way they are never surprised at the end of the month with a large, unexpected bill that they might have trouble paying. Once callers exceeds $100 in 900 service charges, they are informed via a recording that they have exceeded $100 in charges for the calendar month. When they reach $250 they are informed that they have exceeded $200 in charges and are not allowed further access to 900 services for that month.

Callers can contact the phone company and negotiate a higher limit if they wish, and a handful have done so. Most people, however, seem to be satisfied with this policy and really don't want to spend much more than $200 on 900 services in a given month. According to Harvie, many people just don't realize how quickly the higher per-minute charges can add up, and this reminder really helps prevent that from happening.

This system also maintains a "deadbeat" file of callers with a history of chargebacks, and they are prevented from getting access to any 900 service. Harvie's statistics show that 65% of the chargebacks are caused by only 6% of the callers. These are obviously intentional abusers that shouldn't be allowed to continue stealing from service providers with impunity.

What make this service unique is that it is provided by the phone companies at the network level. Bad credit risks are not allowed access to the telephone network when dialing 900 numbers. The Canadian telephone companies have taken a proactive role in trying to help reduce chargebacks even before they become a problem. The IPs and the service bureaus get some very real and valuable help from the telephone companies, who are truly earning the fees they collect for billing and collections. Harvie takes pride in *earning* his 10% billing and collection fee, and feels that all phone companies should be extending the service provided by RMS.

The Risk Management System is a big success. Chargebacks were averaging 12% before RMS was introduced on June 1, 1995. Since the inception of the program the chargeback rate has dropped to about half that rate. There is no question that this system works.

An interesting consequence of RMS has been the chargeback experiences of the Canadian phone companies that have not yet joined the system. Since the RMS was instituted, non-RMS telcos have seen their chargeback rates *increase*. This is likely the result of the intentional abusers migrating over to carriers that haven't yet cut them off.

Snake-Oil Hucksters

There are still plenty of fast-buck artists and less-than-reputable players in the 900 industry. As government legislation and industry self-regulation begins to clean up the industry, some of these individuals appear to be shifting their focus from ripping off the calling public to picking the pockets of would-be IPs.

Maybe you have seen an ad or attended a seminar with statements like, "acquire your own 900 number before the government limits the amount of numbers," or, "purchase the rights to one or more 900 numbers and lease the rights to others for monthly profits." These statements are generally accompanied by a hard sell for you to part with a substantial sum of money before it's too late.

Here's a verbatim statement from an actual seminar flier: "Ordinary people like you and I are making billions of dollars from 900 numbers." The entire 900 industry hasn't yet reached the billion-dollar mark, so it's kind of unlikely that any one individual is doing quite so well. Also, these seminars rarely mention the advertising expenses that would be required to achieve the call volume they proclaim is so quick and easy to get.

Back in July 1993 I received an invitation in the mail to attend a two-day Home Business & Technology seminar at the Marriott Hotel in Providence, Rhode Island. Because 900 was one of the topics I decided to attend. I sat through two presentations on the first morning. There were probably 300 people in the audience. The first segment was about joining an organization where you could purchase distressed or close-out goods at a fraction of the retail cost and re-sell them at a huge profit. It sounded pretty interesting, and they managed to sign up at least 50 people at $495 each.

The second presentation was about a new way of teaching math to kids, and the business opportunity was to hold classes in your home using this system. This system was very interesting, fascinating actually, but no mention was made about zoning, licensing, insurance or any other hurdles to teaching children at home. Again, the cost for this system was around $500, and another 50 or so converts rushed to the table at the back of the conference room to sign up.

I was beginning to get the uneasy feeling that these people could make a septic tank cleaning business sound like the most glamorous business opportunity of the century. These guys could sell sand to a Saudi or ice to an Eskimo.

After lunch, I was convinced. The third presentation was about making a fortune in 900 numbers. Well, I thought, now they're talking about a topic I know something about, so we'll see how accurate they are.

I can't honestly say that there were any blatant lies. Some of their statistics were wrong, such as that the 900 industry revenues had exceeded $2 billion dollars in 1992, when in fact the actual number was less than half that amount. Nonetheless, it's possible that some of these inaccuracies were not intentional misrepresentations. It's only fair to note that a certain degree of "puffery" should be expected from people trying to sell you something, and it's quite natural to emphasize the benefits while downplaying or ignoring the shortcomings. All advertising is done this way. When was the last time you saw an ad that mentioned the shortcomings of the featured product?

You should be aware, however, that 900 has been oversold as a get-rich-quick business opportunity because it can be made to sound so easy, and the unique benefits we discussed earlier are very real. At the seminar I attended, the guy making the pitch did a masterful job of exaggerating those benefits, such as giving an example of a program that generated a zillion calls, but leaving out a minor detail on how much advertising was spent to generate that call volume. I guess he didn't think the audience was smart enough to understand the difference between gross revenue and net profit, so he just kind of skipped over such an inconvenient detail. IBM has gross revenues in the billions of dollars, yet it has still managed to *lose* millions of dollars in the past. Few of us can afford to lose hundreds of dollars, let alone millions.

Anyway, they were offering a package of three passive 900 lines where you had to charge $2 or $3 a minute for a *recorded* message, not even a turnkey program where you can use an established dating or sports line. No, the IP had to come up with a recorded message that would be sold for $2 or $3 a minute, an impossibly high amount.

To create a sense of urgency, the audience was warned that they had better buy their 900 numbers before the government placed limits on them, and another 50 or more people rushed back to sign up for a $500 package of 3 lines (passive program only) and an instruction manual consisting of a three-ring binder filled with information of dubious value.

Here's what Bob Bentz says in his book, *Opportunity is Calling* (Appendix C), about the snake-oil business: "I've heard of some travelling carpetbaggers who sell 900 line extensions at seminars in local hotels for as much as $695! Part of the pitch is that 900 numbers are in short supply so you'd better buy one now. Not! There are currently 10,000 900 lines operating and AT&T alone has over 170,000 different 900 numbers available! They are not in short supply. And, if they ever get close to running out, they'll surely make others available."

This is not to say, however, that all 900 seminars are worthless. The publishers of *Audiotex News*, Jerry and Carol Ginsburg, put on an excellent educational seminar through the Learning Annex in New York City and in Washington, DC. Antoinette (Toni) Moore, a 900 consultant and author of *Dialing For Dollars*, conducts valuable seminars for serious IPs in the San Diego area. Keith Mueller of the 900 Advertising Club gives a good one-day seminar about how to market a 900 program. See the Resource Guide for further details about the products and services offered by these experts in the 900 industry. Other seminars emphasize the business and marketing training that are required, and some are genuinely trying to help new IPs learn how to be successful with a 900 program. Some even include this book or my other book, *Money-Making 900 Numbers*, as part of the course materials. Anyone giving away, selling or recommending honest books about the business is helping to point you in the right direction.

Just be aware that by its nature it's easy to oversell the 900-number business. It does indeed have some powerful and unique advantages can be played up while the shortcomings are ignored. In this respect it's a lot like the mail-order business, which has been oversold as a business opportunity for decades. I wouldn't be surprised if 10 years from now 900 (or pay-per-call) is still being touted as a hot get-rich-quick business opportunity.

Dishonest Service Bureaus

We will be discussing service bureaus later in Chapter 7, but it should be mentioned here that a disreputable service bureau can cheat an IP out of a lot of money. They do exist, and you should obviously avoid them. This is particularly problematic if there is no independent or automated means of verifying call counts. If your call count information is limited to a weekly or monthly written report generated by the service bureau itself, there is no way you can independently verify the accuracy of the numbers.

The better service bureaus generally offer automated 24-hour access to call counts, often with a toll-free 800 number. Also, they will often include a copy of the monthly long-distance carrier report (i.e., AT&T, MCI, Sprint) of call volume to the 900 number. These are obviously good features to look for in selecting a service bureau.

900 is No Free Lunch

According to Warren Miller at Telecompute Corporation (Appendix D), who is building a database of all 900 numbers (application category; the name of the IP; etc.), between AT&T and MCI there were about 31,000 900 numbers in June 1995, which accounted for the vast majority at the time. Strategic Telemedia, an industry market research firm, pegs 1995 revenues at $750 million for the telco-billed part of the 900-number industry. By simple division we can calculate the average annual revenue for each 900 number:

$$\$750,000,000 \ / \ 31,000 = \$24,194$$

This number represents the average gross revenue for each 900 number, so we still need to subtract transport charges, service bureau fees, chargebacks, operating and advertising expenses. You can readily see that the average numbers involved aren't quite as exciting as you may have been led to believe. Earning a respectable profit isn't automatic in this business.

According to Bruce Kushnick, the former president of Strategic Telemedia, "80% of IPs do not make their money back. 900 services have attracted entrepreneurs and IP wannabes who see a pot of telecom gold at the end of the phone line. The entry costs to 900 programming are low, and the false promise of getting rich quick has been perpetuated by the industry itself. In most cases, basic marketing principles are often ignored by the entrepreneur."

Success in the pay-per-call industry is by no means guaranteed. You must know what you're getting into, and it will be just as challenging as launching any other kind of business. Sure, there are people making good money in this business. But no one is raking in millions of dollars without expending any significant effort. There is no free lunch with any business, and pay-per-call is no exception.

Chapter 4
Getting Started

The most important decision you will make as you get into this business is deciding what kind of program to offer. This may sound obvious, but a lot of people go about this whole process somewhat backwards. First, they decide to get into the 900-number business, then try to figure out what program to offer. Like deciding to get into the retail business before you have any inkling about what kind of store you want to open.

Remember, you're not getting into the "900-number business." The 900 number is simply one of several ways of delivering your service to your customer. Your actual business is selling some kind of information or entertainment.

I get calls on my 900 consulting line (see back page) all the time from people who have just purchased a 900 number, and are now wondering what to do with it. I tell them that having a 900 number is of no importance whatsoever. It's completely useless without a marketable service to sell. Getting the number before having anything to sell is like getting a post office box before deciding to start a mail-order company. It certainly doesn't make sense to rush out and get it before doing anything else, because it's clearly of minor importance to the business as a whole. Sure, you'll need the 900 line (or post office box) eventually, but that is a relatively minor detail that deserves only passing attention.

The smart entrepreneur starts the process already knowing *what* he or she is going to sell, and to *whom*. The nature of the business – retail, manufacturing, service, 900-number information service or mail order – is usually of only incidental importance. What is most important is *what's* being sold, not the *means* for getting it to the customer.

Nonetheless, many people will choose a certain type of business they wish to start first, before focusing on the options within that category. Joe Gladhand decides to get into retail because he loves contact with people and working on weekends. Mary Mailer gets into mail-order because she wants to work from home and stay near the kids.

Because you're reading this book you are at least interested in learning more about this business. Maybe you haven't yet zeroed in on a specific idea. This chapter will help you focus your efforts in the right direction.

Research

When you start any new business you begin by collecting as much information as possible. The 900 business is no exception. Appendix C lists several publications that you should purchase. *Money-Making 900 Numbers* will give you a good overview of the kinds of programs that are out there. *Opportunity is Calling*, by Bob Bentz, is written from the perspective of a service bureau marketing director who has seen thousands of 900 applications, from the success stories to the failures. *The Audiotex News Resource Guide* is another invaluable resource, including lists of service bureaus, 900 advertising agencies, 900 consultants, and other sources for audiotex products and services.

You should also subscribe to one or more of the leading trade magazines or newsletters in order to keep current. Also, attending a trade show is a quick way of making contacts and learning about the business. You will meet and talk to people from service bureaus, long-distance carriers, equipment vendors, 900 advertising agencies, and program sponsors, to name just a few. You will also learn about what kinds of programs are out there, how are they marketed, and where to go for help. This will be your fastest and most direct method of gathering valuable information about the 900 industry.

At the same time, pay attention to media advertising for 900 programs. Get a good feel for the types of programs being offered and where they are being advertised. Vary your TV viewing and radio listening habits, perhaps even recording a good sampling of 900 commercials. Make a habit of buying different publications and clipping out print advertising. Develop a file of 900 advertising, paying particular attention to repeat advertising, because this usually indicates a successful program.

Study what appear to be the most successful ads – how are they different? How did they grab your attention? For radio and TV, what time of day or night do they normally appear, and on what networks or stations? We'll talk more about this in the next chapter about market research, but suffice it to say, pay close attention to the ads which are repeating regularly over a long period of time. The advertiser has already spent a considerable amount of time and money testing different media and ads, so you might as well learn something from his or her experience and investment of advertising dollars.

Call several kinds of 900 programs. Hear what type of information they offer, and how they handle the interactive menu selections. No amount of verbiage from a book such as this will give you a true picture of how these programs can work. Call them, and you will get valuable ideas on how interactive programs can be designed.

Now there is a way to find out how many competitors you are likely to run up against in any given program category. Telecompute Corp., a service bureau based in Washington, DC (Appendix D), maintains a database of some 40,000 active 900 numbers, including the IP name and address, program category and price. The database can be searched by any of these criteria and a custom report generated. For example, you could ask for a list of California-based IPs offering voice personals programs charging callers less than $2 per minute. This is one method of quantifying your potential competition before launching your program.

If you don't already have an idea for a program, don't make a hard commitment to any specific 900 application until after you have completed your preliminary research. Having some general ideas is fine, but financial commitment might not be. Finish reading this book, then get some of the other publications listed in the appendices. Talk to people at service bureaus, and attend a pay-per-call conference. Then read this book a second time — with a little bit of wisdom, some of the advice may take on an entirely different meaning.

Your 900 Idea

What if you have this great idea, and after reviewing all the most logical media sources for possible competitors, you find none. No competition. This could mean one of three things. First, your idea is so unique and revolutionary that no one else has thought about it yet, or at least their programs haven't yet hit the streets. Second, your idea simply won't work or has been tried and failed. Or third, you idea is in fact already being used, but it's being advertised in specialized media that you haven't been exposed to yet.

Be careful about the first conclusion. There are scores of very imaginative entrepreneurs in this industry, and the fact that your idea hasn't been tried should be a danger signal — not an invitation to plunge headlong into a program that might flop miserably. This does not mean, however, that you should discount any novel application simply because there's no competition. That's not being very entrepreneurial! It simply means that you need to do some further digging until you are completely satisfied that there is no good reason for the lack of competition.

Make sure that your idea is suitable for a 900 application. Is there an easier or cheaper way for your target market to get the information? Will someone actually pick up the phone and pay his or her hard-earned money for your information or entertainment service?

As mentioned earlier, weather information is timely, and seems to fit the criteria for a successful 900 application. But what are the potential caller's other sources for this information? If he has cable TV, he can tune into the Weather Channel. If he has a boat, he tunes his radio into the marine weather frequency. Or maybe he simply calls his local weather bureau. If he's travelling by car, he listens to the radio. It is doubtful that you can compete with those free sources of information by offering general weather information.

But how about some truly unique or specialized weather information? In California, you can call a 900 line to get the latest surf conditions at the beach. For the avid surfer who lives 50 miles from the beach, this is very valuable information. It can save a wasted trip, consuming valuable time and gas only to find out that the surfing conditions are pathetic.

Offering specialized weather information to a small specialized market will not work in a small town. There just aren't enough people to generate sufficient call volume. But it will certainly work in a large metropolitan area such as Los Angeles or Miami. And it's pretty easy to get the word out to your market through the area surf shops or radio stations.

How's this one for a great idea: a specialized 900 service that offers up-to-the-minute information on nightlife, restaurants, tourist attractions, sporting events, and cultural activities for visitors to your city? Great idea, right? Wrong! Tourists stay in hotels, which do not offer 900 calling services from the rooms. And trying to get them to call from home prior to leaving on the trip will require extensive regional or national advertising to reach them, and then it's unlikely they will want to plan that far in advance anyway.

This is an example of a good idea, with a good targetable market, but with a fatal flaw: There is no way for the target market to purchase your service when they are most likely to need it. At least via a 900 number. This application might work with a prepaid telecard, as discussed in the previous chapter, as long as you can market it effectively.

Good ideas are plentiful and easy to dream up. It's the successful execution of a good idea where the real challenge and talent come into play. This is what separates the dreamers from the doers.

Turnkey Programs

Instead of investing lots of time, money, and effort in developing a brand-new untested program, the budding infopreneur has many opportunities to share existing programs that are already established and successful. For a share of the call revenue, the infopreneur is given an exclusive 900 number (or extension) to promote as he or she sees fit, which taps into the existing 900 program owned by the sponsoring IP, or program sponsor. Many service bureaus offer in-house packaged programs in this manner. Such established programs are also known as "canned" or "turnkey" programs.

Calls to each number are separately accounted for, and revenues are split on a predetermined basis between the infopreneur and the program sponsor. The program sponsor may require a minimum monthly fee to cover the incremental costs associated with adding another 900 line to the program, but this amount is usually much less than what the infopreneur would pay by going it alone.

The program sponsor may also help with marketing efforts or advice. After all, it's a win-win situation for both parties, and higher call volumes benefit both parties. The program sponsor already has a great deal of experience in promoting the program: what type of ad copy works best, and which media pulls in the most calls at the lowest cost-per-call.

There is also strength in numbers. This is particularly true if the program has a recognizable name and everyone uses similar, standardized advertising copy. For example, "Madame Zarra's Horoscopes" or "The Ski Connection" could develop a healthy recognition factor if promoted widely in various media by many infopreneurs. Because repetition breeds credibility, the effort of the group as a whole benefits each individual participant. The fact that the telephone numbers are different is of little consequence. The caller isn't likely to notice, and will simply dial whichever number is immediately at hand.

Program-sharing opportunities run the gamut of 900 applications, including weather, sports, games, jokes, soaps, and horoscopes. This is a trend that will continue to be popular, because everyone is a potential winner. The program sponsor is able to inexpensively broaden his market while spreading out his program and marketing costs, reaching a much larger audience than what he could possibly afford to reach alone. For the participating infopreneur, it's a simple, inexpensive way to get started in the business, while benefitting from the marketing experience of the program sponsor, saving a lot of money on potentially ineffective advertising.

Where can you find out about program-sharing opportunities? Check out the ads in the relevant trade magazines or the Business Opportunity sections of major newspapers or business magazines. Many of the service bureaus listed in Appendix D offer turnkey programs, so ask what types are available. Indeed, many service bureaus are nothing more than IPs that own their call-processing equipment, with excess capacity to handle additional programs for other IPs. Most of these companies actively seek IPs to help promote their programs.

Beware of significant up-front costs. The cost of adding a separate 900 number to an existing program is quite modest. It would not be unreasonable to charge something to cover programming, administration, and accounting costs, so a modest monthly charge would be reasonable.

On the other hand, if the program sponsor is simply offering a separate extension to the 900 number, this normally costs the program sponsor nothing, and a set monthly charge, if any, should be minimal. Although less expensive, the use of extensions cheapens the product, and may not be the best way to promote the program.

Another consideration is call-count verification. Most major service bureaus offer automated access, via telephone, to current call counts to the program, often with a toll-free 800 number. In some cases, the service bureau is a separate, independent entity from the program sponsor. If the infopreneur is given access to call counts to his or her 900 number, through the use of an exclusive access code, it serves as an independent verification of the call volume from the service bureau. This is easily achieved if each infopreneur is assigned a discrete 900 number, but is not generally available when extensions are used (some of the most sophisticated services bureaus, such as West Interactive in Omaha, Nebraska, can track call counts by extension). With extensions, you usually rely exclusively on the honesty of the program sponsor in accounting for calls to your extension.

Besides independent call-count verification, instant telephone access to call counts is very helpful in measuring the success of advertising strategies. Waiting for a two-week-old written call summary report can result in expensive marketing mistakes or lost opportunities.

In general, it is best to avoid programs where call counts cannot be accessed instantly by using an automated interactive telephone program. The notable exception would be where the 900 number spells a highly recognizable word or phrase. In this case it would benefit the infopreneur to use the same 900 number with a separate extension. Just make sure you check out the program sponsor.

The revenue sharing arrangements can be structured in many ways. The program sponsor will be interested in covering his incremental costs for each additional line or extension, but should also want to give the infopreneur sufficient incentive to aggressively market the program. For example, the monthly fee could be "$250 or $0.15 per call minute, whichever is greater." Or a sliding percentage scale could be used based upon monthly call-minute volume, with the infopreneur receiving a greater percentage as volume increases. Regardless of how it is structured, the party doing the marketing – the infopreneur – should receive the largest share of call revenue because marketing is the largest cost component of any 900 program. Be careful with any program that offers a 50-50 or less split, because it may not be a fair division of revenue, unless the program sponsor is also providing significant marketing assistance.

Does anyone actually make any money with the canned programs? Not many. There are only a handful of generic types out there – psychic, voice personals, adult and sports, to name the more popular programs – with a lot of small IPs competing directly with big IPs, like the host newspaper, for a tiny slice of the market. I can't imagine how a small classified add for a voice personals program can possibly draw any calls away from the newspaper's own in-house version that gets four full pages of coverage, along with the credibility of the newspaper itself behind it.

An exception is with adult programs. The design of the ad becomes more important than just about anything else, making it possible for a start-up to compete with the entrenched IPs, as long as he invests enough in attractive display advertising and doesn't make too many marketing blunders early on.

Does this mean that all the other turnkey programs are worthless? Not in the least. A canned program is a low-risk way to get into the business quickly, with little money, and to learn the ropes. A handful of people have indeed made money with turnkey programs, but these are tenacious entrepreneurs who will be successful doing almost anything.

Even if you don't make a lot of money, you won't risk losing much either. It's like investing: the greater the risk, the higher the potential return; lower risk, lower return.

The existing canned programs are targeted to large markets that cost a lot of money to sell to effectively. It is theoretically possible to be successful marketing a canned program to a large homogeneous audience, as long as you have enough money to do it properly. Most start-up IPs don't have those kinds of resources. If you did, you would probably want to start your own custom program, one that you own and control exclusively.

The concept of a turnkey program is a good one. There is no reason even a start-up IP can't take advantage of "canning" his or her program in order to spread out the marketing costs among other like-minded entrepreneurs. The existing canned offerings out there may be a little tired and lacking in promise, but that doesn't mean other more imaginative offerings wouldn't be good investments. We're just waiting for creative entrepreneurs like you to offer us some better choices in turnkey programs.

What Works for 900?

As discussed in Chapter 2, the most obvious fit for a 900 program is timely or specialized information. Timely information changes quickly — weather forecasts, stock prices, sports scores, horse races, currency exchange rates, or flight information. Existing 900 programs already run the gamut of timely information applications, and you will have to use your imagination to come up with original applications in this area that would have broad market appeal.

The options for specialized information, on the other hand, are still wide open. Possible information categories are endless. Here is a small sample:

LAW	HORTICULTURE
ACCOUNTING	COMMUNICATIONS
INSURANCE	TRAVEL
MEDICINE	ENTERTAINMENT
FINANCE	LITERATURE
MANUFACTURING	DIPLOMACY
TRADE	HISTORY
MARKETING	BANKING
CONSTRUCTION	HOBBIES
REAL ESTATE	SPORTS
ENERGY	EDUCATION
POLITICS	RETIREMENT
MUSIC	BUSINESS
CINEMA	TRANSPORTATION
PUBLISHING	APPAREL
INVESTING	FASHION
CHILD CARE	FOOD
FITNESS	SPIRITS
WEALTH	HOME
COMMERCE	ENGINEERING
AGRICULTURE	ARCHITECTURE

This is only a brief listing, and there are hundreds of sub-categories under these headings. Try this for an exercise: Go to the reference section of your nearest large library (or college library) and browse through the reference books. You will find hundreds of information classifications that are obviously useful to someone – or the books would never have been published!

Now, going to the library to dig out a reference book to look up specific information is a time-consuming chore. This is where a 900 program can excel. It's a whole lot more convenient to pick up the telephone, from the comfort of home or the office, at any time of the day or night, and get exactly what you need, when you need it.

Don't forget about business customers — particularly small businesses, many of which lack the staff or resources to have easy access to the wide range of information they need every day. Business customers are easy to target, and they will pay a reasonable fee for convenience.

Too many start-up entrepreneurs limit their thinking to selling to the general public – probably because they're members of that group, along with everyone else. That isn't necessarily the best way to go when starting a new business. Much better to be specialized, offering something of real value to a specialized group that really needs what you are selling in order to succeed. It's easier selling tongue depressors to doctors than selling toothpaste to the masses.

Figure out what will be most valuable to your market. Convenience will always be important. In his book *How to Make Millions With Your Ideas* (Plume/Penguin, 1996), marketing expert Dan Kennedy says, "The most precious commodity of the 1990s is not money, gold, silver, or diamonds — it's time. That's what we have the least of; that's what we'll cheerfully pay to preserve. . . people will pay money for convenience. If you can give people time, you can make a fortune."

Live or Recorded?

If you're going to offer expert advice on WordPerfect® software, you will have to talk to your customers. You will also have to be an indisputable expert in WordPerfect®, and you will be tied to the phone during business hours (accounting for all four U.S. time zones if you're offering your services nationally). You will also need a computer at hand so you can walk through any specific problem with your caller.

Callers expect to pay more for live technical advice, so you may be able to charge $2 to $5 per minute. You will probably get repeat calls until that caller becomes proficient in this software.

There is a limit to how much money you can earn, at least by yourself. A very high call volume would realistically tie you up on the phone 50% of the time during a 10-hour day. You can't possibly talk continuously for that long, and at 50% usage many callers will be getting busy signals or will have to wait in queue.

Say you're charging $3 per minute. The most you can gross in a day will be $900 (10 hrs x 60 min/hr x $3 x 50%). After telephone company and service bureau charges, your net will be between $550 and $600 per day, before advertising and overhead expenses. Not a bad income, but there's no potential to make any more money unless you hire additional operators with the same level of expertise as you.

With a live program, you miss out on some of the strongest advantages of a recorded interactive program: *the ability to earn money around the clock with no upper limit on the number of calls you can handle*.

Yes, you have to spend time collecting your program information and periodically updating the program content. But this certainly won't tie you up for 10 hours a day, and you can choose your working hours as you see fit. And your 900 program can handle hundreds, even thousands, of calls simultaneously. Why limit yourself?

By the way, fax-back and voice mailbox classified advertising applications are variations of recorded interactive programs – there is no need for a live operator. Fax-back programs, where a caller with a fax machine can instantly receive a hard copy of very specific information (charts, graphs, schedules, directories, reports, etc.), has great promise. Again, small businesses are the prime target market for this application, and most have fax machines.

What are the Best 900 Opportunities?

The best opportunities for start-up IPs that don't have huge marketing budgets will be with specialized information that can be precisely targeted to a specific niche market. Again, the information classifications are nearly unlimited. Virtually any kind of information can be categorized, packaged and delivered in such a way as to be useful to a given target audience.

The future in 900 is in serving easily definable and targetable niche markets. The large, reasonably homogeneous markets are already served by numerous 900 applications: sports lines, weather lines, horoscope lines, voice personal dating lines, stock and commodities lines, and soap opera update lines, to name just a few.

Although the markets for these types of 900 lines are potentially huge, they are not easy to target with cost-effective rifle shot advertising, a topic that will be addressed in detail later. The successful IPs serving these homogeneous markets are spending tens of thousands – even hundreds of thousands – of advertising dollars to reach their market. And in many cases, these 900 programs do not offer critically important information that is immediately valuable to the given market – the advertisers must rely on impulse purchasing, which is very expensive to achieve, requiring big splashy display ads or attention-grabbing TV commercials.

The novice IP simply doesn't have the financial resources to go after such a large homogeneous market. You must identify a very specific market with very specific information needs. Ideally, information that is critical to achieving a very important personal (or business) goal or objective. You cannot rely on one-shot impulse purchases of your information service. You will likely lose money on the first call because the advertising costs are often not recovered with only one call to your service (the 900 equivalent of a loss-leader). You need your customers to call your service again and again. You need to offer information with high perceived value that your market will need on an ongoing basis.

The point I'm trying to make actually applies to starting any kind of business with limited capital. You don't usually launch a business by taking on your biggest, most established competitor head-on. You will lose. For example, you wouldn't start a mail order catalog operation in direct competition with L.L. Bean unless you're willing to spend millions of dollars. You start by narrowing your focus and your market. Maybe you start with distinctive hunting jackets and outerwear, items that can be targeted precisely toward hunters and hikers.

Every successful 900 IP will tell you that his or her single largest expense is advertising. All other business expenses pale in comparison. This is why you need to get the biggest bang for your advertising buck. A well-defined niche market is easy to reach in a cost-effective manner. It will be served by one or more specialized periodicals, or media, and your advertising dollars will not be wasted on people who have no interest in your information service. And hopefully you will have a program that offers information they will need frequently, so they will become steady customers and continue to call your 900 service despite the frequency of your advertising.

How Do You Find the Right Niche Market?

Begin with your own skills, interests or hobbies. In all likelihood, you already belong to more than one niche market yourself. Make a list, including the specialized publications you read. You may discover a likely information need that could be better delivered with a 900 number.

Be careful, however, about choosing a niche market that is too small. For example, collectors of World War II airplane propellers are a very definable market, but they probably number under a dozen people (if, indeed, there are any at all!). You obviously cannot achieve sufficient call volume to justify a 900 service for this market. Stamp collectors, on the other hand, number in the hundreds of thousands, and would be an adequate-sized niche market for a 900 program offering information these collectors need.

Keep in mind that you are offering a relatively low-cost service, probably well under $10 total, and you will need a fairly decent volume of calls to make your efforts worthwhile. You must know the size of your market and how frequently each person is likely to call. Repeat callers will be very important to the success of your program, so it will be best to offer information that changes regularly. Getting the most up-to-date information available will be the primary motivation for inducing your customers to call repeatedly. Specialized information with an element of timeliness: This is where a 900 program can truly excel.

Where can you get ideas for possible niche markets? Go to the library and look through the following reference volumes. You will find specialized periodicals and organizations that serve specific niche markets. Indeed, you will find many publications and markets you never knew existed!

Encyclopedia of Associations, published by Gale Research. Includes thousands of associations and organizations by subject category, many of which publish newsletters for their members.

Hudson's Subscription Newsletter Directory. Lists thousands of specialized newsletters covering every conceivable subject.

The Standard Periodical Directory, published by Oxbridge Communications. This is the largest annual directory of magazines, trade journals, directories, newsletters, etc.; published in the U.S. and Canada.

Ulrich's International Periodicals Directory, published by R. R. Bowker. Includes 65,000 periodicals published internationally.

Directory of Directories, published by Gale Research. Includes directories and databases.

Gale Directory of Publications and Broadcast Media. Lists 35,000 magazines, newspapers, radio and TV media.

Standard Rate & Data Service (SRDS). A multi-volume reference series including business & consumer magazines, newspapers, TV, radio and mailing lists.

Legal Advice

You may need legal assistance in setting up your 900 program. This is a fairly specialized area that may require the services of a firm with such experience. Some firms stay on top of the regulatory issues and the confusing array of individual states laws that pertain to the 900 industry. Two firms in particular are well-known in the industry:

Ginsberg, Feldman & Bress
1250 Connecticut Ave., NW, Washington, DC 20036
202-637-9000

Hall, Dickler, Kent, Friedman & Wood
909 Third Avenue, New York, NY 10022
212-838-4600

Another option is to call Tele-Lawyer, one of the longest-running live 900 services in the country, started by attorney Michael Cane (see 900 Roundtable, Chapter 9), winner of the 1996 Alex Award for lifetime achievement: 900-TELE-LAW ($3 per minute).

A Working Example

I have always felt that the best way to illustrate a process is to use a specific example. Something we can really get our teeth into. So I'm going to use my own knowledge and come up with a 900 program that relates to my background in writing and publishing.

It will be a program that, as far as I know, has never been attempted. We don't want to copy an existing program, we want to conceive and design a unique new 900 information service that doesn't yet exist. You can follow the exact same process in coming up with your own idea for a 900 program. The process of conceiving and designing any 900 program will follow the same steps we outline here.

Conceiving the Program

In conceiving our 900 program, we must first answer the following questions:

❏   Who is our target market?
❏   What size is the market? Will it be large enough to support a specialized 900 information service?
❏   What are the market's specific information needs? Better yet, what kind of information does the market need to help achieve its most important goals?
❏   How is the market currently getting this information?
❏   Can a 900 program better serve these needs, with more timely or better organized information?
❏   Can this market be easily reached through well-targeted media?
❏   Where do I find the source information necessary for the 900 program?

In answering the first question, let's start with *writers*. However, simply *writers* may be too broad a market. After all, there are fiction writers, poetry writers, mystery writers, lifestyle writers, article writers, how-to writers, novel writers, textbook writers, technical writers, aspiring writers, veteran writers, and so on. And there are literally thousands of information categories that writers write about.

Should we narrow down our market to a more specific niche? If so, what is the size of this niche? Before we decide, let's go through the rest of the questions.

What are some specific information needs of writers? Well, writers need all kinds of information in order to produce their work. Many spend a lot more time on research than on writing. But the information categories they need are virtually unlimited. It may be way too ambitious to consider offering research-oriented information.

What other information might be even more important to writers? What will help them achieve their most important goals? Well, getting published — and getting paid — is certainly important. Few writers enjoy slaving away for little compensation. Can we offer timely, helpful information that will help them sell their work? Of course we can.

Where do writers now turn for this information? *Literary Marketplace, Writer's Market,* and some of the reference volumes listed earlier are some of the sources they would use. Most of these are fairly expensive publications, however, and few writers actually purchase them. They go instead to their local library. And, although most of these publications are updated annually, they cannot keep up with the fast-paced changes always taking place in the publishing industry. And all libraries are on tight budgets, so they may not even have the latest editions available, if they have them at all.

Can a 900 program better serve the writer's needs by offering more up-to-date information that is more easily accessible? Absolutely! Indeed, we might be able to improve upon what already exists by making timeliness our strongest advantage. For example, we could get publishers involved in the program by giving each one a voice mailbox slot, with access via a toll-free 800 number, so that each participant can leave a message outlining the exact types of books or articles being sought at any given time. The message could be changed daily, weekly or monthly. We have created a true information exchange for publishers and writers to connect with one another.

This is how to use the powerful capabilities of voice processing equipment. We can be much more responsive to the immediate needs of our market than any annual printed publication could ever hope to be. And the best part is that one of the most unique and helpful features of our program, the publisher's message, is automatically input into our program directly from the source. We simply start the program and let the publishers help us keep it up-to-date.

There's no question about it – a 900 program can be designed that would be highly useful to writers. Publishers too. And it could incorporate features that would be both unique and timely. Very possibly a real winner.

Can our market be easily reached? *Writer's Digest* is a monthly magazine that no aspiring writer worth his salt can afford to ignore. It has a circulation of 234,000 — mostly writers who need to sell their work. And if we go through the reference sources listed earlier, we will be sure to find other periodicals that are also targeted to writers. It appears, therefore, that we will have little difficulty reaching our market through well-targeted publications and media.

And to keep the information truly timely, we could run small ads in *Publishers's Weekly, Folio Magazine,* and *The Newsletter on Newsletters,* asking all publishers to keep us up-to-date. Indeed, they could get very specific about the books or articles they are looking for, making it very easy for both sides to communicate with one another.

Where do we get the source information for our 900 program? The same place our aspiring author would go: *Literary Marketplace, Writer's Market,* and the listing of directories mentioned earlier.

However, we soon discover that there are tens of thousands of publishers and periodicals. It would be a Herculean task to input all this data into our program. The voice storage requirements would be enormous. We need to further narrow our market to make this a more manageable task.

We return, therefore, to defining our market. We know that repeat callers will be important, so what kinds of writers will need our services on a regular basis? Writers who create articles or short stories for periodicals. Thousands and thousands of periodicals publish tens of thousands of articles every month. This is obviously a good place to start, and we can immediately eliminate book writers and publishers from consideration.

Many periodicals don't use outside, unknown or freelance writers for their articles, so we needn't concern ourselves with these. And many experienced writers already know how to sell their work, or it's sold before it's even written, so our target market can be further narrowed to aspiring, beginning writers in search of receptive publishers. We can eliminate highly specialized technical writers and their journals, because they already know who is going to publish their learned (yet often incomprehensible) writings.

We are actually talking about two potential markets here: aspiring authors and those publishers who actively want their work. If we can bring the two together we will be helping both achieve their goals. We might even be able to get publishers to call a separate 900 line to update their specific messages about what kinds of submissions they are seeking. We must be careful about this, however, and remember who is best served by our program. If publishers resist paying for updating their messages, few such updates will be forthcoming, and the value of the program to aspiring writers will be diminished, perhaps fatally.

An interesting parallel can be found with the personal classified dating lines. Many IPs allow women to advertise for free, via a local number or a toll-free 800 number, because women advertisers generate virtually all the heavy call volume from all those lonely guys out there. Call volume is the name of the game, and these IPs recognize that men constitute the vast majority of their market. The more women advertisers, the more men are going to call. Repeatedly. We don't want to kill the goose that lays the golden egg!

Designing the Program

Okay, now we have an initial concept for our program. It will target aspiring authors of articles or short stories. The purpose of our program is to help our target market find publishers who accept unsolicited manuscripts — and who will pay for their work. Our objective is to offer a uniquely responsive service that will truly help writers achieve their goals efficiently, generating lots of satisfied customers and repeat callers.

How do we design such a program? First, we must list all of the specific information our hopeful Hemingways will need to achieve their goals:

❏ Which periodicals, by subject category, are seeking unsolicited submissions or proposals. Obviously, periodicals will need to be categorized in some coherent fashion by general content.

❏ The current address and telephone number of each publisher.
❏ The current names and titles of editors, by specialty, at each periodical (for addressing a specific submission).
❏ A brief outline of submission requirements (subjects, number of words, SASE, etc.).
❏ Standard payment terms.
❏ Publisher's message. Again, this would be a voice mailbox for the publisher to use for soliciting very specific submissions, or even advising against certain subject categories. It could also be used for alerting authors to address or personnel changes, or for describing a new publication planned to be launched in the future.

The above information is what our caller will receive once she reaches her *destination* in our program. This is the end product. We can't possibly expect her to sit through a three-hour recitation of every publication in our program. She must be able to zero in on those specific publications that will be most likely to want her article.

This is where the menu tree comes in. This is a unique feature of interactive audiotex services, something no reference book can possibly emulate. We can organize our publications into numerous very specific subclassifications, and we can quickly guide our caller to the most appropriate grouping of periodicals for her purposes.

Remember, we want to serve our callers as best we can, which means allowing them to reach the information they require as quickly and efficiently as possible. A well-designed menu tree is a must. This is where we have to exercise our creativity in designing the most effective, easy-to-follow pathway to the end-product information.

A menu tree is simply a hierarchy of classifications, beginning with the broadest possible divisions and ending with very specific divisions. The number of menu levels between these two extremes will depend upon the nature and number of information categories in our program.

In general, the fewer the menu choices at each level, the better, particularly at the beginning. We should never exceed five at any level, because once the caller hears the last choice, she may have already forgotten the first choices.

Our example menu tree may require up to six levels, and might look like the following example, which shows only one possible sequence of selections by our caller (the selection path is indicated by *bold italics*):

Main Menu:
1. Newsletters
2. *Magazines*

Sub-Menu A:
1. Fiction
2. *Non-fiction*

Sub-Menu B:
1. *Adult*
2. Teens
3. Children

Sub-Menu C:
1. Business/Industry
2. Entertainment
3. *Lifestyle*

Sub-Menu D:
1. *Home*
2. Crafts/Hobbies
3. Travel
4. Fashion
5. Health/Fitness

Sub-Menu E:
1. Cooking/Food
2. Decorating & Remodeling
3. *Gardening*
4. Family
5. Pets

Using this example, once our caller selects "Gardening" under sub-menu E, she would receive the information end-product: a recorded list of magazines that deal with gardening, plus the information, outlined earlier, about each publication.

Remember, this example demonstrates only one possible menu path. The complete menu tree will likely be quite complex, with dozens of classifications at the lower menu levels. In the interest of brevity, however, we will not attempt to design the entire menu tree here. I'm simply illustrating the design process.

Scripting

Now that we have designed our proposed menu tree, we need to write the script for our program. We need to identify what information needs to be exchanged at each level:

1. The Introduction.

a. The preamble. This is a mandatory message giving the name of the IP (company name), a brief description of the service, and the cost of the call:

Welcome to the Writer's Marketplace, presented by Aegis Publishing Group, where you will locate periodicals in different subject categories that accept submissions from freelance writers. This call will cost $1 per minute, unless you hang up within three seconds after the tone.

b. Other instructions. Before reciting the main menu, we may wish to offer additional instructions or information. For example, we could offer a customer service telephone number for callers who encounter problems with the program, or offer to send a copy of the full program menu (plus some compelling sales literature!). Or we may want to make it easier for frequent callers to go through the menu levels more quickly:

If you have any problems with this program, or would like to receive a copy of the full menu of options, please call 800-555-RITE. You can return to the main menu at any time by pressing the star key. You do not have to wait to hear all menu choices if you know the menu selection, which can be pressed at any time.

2. The Main Menu. The next message heard will be the main menu. The caller will also be returned to the main menu whenever she presses the star key:

The main menu. Press 1 for newsletters, press 2 for magazines.

3. The Sub-Menus. In our example, it may be advisable to title the sub-menus so frequent callers, or callers with a printed copy of the full menu (sent to them or published in a display ad), can easily follow the menu path. It might also be a good idea to allow our caller to go backwards to the previous menu, and to confirm where she is located within the program:

Sub-menu B, non-fiction magazines. Press 1 for adult, 2 for teens, 3 for children. Press the pound key at any time to return to the previous menu.

It would be a good idea to repeat the instructions given in the introduction in case our caller has forgotten them; or to allow our caller to hear the menu again:

Press the star key to return to the main menu at any time; press 9 to hear the menu again.

4. The Information End-Product. Once our caller selects the "Gardening" category, she will hear a list of publications along with address, editors, submission requirements and a publisher's message. Because there could be several publications in each destination category, we should allow her to skip through our listings. Also, because she will be writing this information down, we need to give her the ability to control the pace of the information flow:

Gardening. You will hear the name, address, phone number and submission information for each publication in this category. Press 2 at any time to skip to the next publication. Press 1 at any time to return to the beginning of the message for each publication. Press 3 at any time to pause, and press 3 again to resume.

At this point the recorded information for each publication is given. If there were five magazines under this classification, all five would be given, one after the other, unless the caller skips ahead (#2), returns to the beginning of the publication recording (#1), returns to the previous menu (pound key, returns to sub-menu E), or returns to the main menu (star key).

5. The Conclusion. After the caller hears the information about the final publication under "Gardening," we need to tell her there are no further listings, remind her what to do to find other classifications, or conclude the program and thank her for calling:

There are no additional listings in this category. Press 1 to hear the last publication. Press the pound key to return to the previous sub-menu, or press the star key to return to the main menu. Thank you for calling the Writer's Marketplace.

This same scripting process will have to be followed for every possible menu path in our program. In some cases, there will not be six menu levels, or there may not be any end-product information at the end of a certain path.

It is also apparent the sub-menu classification will vary depending upon the menu path. Sub-menus A and B might remain constant, but sub-menu C and beyond must be responsive to the path chosen. For example, the following path:

Main Menu: 2. Magazines
Sub-Menu A: 1. Fiction
Sub-Menu B: 1. Adult

might result in the following sub-menu C classifications:

1. Mystery/detective
2. Science fiction
3. Western
4. Adult
5. Romance

This particular menu path may not require any further sub-menus beyond level C.

By the way, our proposed menu tree is not necessarily the best possible design. For example, newsletters always contain topical news, never fiction, so it would be better to revise sub-menu A, at least after the newsletter path is chosen. Again, a lot of creative effort needs to go into designing the most responsive menu tree, and we might end up going through numerous variations until we get it right.

Although this process may appear somewhat complex and intimidating, don't despair. Your service bureau, if you've picked a good one, will help you every step of the way in designing your program. They will tell you what can and can't be done.

Data Input

Now we need to fill our program up with all the end-product data. This is the meat of our program, the reason callers are paying $1 per minute to hear our information.

How is the information physically put into our program, and how is it updated? A dedicated program editing line. An interactive telephone program, using a local or toll-free 800 number, would be designed along the same lines as our 900 program, except to input the voice data. Using an interactive menu and voice prompts for each information category, we can load the entire program from our telephone. Or revise it after it's up and running.

Now, we have three options as to how the information gets loaded into our program:

1. We input all of it ourselves. This may have to be done over numerous sittings spanning several hours to record all the necessary information.

2. We get publishers to do all the work for us. We give the editing line number to publishers and encourage them to input the information about their publication. The disadvantage to this approach is that we must get the word out to all prospective publishers well before the program is operational, and then we must rely on them to input all the data correctly and on time. And since the editing line will be somewhat complicated, and we have no control over whether or not the publishers will actually respond, this option doesn't have much promise of working.

3. A little of both. We input all initial data to get the program off the ground. Then we provide publishers with a simple editing line for updating their information and leaving their "publisher's message." For example, we could assign each publisher a voice mailbox number for recording messages and any changes to the other publication data, such as address changes, personnel changes or new submission requirements. Then we control the transfer of this information to the actual 900 program, transferring it directly or by recording it ourselves.

When gathering your source information, make sure you get all the necessary permissions you need, such as copyright or a license to use the information in your program. Instead of paying for the right to use such information, we might consider proposing a joint venture with one of the leading sources for such information, such as *Literary Marketplace* in this example. The resultant name recognition would be quite beneficial to the program's success.

Will Our Program Work?

Say our caller has written an article about herbal gardening, and wants to identify all possible publications that might be interested. In addition to the menu path indicated, she may also select the "Cooking" and "Health & Fitness" categories as well. She may end up spending six or eight minutes on the telephone.

At $1 a minute (a very common charge for recorded interactive programs), she will spend $6 to $8. Was it worth it? Well, this information is available at good-sized libraries, but our Martha Stewart must drive 30 minutes to get there. And then spend another 30 minutes digging through the appropriate reference volumes. An hour and a half, minimum, plus the cost of gas, parking, and the babysitter, which could easily exceed the cost of the 900-number call.

And the reference volumes might not be current. Libraries have tight budgets. Because we can update our 900 program daily, we were able to add a new gardening magazine that was launched only two months ago.

Our author certainly appreciated the convenience of the 900 program. With a full-time job and two kids, it is very hard for her to find the time to go to the library. And she would never have learned otherwise about a new gardening magazine that is eagerly looking for submissions.

She might be so happy with the 900 service that she begins using it in order to find out what topics publishers are seeking *before* writing her next article. The 900 program is truly helping her achieve her goals: selling her work and getting published.

What, in effect, have we actually done? We have taken existing information and simply repackaged, sorted, and organized it in such a way to allow our callers to quickly find the information they need. We have done all the research, making it instantly available by telephone. And as a finishing touch, we added *value* to the information with the publisher's message.

This is just one example of the kind of 900 program that can work. You probably have knowledge of or interest in other areas that lend themselves to similar 900 programs. Find an information need within an easily identifiable and reachable target market, then design an information program that is superior to all the other alternatives. Provide information that makes it easier for your callers to achieve their most important goals. Help them, and they will help you by patronizing your service.

Chapter 5
Marketing

Okay, you have now come up with a promising 900-number application. How do you get people to call your number? Simple question — however, by far the most important one you must answer. Your success depends on it.

First, let's do an initial cut and eliminate some market segments that are unlikely to call *any* 900 number. The conventional wisdom is that the over-50 crowd does not call 900 numbers. At least not yet, with few programs appealing to this age group. Back in Chapter 3 you read about the survey that showed that 70% of the respondents wouldn't even consider calling a 900 number, and only 12% have ever used 900 services. This kind of narrows down the potential market. The under-30 generation, who have grown up in the electronic information age, are the most likely people to call a 900 number.

Because interactive 900 services require a touch-tone telephone, 38% of the population that are still using rotary phones are unlikely callers. Fortunately, they are probably already included in the over-50, 70% segment that wouldn't call anyway, so we shouldn't count them twice.

This might tell you that a 900 program offering valuable advice on Medicare or Social Security benefits would be a miserable failure. Anyway, targeting seniors is swimming against the tide. At least for now, while 900 is still working on its image.

There are exceptions, however. My 80-year-old father calls 900-number stock and commodity lines for instant market price quotes. However, he may not be representative of his peers (he still flies his own airplane and recently did a parachute jump for the first time!). It is surely more a function of information content than anything else. Seniors have a lot of investments in their portfolios and the time to manage them, so perhaps the value of the information will overcome any initial negative perception about the overall industry.

Not all telephones are created equal. Access to 900 dialing isn't available from most college dorms, businesses, hotels, or from public telephones. It makes little sense, therefore, to target anyone who doesn't have ready access to a residential telephone. And now that call blocking is readily available to all residential customers, we will probably see many families with young children elect this option to keep the kids from running up the phone bill.

Who's left? Educated young singles, Yuppies and Dinks (dual income, no kids), to name a few. But don't be mislead by cute titles. Plenty of people who call the soaps and 'scopes lines don't necessarily fit these classifications — yet these kinds of lines can be very successful. In general, however, it is safe to assume that the largest overall market for 900 services is young, fairly sophisticated, and generally childless.

The Target Market

Based upon your chosen 900 application, you now need to further identify your market with as much precision as possible. Why is this so important? Because if you don't know who they are, you will have a very hard time reaching them. And if you can't get your message to them, they are not going to call your number.

Use the following demographic questions as a guide:

1. How old are they?
2. Are they male or female?
3. How much education do they have?
4. Do they live in apartments, or houses?

5. Are they in cities, the suburbs, or out in the sticks?
6. What kind of jobs and income do they have?
7. Are they married or single?
8. What do they do for fun and relaxation?
9. Where do they shop?
10. To what clubs and organizations do they belong?

Which all leads up to the most important question,

11. **What media do they watch, listen to, or read?**

Once you come up with a profile and get to know the kind of people they are, you will be better able to identify the most effective ways of reaching them. If you're offering a fairly specialized program, there will likely be specialized media targeted specifically at your market.

Say you're offering a voice mailbox classified advertising program for coin collectors, where callers can either leave recorded ads or listen to ads in various classifications, then make direct contact with each other for buying, selling or trading rare coins. These same people probably subscribe to magazines that specialize in rare coins, so it is very easy to reach this market through print advertising in these publications. This is known as "rifle shot" marketing, because you are able to devote all your advertising dollars to reaching the exact market you need to reach.

The converse is "shotgun blast" marketing. An ad in a general circulation daily newspaper may reach the target market in the circulation area of the newspaper, but you are also paying to reach everyone else who reads the paper, including those who are not interested in your message. Because advertising costs are based upon circulation, or the size of the audience, you pay a lot of money reaching people who will never respond to your ad.

Of course, rifle shot marketing only works with a very well-defined target market which is served by specialized media. A more general 900 program, such as sports or weather, doesn't permit such precision. Nonetheless, keep in mind who, in general, calls 900 numbers, and you still may be able to narrow down the media focus to your general target market.

For example, alternative weekly newspapers are well-read by the potential 900 market: young, educated readers. It follows, therefore, that a general 900 application would be more successfully and cost-effectively marketed in such a newspaper than in the major daily newspaper in the same city. The alternative weekly newspaper has a smaller circulation, so advertising costs are lower. Yet the audience is much more likely to call your 900 number because many have probably already used other 900 services. This results in much more cost-effective advertising. The cost per response is much lower. We'll talk more about this later.

The Advertisement

It's beyond the scope of this book to get into the art of creating the actual advertising — the layout, design and copy. There are many excellent books that are entirely dedicated to the subject, and they do a much more thorough job than I could possibly hope to do here. Nonetheless, there is one simple formula that should guide the creation of any ad: the AIDA principle. Attention, Interest, Desire, Action.

Attention. First you must get your customer to stop and notice your ad. This is accomplished with a headline, a photo, a graphic, a cartoon, a bold statement on the envelope, or anything that commands attention.

Interest. The only thing that really interests anyone is something that benefits him or her in achieving an important goal or solving a problem. What is important here are benefits, not features. A man buys cologne because he wants to be attractive to the opposite sex. The actual smell is merely a feature of the product, which is quite secondary. If women were attracted to the odor of skunks, you better believe that men would enthusiastically drench themselves in copious quantities of eau-de-lepeau!

Desire. Now you've got him hooked, but you need to do some more convincing so he'll buy your product, and not someone else's.

Here's where some features might come in, like the uniqueness of your scent, extracted from only the most virile of skunks. A testimonial or two — from lucky guys who used the scent and were attacked by mobs of beautiful women — would be a nice touch. More about testimonials in the next section.

Action. You haven't made the sale until your customer actually calls and orders your product. Don't expect him to do that without some encouragement. This is where you use words like CALL NOW, or ORDER TODAY, or WHILE QUANTITIES LAST, or any other method of getting him to act immediately. Incentives for immediate orders are always effective, such as BUY ONE GET ONE FREE UNTIL DEC 31ST!

These basic principles can be used for guidance in creating any kind of ad, or inducement to buy, whether it be for print, TV, radio, classified, brochures, sales letters or any marketing communication you write. Forget them at your peril! I am continually amazed at how many companies — and it's usually the biggest ones — completely ignore the AIDA formula in their marketing. They are throwing a lot of money down the drain. If it doesn't motivate your prospect to buy your product or service, the cash you spent is gone forever.

Advertising Copy

Anyone getting into the 900-number business must learn how to write compelling advertising copy. You'll be doing it all the time, not just for your advertisements, but also in sales and cover letters, brochures, fliers or any other type of marketing communication that leaves your office. Writing good ad copy takes practice. After doing it for awhile, with conscientious effort, you will get the hang of it.

As I said before, the key is to emphasize benefits, not features. Everyone is self-interested. The only thing of interest to anyone is what benefits will be derived from using the product or service. Will it save money, improve health, improve appearance, enhance intelligence, entertain, or increase wealth? **Always write about benefits.**

Begin by writing them down. Then prioritize, beginning with the most important. For example, what would be the benefits associated with a stock price line? Let's make a list:

- ❑ Instant Information
- ❑ Convenient Access (by phone)
- ❑ Inexpensive
- ❑ Improved Trading Timing
- ❑ Avoid Losses
- ❑ Identify Opportunities
- ❑ Make More Money

Notice how this list starts with the more obvious pluses and leads to the more important resulting benefits. If we were to prioritize, it would be reversed:

- ❑ Make More Money
- ❑ Identify Opportunities
- ❑ Avoid Losses
- ❑ Improved Trading Timing
- ❑ Inexpensive
- ❑ Convenient Access
- ❑ Instant Information

In the final analysis, the ultimate reason for calling the line is to help make more money trading stocks. The benefits at the bottom of the list simply lead to achieving the ultimate benefit of making money. Indeed, it could be argued that Instant Information and Convenient Access are really more like features than benefits.

After going through this exercise you might even decide to modify your program in order to provide even more powerful, concrete benefits for using your service. In this example, perhaps we would add a feature that tracked all stocks that have changed price more than a certain percentage over a short period of time.

The caller would be better able to identify buying and selling opportunities.

If you go through this exercise and can't identify any solid benefits to using your program, you have a real problem. Either your idea is totally worthless, or you are not endowed with much of an imagination. Either way, you probably shouldn't quit your day job.

The other thing to keep in mind when writing ad copy is the viewpoint. Don't use the words "I" or "we." The reader really doesn't care about you. She cares a lot about herself, and what you can do to improve her life. Use the "you" viewpoint as much as possible.

Here's an example I dealt with recently, involving my mother. She has her own custom window-treatment business, which she operates out of her home. She will often send letters to new homeowners in the area, a smart way of targeting an audience that is ripe for her service. She faxed me a copy of the letter she was using and asked me to improve on it:

Congratulations on the purchase of your new home.

I design and make window treatments and accessories myself. I would be grateful for the opportunity to assist you in these decorating ideas with a free in-home consultation.

Cordially,

Marilyn

What's wrong with this letter? First, two of three sentences start with "I," and the "you" viewpoint is almost totally missing. And besides the free in-home consultation, there is really no discussion of what benefits are in store for the reader. Finally, "Cordially" sounds too stilted. This is what I faxed back to my mother:

Congratulations on the purchase of your new home. Do you need some affordable help coordinating your window treatments and accessories? I will be happy to help you put your own custom touches into your new home.

You will get the same coordinated, professional look you would get from an expensive interior decorator at a fraction of the cost. I work independently from my home workroom and do all the work myself. You will be pleasantly surprised at how affordable custom treatments can be when you bypass the middleman (decorator).

Please call me today for your free in-home consultation.

Yours sincerely,

Marilyn

P.S. If nothing else, you'll get some good decorating ideas with no obligation to go any further.

This letter is an obvious improvement. It uses the "you" viewpoint almost exclusively, and talks about the benefits of using her services, such as getting a personalized, custom look without spending a fortune. Notice the "P.S." at the end of the letter. For some reason the postscript is almost always read, often before the body of the letter. Always use a postscript for some irresistible inducement if possible. In this case, my mother decided to do the body of the letter on her word processor and the P.S. in her own handwriting, which really helps to personalize the letter. I hope this new letter works better, because if it doesn't I'll never hear the end of it!

This has been a very brief discussion of advertising copy. I hope you now appreciate the big difference between good copy and bad copy. Learn how to do it right. Practice, and read other books on the subject. The following two books have helped me become a better copywriter:

The Copywriter's Handbook
by Bob Bly (Henry Holt and Company, 801-972-2221)

Cash Copy
by Jeffrey Lant (JLA Associates, 617-547-6372)

Testimonials & Endorsements

We already know that 900 numbers come with built-in credibility problems. No amount of effort on your part will convince your target audience that you are the honest, trustworthy individual that *you* know you are. *All* advertising copy is met by a certain degree of skepticism by consumers. Advertising by companies with no brand recognition, that are totally unknown by the consumer, are met with even more skepticism. The 900 industry, which is already widely suspect, gets a double heaping of skepticism.

Before anyone will even *consider* buying your service, they want assurance that they will be getting what they expect, and that they won't be disappointed, or worse, ripped off. As I said earlier, you can try until you're blue in the face, but your words will mean nothing unless you happen to be a respected, nationally-known figure. Since that is unlikely, you need help convincing your audience that the claims you are making are true.

How can you gain the trust of your audience? By getting someone else, who has no interest in furthering your cause, and who is perceived as a disinterested independent person, to back up your claims. It doesn't always have to be a celebrity. A satisfied customer might be willing to say something good about your service. Make sure you get his permission to use his name first, in the form of a signed release.

You've seen this kind of testimonial, which usually lists the name and hometown of the person. Most people believe that these are legitimate statements by the person who is quoted, as they should be. However, it's important to use a full name and the hometown. Although not easy, the statement *could* be verified by someone willing to do some digging. Using only initials or omitting the hometown should be avoided. I usually think such testimonials are bogus, or that the advertiser was too lazy to get permission to use them. And if the testimonial appears to be bogus, you could end up doing yourself more harm than good.

You might get an expert in the field to say something positive about your program. The public may not know who this person is, but his or her title may be persuasive. For example, if you're offering pharmaceutical information, try to get a testimonial from a medical doctor, the president of a hospital, the director of a health maintenance organization or any prominent person with relevant credentials.

Obviously, the more famous the expert, the more powerful the testimonial. Finding a "name" to endorse your service, however, is neither easy nor inexpensive. On the other hand, getting a satisfied customer or a credentialed expert is not that difficult, and is much better than no testimonials at all.

One of the most successful 900 programs is The Psychic Friends Network. You have seen the 30-minute infomercial. Why is this program so successful? *Dionne Warwick.*

This is known as a celebrity endorsement. Dionne Warwick is not a psychic. She simply says good things about the program in a friendly, persuasive way, and the audience figures that if she endorses the program it must be good. At least that's the idea.

Celebrity endorsements are very powerful, and a good substitute for a recognizable brand name. Your spokesperson is so recognizable that brand recognition needn't be an issue.

The best possible endorsement to get would be a celebrity who is a leader in the field. Get David Letterman to endorse your joke line, or get Joe Montana to recommend your sports line. Impossible, you say? Not really, if you know how to do it. And there are plenty of lesser-knowns who will work almost as well as the superstars, for a lot less money. The following company matches celebrities with events, charities, products or services:

The Celebrity Source
8033 Sunset Blvd., Suite 1108
Los Angeles, CA 90046
213-651-3300 Fax: 213-651-3397

According to owner Rita Tateel, they have a database of 4,400 celebrities involved in film, music, TV, politics, sports and business. They will probably come up with several good suggestions you never dreamed about, and will have a good handle on what you can expect to pay for the celebrity's services. You can also try the various talent agencies, such as the venerable William Morris Agency in Beverly Hills (310-859-4501).

If your 900 line is highly specialized a major-name celebrity is not as essential. All you probably need is a well-known person in the subject area of your program. In the investment arena, for example, many people know Richard Young, who writes an investment newsletter. However, the vast majority of people who don't know the difference between a debenture and a debutante have never heard of Richard Young, and probably never will. It doesn't matter, however, if your market consists of savvy investors who would be impressed by Young's opinion. It matters little that people who would have no interest in your message never heard of him.

Whether you get testimonials from customers or a well-known celebrity spokesperson, get others to endorse your service. This is the only way you can establish unambiguous credibility. I cannot overemphasize how important this will be to the success of your marketing plan.

The Media Choice

Once your target market has been defined and profiled, you need to find out what types of media best reach your intended audience. If you can get a rifle shot media source, go for it. You should select likely sources and contact them for media kits, which include information on circulation and audience size, advertising rates, and most importantly, the demographics of their audience.

Also, make sure they accept 900 advertising. The lingering negative perception about 900 numbers has resulted in the exclusion of such advertising by some media companies.

Print

There are literally thousands of print media sources to choose from, from huge daily newspapers to very specialized monthly magazines. Newspapers are usually read by a broad, general audience and are unlikely to be a cost-effective choice for many pay-per-call programs. Nonetheless, there are exceptions. The national sports newspapers are targeted to sports fans. The national tabloids may be a good choice for horoscope or soap opera lines.

And, as I mentioned earlier, the alternative weeklies are good prospects for 900 advertising. Paul Twitchell, director of marketing at Tele-Publishing, a service bureau serving numerous alternative weeklies with 900 programs, says, "The typical reader is a socially active, college-educated professional between 18 and 35 years of age, with a high disposable income. Many IPs are turning to alternative weeklies as a more efficient means of reaching their target audiences."

What makes the alternative weekly unique is that it is often the most comprehensive source for local arts, entertainment and cultural activities, which means it is being read when the reader is in a relaxed, fun-loving mood. This could be particularly auspicious for 900 game, contest or entertainment lines.

Magazines require a much longer lead time for ad placement than newspapers, often a few months or more, but the variety of specialized markets is truly impressive. There seems to be a special magazine for just about every sport, hobby, profession, trade group, or interest imaginable. The potential for rifle-shot target marketing is very good with specialized magazines. The reference section of your local library should have some of the reference volumes mentioned earlier in Chapter 4, listing all periodicals published in the U.S. and abroad. You should definitely review some of these, because you will find many magazines you have never even heard about, and some could be good prospects for your 900 advertising.

With any print media choice, the size and placement of your ad will greatly influence the rate of response. First, you must grab the reader's attention, and only then can you induce him to call your number with compelling benefit-laden copy. If the reader doesn't first notice your ad, the best copy in the world can't save it from being ignored. The right-hand page, top outside corner, is considered the best position for a display ad that isn't a full page.

Classified advertising, although relatively inexpensive, will not generate calls if you need to thoroughly explain your message in order to induce a call. A trivia contest or a music review line will not work with classified. For classified to work, the benefits of calling must be fairly obvious to the reader, without having to explain it in the ad copy, and the cost of the call should be quite low. The content of a Dow Jones stock price line is obvious and needs little elaboration.

People in the mail-order business are often successful with a two-step classified ad, which doesn't ask for money, but offers to send free information. Then, a very detailed mailing piece is sent, which can do a much better job of inducing the purchase decision. This same concept can be tailored to pay-per-call marketing, with the added advantage of compiling a database of inquirers for regular follow-up mailings. Indeed, the first step of the classified ad could be to call a toll-free 800 number, where the caller hears a convincing message that motivates him to call the 900 program. Much more information can be conveyed verbally in 30 or 60 seconds than can be printed in a classified ad, and the printed word will never convey a reassuring or enthusiastic tone of voice.

With most publications, you're not limited to just display or classified advertising. Many will accept printed inserts, which can be quite cost-effective. You can print up a colorful insert, on both sides, and get better exposure than with a full-page ad for less money. Inserts also dovetail nicely with a fundamental feature of the 900 business: if a potential caller doesn't have your 900 number readily available, he or she isn't going to call. An insert can be put aside or stuffed into a pocket for later reference without destroying the publication by tearing out the page. It makes it easier for the potential caller to save your promotional message and telephone number.

Because print media is a relatively low-cost advertising vehicle, often permitting fairly precise target marketing, it is usually the first choice of many start-up 900 programs. Indeed, the ability to rifle shot the marketing with low-cost print advertising should influence the final selection of a 900 program.

Radio

Radio is another medium that can be fairly accurately targeted to a given market. A significant shortcoming, however, is the fact that a very large percentage of radio listeners are in their automobiles, with no access to a regular land-line telephone. You cannot currently call a 900 number from a cellular telephone. This problem can be partially offset with the use of a very recognizable telephone number, or a vanity number that spells a word or phrase, which can be easily recalled later when the customer is near a land-line phone. Nonetheless, response to 900 advertising is usually immediate and spur-of-the-moment, and many potential callers will be unable to respond to your message. It's not enough to target the market. You also want to reach them at a time and place where they will be most likely to respond.

This doesn't mean that radio should be ignored. After all, it can be quite inexpensive. Talk radio has been effective for some 900 programs, particularly live ads by a popular DJ. Just keep in mind the limitations, and test carefully before making any major financial commitments.

Television

Television is probably the most effective medium for mass-market 900 advertising, particularly entertainment-type programs. TV viewers are a captive audience, and a good, attention-grabbing commercial will be noticed by a large percentage of the viewers. Tune into various cable channels or the Fox Network, especially after 11:00 p.m., and you will see many 900 commercials. The fact that many of them have been airing over a long period of time indicates that they have been effective. You will also see many direct-response 800 commercials on TV. Direct response works on television, and 900 is a direct-response information or entertainment service.

As a start-up IP, you may automatically assume that TV advertising is way beyond your budget. Not necessarily, because you don't have to start by trying to reach a huge market on a national network. Local cable channels, depending on the size of their market, can cost as low as a few dollars a spot. The cost of producing a good commercial will run from $3000 to more than $10,000, but once it is produced it can be used for a fairly long period of time on various cable channels or networks.

The actual production of any TV commercial should not be undertaken by novices. Too much money is at risk. According to Jeffrey Price Michelson, president and creative director of Media Wizard Productions, an experienced producer of 900 TV commercials, "Production values, which didn't matter so much in the beginning, are all-important now. I remember the days when just being on TV was enough. There was the novelty factor, fewer players, lots of first-time impulse buyers, and no recession!" Well, those days are over, and to protect your investment and to ensure success, you must seek out the help of experts — preferably ones with experience in 900 television advertising.

You have probably noticed TV ads for local businesses on your cable channels. This is obviously a cost-effective advertising vehicle — and they certainly don't have huge ad budgets. Check out the rates with your local cable service provider.

Another advantage with cable is that there is the ability to focus the market a little better than network TV advertising. The more affluent, educated viewers tune into the news channels while sports fans tune into ESPN. Your Spanish language horoscope line will get a better response on the all-Spanish Univision cable channel.

Direct Mail

Direct mail is the most precise rifle-shot marketing available. There are specialized mailing lists for just about any kind of demographic group imaginable. Plus, there is a lot of valuable statistical science associated with good mailing lists. A direct mail piece allows a comprehensive message which can be precisely tailored to the target market. There is virtually no limit to the length, size, or complexity of the advertising message included with the mailing.

Direct mail, however, is a fairly expensive rifle. A mailing piece can cost up to 35 or 45 cents each — including list rental, creative and production, printing costs, and postage. A typical 900 line might net only a couple of dollars a call, so the response rate from the direct mailing would have to be extremely high in order to be successful. Much higher than industry averages.

Direct mail should be considered only for higher priced 900 services. For example, a computer software help line staffed by expert live operators, netting an average of $10 or more per call, could work very well. Particularly if the IP was able to rent a mailing list of recent software purchasers from the vendor. A true rifle shot without a penny wasted reaching the wrong people.

A unique advantage of direct mail is the ease and confidentiality of testing. You can try small mailings without investing a lot of money to measure response rates. You can test different messages, prices or lists. And you can do this while keeping fairly low key, so your competitors will be less likely to find out about your program or your methods.

Most direct mail professionals don't even expect to break even on their first mailing. They view it as a means of building their in-house list of buyers, and don't expect to actually make any money from these customers until they have purchased the second or third time.

It is usually better to employ a mail-order *campaign* as opposed to a one-shot effort. Instead of one mailing to 5,000 prospects, do five mailings to the same 1,000 people over a six-to-12-month period. It works a lot better.

Where do you find a good mailing list? It depends upon your target market. There are dozens of mailing list companies that maintain all kinds of lists broken down into all kinds of categories and sub-categories. Or you can often acquire a mailing list from a specific association whose membership is the same as your target audience. Or a magazine whose readers are a perfect match. These are known as compiled lists, because they are nothing more than a complete compilation of everyone in the given category, without regard to whether or not they have actually ever purchased anything via mail order.

In general, a "response" list is better. This kind of list consists of people who have purchased something similar to what you are selling by mail. By their action they have demonstrated that they are open to mail-order offers. Let's face it — not everyone is comfortable shopping by the mail, and these people may be a waste of advertising resources.

In some cases you can get a compiled list that is further qualified by response. Whatever you do, don't try to save money by being cheap. Mail order is expensive, and you want to start out with the best possible list you can get. Don't settle for ACME Fly-By-Night-Number-One List Company. Get recommendations from the Direct Marketing Association (listed later). Or try the list company I have used (specializing in compiled business lists):

Dunhill International List Co., Inc.
419 Park Avenue South, New York, NY 10016
212-686-3700 Fax: 212-213-3269

Mail order is very similar to 900 numbers in many ways. Both are direct-response sale methods, where you are trying to convince the customer to make the purchase decision RIGHT NOW. This is much different from image advertising or building brand loyalty or getting the buyer to run down to the local store to buy your product.

I will often compare 900 programs to selling by mail order because the parallels are appropriate. You can learn a lot from the many years of experience that mail-order experts have to offer. Even if you decide that direct mail is not the best way to sell your 900 service, you will learn a lot about direct-response selling from the following books:

Building a Mail Order Business
by William A. Cohen (John Wiley & Sons)

Successful Direct Marketing Methods
by Bob Stone (NTC)

For even more information contact the Direct Marketing Association and ask for its catalog of books and resources:

Direct Marketing Association
11 West 42nd St., New York, NY 10038-8096
212-768-7277

Other Media

So far we've talked about the most logical advertising media. It's possible that none of these will be the most suitable or cost-effective way of promoting your particular 900 program. What else is there? Billboards, cocktail napkins, coffee mugs, matchbooks, keychains, or other novelties. Imprinted items and novelties are known as "advertising specialties," and distributors for such items can be found under that heading in the Yellow Pages.

Hand out fliers at shopping malls, sporting events, or music concerts. Have your message displayed on the electronic scoreboard at the football game, or have it printed or inserted in the game program, or hire an airplane to tow the message over the stadium!

Contact the manufacturer or mail-order distributor of a product that your target market regularly purchases, and see if you can insert a flier in its package. This is called "piggyback" advertising, and can be just as effective as direct mail at a fraction of the cost. See if your local pizza parlor will include your message on its pizza boxes, in return for help with the cost of producing the boxes. If it works, try a national pizza chain next. Promote your 900 program on someone else's related 900 program. This will target proven callers to 900 numbers.

Always think about what your target market is doing when he or she is most likely to call your program. Eating a pizza, watching

TV, working on a laptop computer, enjoying a beer, or hanging out with a group of friends? Keep your eyes and your imagination open to creative new ways of reaching your target market during these times, or making your message easily accessible when they might need it. Keep the needs of your audience foremost in your planning, and they will reward you by patronizing your services.

Advertising Agencies

A good advertising agency, particularly one with experience in direct-response marketing, can do all your marketing legwork while saving considerable money by staying away from ineffective advertising buys. These are experienced professionals who can be immensely helpful in designing and executing your marketing strategy. They eat, sleep and breathe advertising.

Nevertheless, few advertising agencies have a lot of experience with the 900 industry, so you must choose carefully. Also, be careful with agencies that specialize in only one medium, unless you have already decided that this medium is best for you. Don't abdicate your responsibility in evaluating all possible media options, and trust your judgement when considering which is best for you. No one understands your program as well as you, and there are many horror stories around the 900 industry about IPs who have lost a lot of money by starting out with the wrong agency.

Because marketing is the most important part of any successful 900 program, it makes little sense to completely relinquish control to an advertising agency. There is no substitute for the hands-on learning that comes only from doing it yourself. As a start-up IP, you should at least try out the lower cost media and techniques yourself, and perhaps use an ad agency for the more complex and expensive advertising, such as television. Remember, if you are launching a novel 900 program, both you and the ad agency will be going through a learning curve together.

If you can team up with an agency with extensive 900 experience with programs similar to yours, it will be a source of extremely valuable help. Even if it handles only one segment of your marketing, it will usually be happy to advise you on those areas you plan to handle personally. And after learning the ropes, you may wish to turn over all marketing work to the agency.

How do you find an advertising agency with experience in the 900 industry? A good place to start is through the listings found in the *Audiotex News Resource Guide* (see Appendix C). Another good source would be recommendations from your service bureau. Books and periodicals about direct marketing, such as *DM News* and *Direct Marketing Magazine*, will list agencies with experience in direct response marketing. Ask for a sample copy:

Direct Marketing Magazine
Hoke Communications
224 Seventh St., Garden City, NY 11530-5771
516-746-6700

DM News
19 West 21st Street, New York, NY 10010-8888

Although not technically a full-service ad agency, you might want to check out The "900" Advertising Club. This company was started in 1991 by Keith Mueller, an experienced IP and former NBC producer who understands advertising and the 900 business. He uses bulk purchasing to get better ad rates for members, offers per-inquiry programs, and publishes *Teleletter*, a helpful newsletter on 900-number marketing techniques:

The "900" Advertising Club
P.O. Box 5048, Newport Beach, CA 92662
714-721-9280

Mueller recently launched a new World Wide Web site, available to both consumers and industry veterans, at the following address:

http://www.infoguru.com

The web site features "some of the best 900 numbers available, including information on sports, music, entertainment, job openings and business news," says Mueller. Additionally, the site serves as an industry clearinghouse, with information on service bureaus, industry seminars, advertising resources and other industry contacts.

Some advertising agencies that are experienced with direct response and the 900-number industry:

Ad Partners
Contact: Bruce Kennedy (see The 900 Roundtable, Chapter 9)
9000 Sunset Blvd., Suite 525, Los Angeles, CA 90069
310-247-7703

Arch Communications
Contact: Steve Hearne
3700 South Las Vegas Blvd., Suite 1000, Las Vegas, NV 89109
702-597-1829

Paramount National Media, Inc.
505 South Beverly Dr., Suite 1133, Beverly Hills, CA 90212
310-282-8317

Paramount National Media is an agency started by industry veterans Glen Chazak and Deborah Hinderstein, each with more than 10 years experience as successful IPs in this business. As I mentioned earlier, see the Advertising Agency section of the *Audiotex News Resource Guide* for a complete, up-to-date listing of ad agencies with experience in this business.

If you end up using *any* ad agency you will be entrusting a lot of advertising money to that agency, so check them out thoroughly. Few agencies will say that they can't handle the job, even when they have little first-hand experience with direct-response marketing. Too many agencies seem to be quite adept at blowing through the advertising budget without generating any significant response. Shop around very carefully and make sure you're absolutely certain that your money will be invested wisely.

The Competition

You don't have to make all your media selection decisions in complete isolation. Simply check out the competition. Or, if there is no direct competitor to your unique 900 program, there will surely be some similar programs which would advertise in similar media.

As I mentioned earlier, pay close attention to repeat advertising. The longer the ad runs, the bigger or splashier it is, the more likely it has been successful.

First, identify all the possible media that are most effective for reaching the target market. And then get creative and try to identify a few which may not be so readily obvious. Then monitor them all to see what programs are being advertised, and how. Learn from their marketing and then gratefully borrow as much useful information as possible.

Don't automatically assume, however, that because you saw a competitor's ad a few times in a given media, that it has been successful. All advertisers constantly test different media, anywhere from a few weeks to several months. You want to watch for fairly long-term repetition. To save some time, call the media advertising department and try to find out how long your competitor has been advertising with them. Or go to the library and go through several back issues of the publication.

In addition to where your competitor advertises, pay attention to the size, layout, or design of his ads. Try to identify the features that make it successful, then incorporate them in your advertising.

Why does Burger King always sprout up across the street from McDonalds? Because they let McDonalds do all the expensive market research in selecting the best location, and then simply play follow-the-leader. Burger King saves a lot of time and money by just watching and following the competition.

This does not mean that you should never conduct your own market testing. You should, and you will, and we'll talk more about this later. But you have to start somewhere, and you may as well benefit as much as possible from other people's experiences in order to get the biggest bang for your advertising buck. The more effective your initial advertising, the quicker you can increase your budget and multiply your revenue.

Strategic Alliances

Advertising is by far the largest expense associated with any successful 900 program. What if we could completely eliminate this expense? Sounds like a reasonably attractive proposition, does it not? It is often possible to structure a win-win relationship between the IP and the media company, also known as a "per inquiry" (PI) revenue-sharing relationship. And, not surprisingly, revenue sharing with media partners is fairly common in the 900 industry.

The media partner already has the advertising vehicle, and often has difficulty selling all its ad space or time spots on a regular basis. The IP has the program, access to the featured information or entertainment, and keeps the program up-to-date and functioning. Put the two together and both come out ahead.

The media partner contributes ad space or time spots which otherwise may have remained unsold, in return for a predetermined share of the call revenue to the 900 program. Although the IP gives up a percentage of potential revenue to the media partner, he doesn't pay a dime in advertising costs. If the program proves to be successful, the media partner may in fact earn more per ad with this arrangement than by selling the space or time to a regular advertiser.

And if the 900 program is compatible with the image of the media partner, the media partner may lend credibility to the program by sponsoring it under its own name. As we already know, the 900 industry lacks credibility, and media partner sponsorship can go a long way toward improving the perception of legitimacy for any given program.

Voice personal dating programs are a good example of an extremely successful IP/media partnership. Thousands of newspapers across the country now have a voice personals section. Once limited to the alternative weeklies, many mainstream dailies now offer them, and the number is growing all the time. The reason for the widespread acceptance of this partnership arrangement is because they make money.

Few of these programs are proprietary, in-house programs that are launched and managed by the newspapers themselves. Established IPs, many of whom have since become full-fledged service bureaus, operate them and have signed up newspapers as media partners. Some of the more successful IP/service bureaus have hundreds of newspaper media partners, representing the most important segment of their business.

Revenue sharing with a media partner is a lot like program sharing discussed earlier. If the IP is using more than one media partner for a given program, each participant should be assigned an exclusive 900 number plus access to independent call count verification. The media partner may justifiably insist on exclusivity in its market area, particularly if it is lending its name to the program. The IP, on the other hand, has a legitimate basis for requiring a commitment to a certain level of advertising to help cover the cost of adding another 900 number to the program.

The revenue-sharing breakdown must be beneficial to both sides. The media partner will want to see projected revenue, at a realistic response level, at least equal what it would otherwise earn by simply selling the space or time to advertisers. Also, the media partner will probably not want to compete with established paying advertisers of similar programs in its media.

Because revenue sharing can be quite lucrative for the IP, you should carefully consider this option for your 900 program. And do your homework before approaching a prospective media partner. It might be prudent to advertise with the company for awhile so that you can unequivocally demonstrate call volume response to advertising in that specific media. Because you will be dealing with an experienced business person, a well-organized written proposal should be prepared. The subjects outlined in your proposal should include the following:

❐ Description of the program.
❐ Your target market (It better describe the potential media partner's audience!).

❏ The proposed functions and responsibilities of both partners.
❏ The revenue-sharing breakdown, including details on per minute/call gross revenue, long-distance carrier charges, service bureau charges, and net revenue per minute/call.
❏ Demonstrated response rates. This can be from prior advertising with similar media or from a test run with the prospective media partner.
❏ Call volume and revenue projections. Demonstrate realistic revenue projections as call volume increases with repeated advertising exposure.
❏ Anything else that gives you credibility. A paragraph about your background, business references, other successful media partners, the capabilities of your service bureau, and anything else that makes the potential media partner feel comfortable about doing business with you.

Don't ask the media partner to invest any money, and don't require a minimum monthly fee. Make your proposal as risk-free as possible, which makes it much easier for him or her to accept. To cover your incremental monthly costs, you may consider dividing the revenue on a sliding scale, with the largest percentage going to you until your costs are covered. And don't tell the media partner that it doesn't cost him anything. It certainly does — especially if he has to turn away a potential paying advertiser for the same space or time spot. Just make sure you structure the revenue sharing so there is a realistic expectation for the media partner to in fact earn more than by simply selling the advertising space or time.

It would also be a good idea to suggest a realistic trial run of three to six months in order to give the program a fair chance of success. As with any other advertising, it will take time and repetition for response rates to increase to an acceptable level.

A profitable marketing relationship doesn't need to be limited to the media. Other companies and organizations will likely be communicating with your target market, so perhaps you can join with them to reach your audience cost-effectively. That's why I titled this section Strategic Alliances instead of Media Partnerships.

For example, if you had a program offering live technical support for PC users, you might try to establish a relationship with computer vendors. Especially the smaller vendors who don't already have their own support lines. You could also go beyond the computer itself, and offer advice on all the peripherals and how they work together, plus the various operating systems such as DOS, Windows and OS/2. Offer their customers a special rate or discount in return for having your literature placed inside the carton. Both parties are winners here. You get perfect rifle-shot exposure, putting your message into the hands of your prospect at the absolute best time possible. The vendor is able to take credit for offering free or discounted services that otherwise would not be available at all. And the customer gets help when he needs it. Everybody wins.

Trade and other associations are another possibility. These are groupings of people in very specific interest categories, and there may be several associations whose members would be particularly good prospects for your service. Offer their membership a special discount on your service in return for distribution of your literature during the next membership mailing or conference.

This is one method I have used to get exposure for my Telephone Area Code Map, which is sold as an advertising specialty with the imprint of the organization giving it away. If you ordered this book from my company you probably got a free sample of this map along with the book. I try to get associations with telephone-related companies as members to distribute the map. If the association is big enough I offer to imprint the association's name and logo on the map. The reverse side of the map has my sales message and pricing for quantity purchases. The association looks good because it is able to give away a useful gift to its members. I get my message out inexpensively *along with a tacit endorsement of a trusted trade association.*

Get into the mindset of always thinking about what you can *give* to someone who can help you. They have what you need:

access to your market. What can you give them in exchange for that access?

Charitable organizations are another possibility. Give something away using the charity as a means of promotion and distribution. You might be able to enlist a large force of volunteers to serve as your temporary sales force. You become a hero while getting your message out — quite effectively.

Low-Cost Advertising

When you get a media kit or price quote from a media source, don't automatically assume that the quoted advertising prices are set in concrete. Just because the prices are formally printed up on an official-looking schedule doesn't mean there's no room for negotiation.

I mentioned before that media companies often have unsold space or time spots. If they cannot sell this advertising in time, they will earn absolutely nothing. Once the lost time or space becomes history, it becomes totally worthless to both advertisers and the media. They will much prefer to get at least something for the space or air time. It's not unusual to be able to negotiate drastic discounts — often less than half the published prices. Or, get them to throw in some free insertions or time spots for an up-front payment. Nothing works as well as the promise of immediate cash in hand.

According to direct marketing expert Dan Kennedy, author of *How to Make Millions With Your Ideas* (Plume/Penguin, 1996) and several other books, "Direct response advertisers need to get space at 50 percent to 70 percent off rate card in order to make money." Discounts of this magnitude are hard to get for individual advertisers, but can often be obtained through media placement agencies, who buy advertising space in bulk (and will often guarantee each publication a certain amount of revenue). Kennedy's book lists several such agencies, and the following are two I am familiar with:

National Mail-Order Classified

P.O. Box 5, Sarasota, FL 34230
813-366-3003

National Response Corporation
13619 Inwood Rd., #300, Dallas, TX 75244
214-458-7625

Also check out The 900 Advertising Club mentioned earlier in this chapter. It buys bulk advertising for its members, serving as a purchasing co-op.

With print advertising, a another good strategy is to wait until the submission deadline date for a particular issue, then contact the media company at the last minute to see what kind of deal it can give you. Explain that you are just starting your program and would like to give them a try, but you simply can't afford to spend more than X number of dollars for testing your ad in their publication. More often than not you will be able to get a significant price break for your efforts. Yes, you may have to Federal Express the camera-ready ad copy to them to meet the deadline, but this will often be worth it. And remember, particularly with print media, their published deadlines are very rarely their true deadlines.

With radio and television you can achieve similar savings by taking advantage of "run of station" (ROS) advertising. You simply contract for a certain number of spots over a period of time, and the station airs the spots wherever they have unsold time. This is a more formalized way to take advantage of unsold time, and gives the media station some flexibility in filling up its advertising schedule. You still might try some last-minute negotiation for better rates if the station already has your commercial in the can. Instead of renewing an ROS arrangement, let it lapse and call periodically for good rates for the next day or two, and you are likely to save even more money.

The only disadvantage with last-minute purchasing or ROS is that you will rarely get the best placement or time slots. A TV ad that airs at 3 a.m. won't be seen by many viewers. Some of your savings in advertising costs may be offset by lower response rates to the ads.

Run of station television advertising is typically aired during the daytime or late at night, during non prime-time periods. But your specific target market may in fact be daytime or late-night viewers, so this may end up working to your advantage. Indeed, many direct response advertisers have been quite successful with late-night advertising. This is likely due to the fact that many late-night programs are reruns, and the viewer may not be quite so glued to the program. Because the viewer already knows the plot, he or she might be more willing to break away and make the telephone call to your 900 number.

The fact is, you can save considerable money by offering to purchase unsold space or air time at the very last minute, when the media company will be eager to get at least something. Don't be afraid to try this technique — it works!

Contests, Games & Sweepstakes

The possibility of winning a prize of value appeals to everyone, and adding a prize element to a 900 program, when appropriate, can multiply call counts significantly. Everyone knows that Publisher's Clearinghouse gives away millions of dollars a year in prizes. You have probably entered its sweepstakes at least once. This promotional technique obviously works very well for many companies, or they wouldn't be doing it with such predictable regularity.

The nature of the program will dictate whether or not a prize feature is appropriate. Telephone games and contests are obvious candidates. Product, service, or event promotions are another likely application. For example, Paramount sponsored a 900 sweepstakes in conjunction with a polling application in order for *Star Trek* fans to select their favorite episodes for an upcoming *Star Trek* television marathon featuring the 10 most popular episodes. In return for calling to register their vote, Trekkies were given a chance for a walk-on part in Paramount's *Star Trek: The Next Generation*.

The entertainment industry in particular has embraced the use of 900 games, contests or sweepstakes in promoting its products and services. New Line Home Video, The Nashville Network, NBC, TBS, MTV, Fox Broadcasting, HBO, and MCA/Universal are just some of the entertainment companies that have developed 900 telepromotions in order to generate interest in their products or services. Very often, the prizes being offered are tied into the product or service being promoted: concert tickets, videos, or promotional novelties.

The long-distance carriers have established some fairly stringent guidelines in allowing 900 programs with contest features. Expert legal assistance will be essential in properly executing any game, contest or sweepstakes. Every state has its own lottery laws, and these laws are constantly changing or being re-interpreted. In some cases, they are applied more stringently to 900 promotions in particular. Needless to say, this is not an area to jump into without some expert legal help.

Promotion law is a specialized field, and it is unlikely that your local attorney will be equipped to help you set up your promotion. The Promotion Marketing Association of America (PMAA) is a valuable source of information for not only legal information, but also for all other aspects of running a successful promotion:

PMAA
322 Eighth Ave., Suite 1201, New York, NY 10001
212-206-1100

The PMAA maintains a list of member law firms with experience in promotion law. Two firms in particular are widely recognized as leaders in the 900-number industry:

Ginsberg, Feldman & Bress
1250 Connecticut Ave., NW, Washington, DC 20036
202-637-9000

Hall, Dickler, Kent, Friedman & Wood

909 Third Avenue, New York, NY 10022
212-838-4600

Measurement & Testing

Even though you have already conducted thorough market research and have selected some very promising media sources for your initial advertising, you can't stop here. Advertising is your largest expense category, and it will pay off handsomely to be able to spend your advertising budget as cost-effectively as possible.

As we'll see later in Chapter 8, even small variations in the rate of response to an ad will result in significant changes in the projected revenue. To get the biggest bang for your advertising buck, you have to be able to somehow measure the effectiveness of your advertising. What we're really looking for here is the lowest cost-per-response.

Advertising measurement and testing is an extremely important function for any business. Hundreds of books have been written about this subject. Many highly educated professionals are paid impressive salaries for their expertise in this field. It is a fascinating science unto itself. But it all boils down to finding out the lowest cost for generating a response or purchase.

Fortunately, the pay-per-call industry has a unique characteristic shared by few other businesses: direct, immediate response. When your 900 program ad hits the streets or the airwaves, most of the responses will be immediate.

Companies such as Coca Cola or General Motors do not benefit from such direct response, and they have to spend a lot of money on measurement information — which is by nature quite subjective. Think about it: Do you remember what specific advertising motivated you to purchase your last automobile? Well, the manufacturer doesn't really know either.

Testing ads of different sizes and types, in different media, and then measuring the results, will eventually result in finding out what works best for your program. Indeed, the process never ends. There are literally hundreds of ways you can vary any given ad, and it takes time to test every possible variation. The measurement and testing process is an ongoing effort for the life of any business.

How is effectiveness actually measured? By calculating the cost-per-response. Say a $5,000 display ad generates 2,500 calls to your 900 program. The total cost-per-response was $2 ($5000/2500 calls). Now let's say we tested a different publication. The ad cost is $3000, and a total of 2000 calls are generated from the ad. The cost per response in this case is $1.50 ($3000/2000 calls). This is obviously a better investment than the first example. Although the total number of calls are lower, you must ask yourself whether it would be better to spend more of your advertising budget on larger ads in this publication while dropping the other publication altogether. Yes, both publications are actually making money, but one of them is making money more cost-effectively than the other.

This decision shouldn't be made too hastily, however. Doubling the size of the ad will not necessarily double the response. It may increase response only slightly, or it could triple response. You won't know for sure until you try it. Or, you may find that a smaller ad is even more cost-effective. A $1000 ad pulling 1000 calls costs only $1 per response.

Another consideration is market saturation. Any specific publication has a relatively static group of subscribers or readers. After an initial rise in response rates, you may in fact experience a gradual drop-off after all of the likely callers have tried your program. This is particularly true for novelty programs such as games. If and when this happens, it might be advisable to switch to a similar publication for a fresh group of likely callers.

If your program features valuable information with many repeat callers, continued advertising to those callers might not be very cost-effective because they are calling despite the ads. You might try stopping the ad for a couple of months to measure the drop-off in call volume.

Advertising Schedule

Accurate measurement is possible only when calls can be reasonably tied to specific advertising. It will be impossible to measure the effectiveness of any given ad if several are published

---

almost simultaneously in various publications or media. There are ways around this problem, however, which will be discussed later. Nonetheless, in the absence of a methodology for differentiating the response, the only way to properly measure results is to space the timing of the advertising such that the response from each ad can be determined before the next ad is published or aired.

Fortunately, each media type has unique characteristics relating to their typical time of response periods. For example, radio and TV are essentially immediate. As long as you know the station's schedule for airing your spots, you will be able to measure response on an hourly basis. Nearly all the response to your spot will occur during or shortly after the ad is aired.

A monthly magazine, on the other hand, will have the longest response period. It may lie around for several months before being discarded, resulting in calls months after the ad first appears. Nevertheless, most of the call volume resulting from a magazine ad will occur during the first two weeks after the on-sale date.

A weekly newspaper will be similar to a monthly magazine, except that most of the response will be experienced during the half-week after the on-sale date instead of the first half-month.

Understanding the different media types, you can in fact run advertising in various media fairly close together. For example, a TV spot which is run a week after a monthly print ad appears will hopefully result in a measurable spike in call volume just after the spot airs. By subtracting the average daily counts from the total for the day the TV spot aired, a reasonable estimate can be made for the TV response alone.

The actual advertising schedule can be a simple wall or desk calendar that notes the on-sale or air dates for all advertising, plus the daily and/or hourly call counts. Tracking call counts by the hour will be necessary only if using TV or radio advertising.

Caution! Do not make any long-term commitments for advertising until you have completed at least some initial testing with that media company. You will be enticed with lower-cost ads for making a commitment to repeat advertising with any media company. You must resist this temptation until you are convinced, through actual testing and measurement, that the response rates justify allocating a significant portion of your advertising budget on a long-term basis.

Testing Strategies

We have talked about several different variables that may influence the response rate to your ad, and it will be instructive to summarize all the variables here:

❒ The medium. Radio, TV, print, or direct mail. Rifle-shot or shotgun blast.

❒ Ad size or length. Full-page or quarter-page, 60-second or 30-second.

❒ Ad appearance or design. How well does it grab attention and induce people to read the ad?

❒ Ad copy. Does the ad copy successfully induce the target audience to take action? Does it follow the AIDA principle? (Attention, Interest, Desire, Action).

❒ Timing. Does the ad appear when your target market is most likely to call? Time of day will be important for radio or TV, whereas seasonal factors might effect response to magazine ads.

❒ Price. The price of the information service will likely influence the response rate, so it may be prudent to test different price points.

Start multiplying out the options for each of these variables and you can end up with hundreds of different combinations. It would take years to test all possible combinations if you had to rely on adequate time spacing alone for proper response measurement. Plus, a true test will take more than one repetition for each ad. How can you streamline the testing process in order to get measurable results more quickly?

First, you can use smaller local or regional media sources before launching a national advertising campaign. In order to measure response, you will simply need to know where the calls originate from. This can be accomplished two ways: Automatic Number Identification (ANI) or Online Call Detail Data (OCDD). Either way, you will know where each call originated, by area code, so you can test different ads in different regions at the same time.

ANI information is provided monthly by the IXC to the service bureau for calls to 800 and 900 numbers, including the originating caller's telephone number, date and time of call, and call duration. A sophisticated service bureau will then collate the data in any way you require: by originating area code, hold time, or time of day. You also receive a monthly report which tells you the origin of your calls. Some of the more sophisticated service bureaus, such as Scherers Communications in Ohio, can give you "last audio played" data, which tells you what segment of the program menu the caller was listening to before terminating the call. This lets you measure which features of your program are most popular with your callers.

OCDD information is not as detailed as ANI, and is typically limited to summarizing call volumes from different telephone area codes or states. Nonetheless, OCDD information is more timely, available weekly instead of monthly, and it is typically less expensive to receive than ANI.

Depending upon how sophisticated you want to get with your response measurement, you may elect to receive both. Make sure your service bureau can provide this service and check out the costs involved.

Either ANI or OCDD permits you to advertise simultaneously in several geographic markets without losing track of which ads draw what response. Another possibility is the use of different telephone extension numbers displayed with each ad. The caller is simply instructed to press the appropriate number, and the monthly call report will break down the calls by extension number. Although less expensive, this option complicates the program and could be perceived in a negative light by the target market.

Unfortunately, testing different price structures for the program isn't quite so simple. Virtually all program preambles are required to include a statement giving the price of the call, and all associated advertising must obviously match this information. The only way, therefore, to test more than one price is to use separate 900 numbers that tie into separate programs with appropriate preamble price information. This results in additional costs associated with adding another 900 number plus any programming costs for using different preambles with the program.

Despite the additional expense, it could be well worth it to test different pricing. Although the net call revenue per minute will be less, a lower-priced service may result in a significant increase in call volume which more than compensates for the lower per-minute revenue. Also, having a second number in place allows you to experiment with other program changes, including the script, voice talent, format, or even adding a promotional incentive for calling.

Customer Database

The ability to know your customers, by name and address, could be quite valuable. They have already called your program once, and a follow-up direct-mail piece could be a cost-effective means of generating additional calls from these people. Perhaps you could include a business card or Rolodex card for handy reference to your 900 service. As long as they have been satisfied customers, your previous customer base is by far the most likely group to call your program again and again. You have already spent a lot of money in advertising to find these people, and now you want to try and keep them.

How do you get the names and addresses of people who call your program? One way is to simply ask. Offer a prize or other promotional incentive, and include a menu slot in the program for the caller to leave his or her name and address.

Another way is by using the ANI data. With ANI you already have the telephone numbers, and now you need to match telephone numbers with names and addresses. There are data service companies that provide this kind of service. One such service, offered by The Times Journal Company, is called Telematch. This company offers computerized reverse matching of names and addresses to telephone numbers.

Telematch
6883 Commercial Dr.

Springfield, VA 22159
800-523-7346

Another option is offered by Telecompute Corp., a Washington, DC-based service bureau, by dialing 900-555-MATCH, at $1.49 per minute. This is an automated system, where you input the telephone number and the name and address are delivered by recorded voice (using text-to-speech technology).

Your in-house mailing list of self-generated leads could become one of your most effective marketing tools. Although unsolicited direct mail is probably not cost-effective for most 900 programs, direct-mail follow-up to previous customers is a different ballgame. They have already called once, and it probably won't take much effort to get them to call again. Repeat business from satisfied customers is the most cost-effective way to build up call volume and revenue.

Further Study

Now you understand why marketing is the most important element in a successful 900-number program. You need to become an expert at all facets of marketing, so you can generate maximum response to your advertising for the lowest cost. As you can see from the information in this chapter, there are many avenues for getting the word out about your program. Not all of them will work. Some will work a lot better than others. In the final analysis, what works best for you all depends upon *what* you are selling, *to whom.*

Give yourself a fair chance for success by taking the time and expending the effort to learn as much as you can about marketing. It will be worthwhile even if you never launch a 900 line. What you learn can be applied to any business, whether it be your own or that of your employer. You can even use your new-found knowledge to help you find a better job or otherwise further your career, by marketing *yourself.* Here's a list of books that have been helpful to me:

Guerrilla Marketing
by Jay Conrad Levinson (Houghton Mifflin). The latest edition of this book is in most bookstores, and you can call Guerrilla Marketing International at 800-748-6444 for a subscription to the *Guerrilla Marketing Newsletter*.

Money Making Marketing
by Jeffrey Lant (JLA Associates, 617-547-6372)

Getting Business to Come to You
by Paul and Sarah Edwards (Putnam, 800-631-8571)

The Ultimate Sales Letter (Bob Adams Publishers) and *How to Make Millions With Your Ideas* (Plume/Penguin), by Dan Kennedy. These books are available in bookstores or by calling 800-223-7180.

The next chapter, about publicity, technically falls under the purview of marketing. As you will see, however, the subject is important enough to deserve its own dedicated chapter.

Chapter 6
Publicity

What is publicity, and how does it differ from advertising? Publicity doesn't cost anything. You supply the media with factual, newsworthy information, and hopefully it gets used in some manner. You, your company or your 900-number service get free coverage in the media. The only possible downside is that you have no control over how that information is used or presented to the public, if at all. The media can be television, radio, newspapers, magazines, newsletters, columnists, wire services or trade journals.

Too many inexperienced entrepreneurs never even consider trying to get free publicity for their business. They are eager to get things going, and the simplest thing to do is to come up with some advertisements and pay to run them. With advertising, you have complete control over the timing and the content of your message. Advertising is actually easier to manage than publicity, and it's a lot more predictable.

But free publicity is much more powerful because it's completely believable. It's the media talking, not you, so the message is perceived as unbiased and truthful. Far more effective than contrived advertising copy. And you can't beat the price!

It's easy to lose sight of alternatives to paid advertising during the flurry of activity surrounding the launch of a new business. A good publicity campaign, however, can bring in tens of thousands of dollars worth of free exposure. Launching a new business is expensive enough, so why not take advantage of the exposure the media will give you for nothing?

When Mary Lynn Bell launched Ask The Pharmacist, AT&T was so impressed with the program that the communications giant used it as a role model for potential 900 service providers — resulting in the equivalent of hundreds of thousands of dollars of free publicity from media nationwide. As a result, she didn't have to spend advertising dollars to start generating calls to her program. This would be a dream come true for any entrepreneur.

Why the potential interest in what you're doing? Because the media is in the business of covering — and selling — the news. If you are doing something newsworthy, they want to hear about it. There are literally millions of pages of print and minutes of air time that need to be filled with interesting or helpful information.

Every day, 365 days a year.

The media is constantly looking for stories that will be of interest to their readers, viewers or listeners. All you have to do is give them what they want. Sounds simple, but for the media to take an interest, you have to give them *NEWS*. More about this later.

The Press Kit

The actual tool for getting the word out is the press kit. The contents of your press kit need not be set in concrete. What's included depends on what information you are conveying, for what purpose, and to whom. The information supplied can either tell your story or provide supporting information that will help the editor do his or her job in reporting it. The following are some of the common elements that can be found in a press kit. Rarely, however, will you find all or even most of them in a single press kit:

The News Release. The news release (or press release) is usually the focal point of a press kit. It's often the *only* element. Because the news release is the most important element, I'll devote a whole section to it later.

Cover Letter. Use a cover letter only when addressing a specific person, when you need to amplify the information in the news release. For example, you might mention how a current event relates to your story. Or you might volunteer yourself to serve as an expert resource for future stories in your area of expertise (including a Rolodex card would be a smart idea). The letter could have some relevant background information that doesn't fit in the news release itself. Do not, however, include self-serving remarks such as, "Your readers will be grateful to get this information." That would be presumptuous, and will only earn you the resentment of the editor. Stick to relevant facts.

Brochure or Flier. It's perfectly acceptable to include a brochure or any other sales piece that helps describe your service, your company or your people. It will often be helpful to the editor in getting a better overall picture. If you are going to spend money on anything, spend it on your brochure. It should be professionally produced and reflect well on you and your company. I always include a one-page flier about the relevant book with every press kit. The front has a nice color graphic of the book and some ad copy, while the reverse side lists other media reviews, testimonials, the table of contents, a photo of the author and a brief biography. This flier serves multiple purposes, as you'll see as you read on.

Biography Sheet. If the story involves a person as its focus or as an expert who has been quoted, you should include a "bio." Keep it brief and factual. Always include the person's hometown plus all salient credentials that will support his or her position as an authority on the subject. Stick with credentials and experience related to the subject of the news release.

Photograph. The print media is always looking for interesting pictures to publish, to break up all the endless type that would otherwise fill up the page. If a particular person is central to your story, send a photo of that person. If it's a unique product, send a picture. Newspapers always want sharp black-and-white glossies. Slick magazines will want color, probably transparencies (35mm slides are common). Have the photograph taken by a professional. If you need to make a lot of copies for a big publicity campaign, you will save money by using a company that specializes in producing prints in large volume. Try the company I use:

Ornaal Glossies
24 West 25th St., New York, NY 10010
212-675-3850

I frequently include a B&W photo of the book's cover in my press kits. I do not, however, send color transparencies or photos until asked, which is rare.

Fact Sheet. This usually relates to a product or service. It is a detailed one-page description of all the features, characteristics or specifications. For my books, it lists title, author, ISBN number, number of pages, dimensions, hard- or soft-cover, retail price, target audience, and a one-paragraph summary of the contents. For a 900-number service it could list the number, price, duration of an average call, purpose of the program, interactive menu, how often it's updated, target audience, and perhaps a sample of the script.

Backgrounder. As the name implies, this piece gives background information about your company or organization. It's a brief one-page summary of your company's structure, history, capitalization, sales volume, and position in the marketplace. It can also list the principals, their credentials and background, and the members on the board of directors. You could also state your company philosophy, objectives and future plans. I never use these only because they're not called for in the publishing business. A 900-number service, on the other hand, has built-in credibility problems to overcome, so an impressive backgrounder can be valuable.

Interview Questions. When sending press kits to the broadcast media, you are usually looking for an on-air interview. A list of suggested questions will help the interviewer. When preparing the questions, don't necessarily list the questions *you* want to handle.

Try to imagine what questions the viewers or listeners would ask if they had the chance. Those are the questions the interviewer will also want to ask, whether you like it or not.

Reviews and testimonials. Reviews and testimonials give you credibility from an independent third party. This helps the person reviewing your press kit: he doesn't have to completely trust your word. He can rely on the opinions of others who have no interest in furthering your cause. He doesn't have to be as careful about trusting your credibility. I always keep up a running one-page list of all reviews and testimonials for every book I publish. When a lot of them pile up, as they have for this book, I go to two columns and small type, and throw out the least impressive ones.

Reply Card. A postcard-sized reply card can be included offering to send follow-up information. Instead of sending a pile of unsolicited materials, send a news release by itself along with a checklist (of some or all of the above items) on the back of a self-addressed reply card. You don't need to put return postage on it. Just make it easy to use. I use a reply card frequently, and the editor can check off whether she wants to receive a review copy of the pertinent book or a photo of the book or the author. Saves a lot of paper while saving a busy editor time going through a big pile of information. If your story is compelling, she will either check the boxes and send the reply card or call for more details. Like two-step advertising we talked about in the last chapter.

Other Stuff. Any other materials that grab attention or support your story. A bumper sticker or a balloon, as long as the message relates to your story. A reprint of an article. Survey results. Include an enticing statement on the outside of your envelope.

Include in your press kit any materials that help describe your story and give you credibility. You can combine the above information into one document where appropriate. For example, combine the bio with the fact sheet or include background information in the cover letter. Don't, however, load up your press package with a lot of extraneous materials that may detract from the main message, which is highlighted in the news release. You will probably never use all the elements we just covered. Put yourself in the editor's position and include those materials that will help her do her job. Make her job easy enough, and it will be hard to pass up your story.

I usually keep my initial, unsolicited mailing quite brief, consisting of a news release, a flier and a reply card, all mailed first-class in a business-size number 10 envelope. Sometimes I will also include a photo of the book. As I mentioned earlier, my flier does triple duty because it also serves as a data sheet, an author bio and a summary of media reviews. Sometimes I'll get coverage as a result of this mailing alone, which usually consists of a mention of the book as a resource. Editors planning a more in-depth review or article either call or return the reply card for more information.

The News Release

Although the news release is a relatively short document, usually only one page long, it is critically important that it be written and formatted properly. Most important, to be considered a news release, it must be NEWS. At the same time it must be INTERESTING.

An announcement about the launch of your new business isn't nearly enough. Honestly now, would you be interested in such information? Now if your new 900-number program solved a real problem a lot of people have, that would be your news "hook." Compare the following headlines:

ABC Company Announces Job Search Line
or
Three Tips For Finding a Job When Nobody is Hiring

It's pretty obvious which hook is the most compelling. The first one is a yawner that will go straight into the trash. The second promises to solve a real every-day problem and will get an editor's attention. By the way, the hook is usually stated in the headline, which is obviously the most important element of the news release. The headline is what gets the editor to take notice and compels her to read on.

You need to identify what problems are solved or what benefits are offered by your service. If it can be tied into current events, so much the better. Always remember that the editor or producer who is evaluating your news release is first and foremost looking out for the best interests of her audience. She is always asking herself, "Why would anyone be interested in this? How will it help them? What makes this unique?" After all, a media company that doesn't cater to the needs of its audience doesn't stay in business for long.

Whether you call it a news hook or an "angle," you must first identify something truly newsworthy to hang your hat on. What do you do if there's nothing at all interesting about your 900 line? What if it's so mundane that there is simply no way to make it exciting?

Unless your service has some truly unique new features that are news in and of themselves, you're usually better off talking about:

❏ Problems solved by the service, or
❏ The controversy surrounding the service, or
❏ Unique benefits offered by the service, or
❏ Current events that relate to the service, or
❏ The stories of the people offering the service, or
❏ A story about someone whose life was improved by the service.

Discuss something interesting and newsworthy that is *related* to your service in some manner. All you need is an excuse to mention your service in the story. The challenge is working in the information *you* want published, which is usually about what you're selling. Just make it fits into the context of the story, and you will get what you want.

Maybe there's news in the people behind your 900-number service:

Unemployed Executive Finds Work
Helping Others Find Jobs

The reasons behind starting your business and the events leading up to establishing the line might be much more interesting than the line itself. People are always interested in hearing a story, specially one with a human-interest angle. It's always much more powerful to talk about flesh-and-blood real people and their specific circumstances than to drone on about statistics and vague generalities.

Another alternative is to stage a newsworthy event yourself:

Free Job Search Offered on Xmas Day

Indeed, your strategy should not be limited to a one-time start-up effort. A good ongoing program will constantly create or seek out newsworthy events. Capitalize on relevant current events:

XYZ Corp. Lays Off 10,000 - Job Line Gears Up

Now you are probably getting an idea of how to come up with a good hook. You will likely come up with several. That's fine, because you will want more than one version of a news release, and you never want to stop at sending out just one. Once you have the hook, the rest of the news release follows.

I will spend days writing one news release. First I identify the target audience and write down all the possible news hooks that will appeal to that audience, choosing the most powerful angle. Then I write the first draft without regard to the length. Then I come back to it every day over the next few days and tweak it a little each time, tightening it up until it fits on one page. I can't overemphasize how important it is to spend the time and effort to compose the best news release possible. *If you can't do it yourself, hire a publicist to do it for you.* It will pay off handsomely.

Don't settle for a one-size-fits-all news release. You need to keep in mind what media you're writing for, and more importantly, who is the ultimate audience. You may use altogether different hooks for different groups. What appeals to the readers of a specialized trade journal will rarely work with MTV viewers. Even at the same newspaper the lifestyle editor and the business editor are serving different readers. Always keep in mind who you're writing for, and make sure it will interest that group.

Why spend all this effort? Because if it isn't done right, any effort will be wasted because it will end up in the circular file — i.e., the trash. Editors get flooded with news releases every day, and only the most compelling ones get their attention. Frankly, most news releases are pretty badly written. That's good news for you, because it means yours has a better chance of being noticed.

Approaches

It is usually difficult to find hard news as the basis for your story. It might sound too contrived forcing your story to fit current events. You may have better results coming at the story from another angle. These are sometimes referred to as feature stories, as opposed to news stories, and can work just as well. The following approaches will help you find several hooks for your releases:

Event. This can cover a future event or a past event. Instead of a simple announcement, it should go into the public impact or benefits related to the event.

The Holidays. Relate the story to Mother's Day, Valentine's Day or Halloween, for example.

Tips. Offer a list of tips from an expert in the subject. This is popular with editors because it helps the reader. See an example of this approach a little later.

How-to Lead. Similar to tips, except it covers one topic, instructing the reader how to accomplish a given task or objective.

Advice. Structured as an interview with an expert.

Survey. This will work if the survey results are interesting or unexpected. Must include details of how the survey was conducted, sample size and details that substantiate the source and the results.

Contest. Announce a contest or report the results of one.

Product (Service) Introduction. Not very interesting unless the product itself is truly newsworthy, which is rare.

Exposé. Use controversy as the hook. Uncover a scam or a charlatan. I have used this one successfully.

Consumer Alert. Similar to an exposé. Cover health or safety issues, for example.

Nostalgia. Tie the story to the past, such as the birth of Elvis or the history of rock and roll.

List. The 10 best (worst, biggest, smallest, longest, shortest, coldest, meanest and so on) list can be humorous, but don't force it. The source of the list should be clearly stated.

The Play by Play. Can work when the details need to be listed chronologically.

Quiz. This gets the reader involved, who will better remember the release. Answers can be given at the end and a scoring system devised.

These suggested approaches are not all inclusive. You may come up with some good ones of your own.

Format

A professionally drafted release will conform to several basic formatting rules:

❑ It must be typed on 8 1/2" X 11" paper. Use a standard serif typeface like the one you're reading here. Do not use legal-size paper. There is disagreement whether or not a news release should be printed on letterhead or plain paper. I print mine on my letterhead, which is quite distinctive with a bold blue stripe going down the left margin. It stands out from the others in the pile on the editor's desk. Others believe it should be printed on clean white paper to facilitate cutting and pasting if it's used. Cutting and pasting doesn't happen much anymore in this age of desktop publishing, so this is no longer a valid argument. Getting noticed and presenting a professional image are more important. If you have a good-looking letterhead that doesn't clutter up the page or otherwise interfere with your message, use it.

❏ The name and telephone number of the contact person should appear at the top of the first page. This will be your publicist, marketing person or you. It should always be an actual person, not a company name. Both a daytime and an evening phone number are helpful, specially if the editor is working on a deadline and needs to talk to you at 7:30 p.m.

❏ I like to title my news release as a **News Release** so there's no doubt what it is at first glance. Editors are real busy, and it doesn't pay to be cute or vague with them.

❏ Also print the release date at the top. Here you are telling the media when it is okay to publish the news. For example, it might be inappropriate to publish the release earlier because your program won't be operational until then. You have two options here: 1) A specific date, or reference to a specific time period, like, "Release Before School Starts," or 2) "For Immediate Release." Use the latter when it doesn't matter. Use the specific date whenever possible because it reinforces the perception of timely news. "For Immediate Release" isn't time-sensitive and doesn't generate the urgency of a certain date. When using a date, give monthly magazines at least three months advance notice, give weeklies one or two weeks and give dailies and broadcast media a week or so. Avoid too much lead time, because your release can get lost in the crush of intervening events.

❏ The headline should be all CAPS, no more than two lines in length.

❏ Double space the text so that the copy can be easily edited. I often cheat a little by using the 1.5 line spacing on my word processor. One page is best, and two pages should be the maximum. I always try to keep to one page. You should try to succinctly state all the necessary facts in one page. If you can't, you're probably rambling and need to focus. If you must use two pages, do not staple them together, because editors don't like to remove the staple to separate them. Type "more..." or "-more-" at the bottom of the first page, and "Page 2 - (Headline)" at the top of the second page.

❏ The dateline. Begin with a location and a date when appropriate. If you are making an announcement about the launch of your program, include the location (of the spokesperson or your company) and date of the announcement: "Newport, R.I., June 15, 1996 --" Don't use the new two-letter Post Office abbreviations; use the old-fashioned ones like "Miss. or Tex." The date should be the same as the "Release Date" at the top of the news release. If your news release is "for immediate release," no date is needed here, just the location.

❏ Always end the news release with three centered ###s. Don't ask why, it's tradition!

Content

It goes without saying that content is paramount. If it's not breaking news, it should be interesting or useful to the ultimate readers. The following are some general guidelines:

❏ If it is meant to be news, make sure it is immediate and timely. Don't wait for several weeks after you launch your program to send out the news releases.

❏ A feature story can be more informative and entertaining than a straight news story. It can employ a human interest angle with some flavor and emotion.

❏ Keep it tight, accurate, factual and not too "pluggy." Watch the flowery adjectives. If it's unique, that will be apparent from the story. Use facts instead of superlatives, and parcel them out one at a time.

❏ Don't get off track. Move the story along with each sentence, covering a key element, supporting what was stated in the lead paragraph.

❏ Use a summary lead style (who, what, where, when, why) whenever possible. Use short, concise sentences with active verbs: subject, verb, object. Grammar and spelling must be flawless.

❏ Spend 80% of your effort on the first paragraph, if not the first sentence. The headline and the first paragraph should grab the reader and tell the story.

❏ Go from the most important to the least important material. Editors usually cut news releases from the bottom (end) up.

❏ Use attribution to make it clear who is saying what throughout the story. It lets the editor off the hook. Use a person if possible, who could be an expert, a company spokesperson or a client. Quotes can be used to help prove the statements you made earlier, and should always be followed by the person's credentials: " 'Too many people get fleeced by the snake-oil crowd,' says industry expert Robert Mastin, author of *900 KNOW-HOW*."

❏ The release should be written in a completely unbiased way so that the media can use it as is without editing. Put yourself in the role of a reporter writing about your company. The media will appreciate you for making their job easier, and will often reward you by running your release exactly the way you wrote it.

Structure

I use a simple formula to write a news release. I learned it from Fred Ferguson at PR Newswire. It is primarily for writing feature releases, but it also works well for a time-sensitive news release. It will be very helpful in organizing your thoughts as you write the release:

Lead Paragraph. Readers who scan (editors) often read only the first sentence of each paragraph. This means the first sentence is critical, and that paragraphs should be short — only 30 words if possible, one or two short sentences (it's okay to have one-sentence paragraphs, because in a narrow newspaper column it's necessary to break up the text more often). Between the headline and this paragraph there should be no doubt what the story is all about.

Second Paragraph. This should authenticate the story. It reinforces and expands upon the premise stated in the first paragraph. The story angle has been established, and now the attribution is introduced, telling the reader the source of the story.

Quotes and actual names don't necessarily get used here. It can be enough to say "industry consultant" or "the president of ACME chemicals." The credentials can be parcelled out over multiple paragraphs.

This paragraph should also be short. The whole story should be told by now, and should stand if the rest were cut out.

Third Paragraph. This is the place to introduce the first quote. The quote can be used to introduce personal feeling or opinion. It can contain superlatives that are inappropriate elsewhere. It can add flavor to the story, but it must explicitly support the story. Use this opportunity to expand upon the person's credentials. This may also be an appropriate place to mention your product or service if you have not already done so, but save details (phone number, price) for the end of the release.

Note: This will sometimes be the last conventional paragraph, and what follows is governed by the approach taken — a series of tips or a list of the top 10 (_____).

Transition Paragraph. If necessary, expand the story further, before introducing another quote. Separate quote graphs with transition graphs. This is a good place to introduce a third-party endorsement. The story can continue for several more paragraphs, alternating with quote and transition graphs.

Now let's put all of this together in a sample news release. The following news release has been used successfully in promoting this book. Notice that it is truly news, with a fairly wide potential appeal. This release follows the consumer alert approach discussed earlier.

By the way, the following examples are formatted to fit on this book page, which is half the size of a normal 8 1/2 x 11 page. Additionally, to save space, these examples are not double-spaced. I promise, this did all fit onto one page!

Aegis Publishing Group, Ltd.
796 Aquidneck Avenue, Newport, R.I. 02842

News Release　　　　　　　　Contact: Robert Mastin
For Immediate Release　　　　　　401-849-4200

BEWARE OF DIALING
INTERNATIONAL PHONE NUMBERS

Newport, R.I. -- Unsuspecting callers to sex lines, psychic lines and other phone services risk losing their phone service when dialing international telephone numbers. The consumer protection available to 900-number callers does not extend to international numbers.

International charges are mingled into the long-distance portion of the bill. They can be difficult to identify and to dispute, and must be paid to maintain phone service. 900 charges are a different story, says industry expert Robert Mastin.

"You can dispute a 900-number bill and by law your phone service cannot be terminated for non-payment," says Mastin, author of *900 Know-How: How to Succeed With Your Own 900 Number Business* (Aegis, $19.95, 800-828-6961). 900 numbers are regulated the Telephone Disclosure and Dispute Resolution Act (TDDRA) of 1992, which includes consumer protection provisions such as full price disclosure in all advertising.

No such protection is available with international dialing. Participating foreign telephone companies inflate the call charges and pay commissions to the U.S.-based promoters who advertise the services, says Mastin. The caller rarely knows how much the call will cost.

You can usually identify an international number by its 011 or 809 (Caribbean) prefix. However, some unscrupulous operators use a 500 number -- used legitimately as a "follow-me-anywhere" number that is programmed to forward to other numbers -- to disguise the fact that the call forwards onto an expensive international number.

This may soon change. The Telecommunications Act of 1996 includes a provision to extend the protection afforded by TDDRA to all dialing patterns. In the meantime, stick with 900 numbers.

"Honest information providers offer their pay-per-call services over 900 numbers," says Mastin, also co-author of *Money-Making 900 Numbers* (Aegis, $19.95), a book profiling some 400 legitimate services. Both of his books are available in bookstores or by calling 800-828-6961.

###

Editor's Note: Mastin is available for interviews.

This release used current events — controversy about the use of international numbers — and turned the story into a consumer alert. Even a negative idea, as long as it is news and it doesn't hurt the perception of your company or service, will help to get your news release published. The more "newsy" the better, and your objective is to get the news release published.

Here's a news release for a different book, *Telecom Made Easy*, using a list of helpful tips as the approach. Again, the strength of this release is how it helps the readers:

Aegis Publishing Group, Ltd.
796 Aquidneck Avenue, Newport, R.I. 02842

News Release   Contact: Robert Mastin
For release March 26, 1996   401-849-4200

SMALL OFFICE -- BIG IMAGE

Pacifica, Calif., Mar. 26 -- Even a one-person business can look like an established, bustling enterprise. Technology has levelled the playing field.

New telecommunications technology is driving the growth of the SOHO (small office/home office) work force, says technology expert June Langhoff. Big-business capabilities such as voice mail are now within reach of the smallest companies.

"A key to success for any business is being close to your customers and easily accessible. New technology offers several ways to stay in touch," says Langhoff, author of *Telecom Made Easy* (Aegis, $19.95, 800-828-6961). She offers the following tips:

-- Fax-on-demand (FOD). Make all printed information -- catalogs, price lists, specifications, product announcements and instructions -- available around the clock with an automated FOD system.

-- Web page. Go a step further and offer interesting content that will attract people to your virtual storefront. Generate more traffic by getting suppliers and other allied organizations to provide links from their Web sites to yours.

-- Interactive voice response (IVR). Go beyond basic voice mail and use an interactive menu-driven system to offer recorded information about your company, such as store locations, business hours, up-to-date pricing or specials. Useful for answering frequently-asked questions.

-- Remote phone line. Establish a virtual presence -- including a Yellow Pages listing -- in any distant city by offering a local telephone number that automatically forwards to your actual location. Often called Remote Call Forwarding, this service is available from the phone company. A talent agent in Holyoke can establish a presence in Hollywood.

-- 900 number. Offer pay-as-you-go technical support. Most people recognize that it is expensive to staff help lines with experts. They will pay a reasonable fee for quick access if the alternative is no help or being put on hold forever.

-- Electronic newsletter. Ask your customers if they wish to be added to your e-mail list (or fax list) for weekly news updates. Less expensive than a printed newsletter and much faster.

"None of these are expensive to implement. Technology allows any business to compete more evenly with its biggest rivals," says Langhoff. Her book, *Telecom Made Easy* (Aegis), is available in bookstores or by calling 800-828-6961.

###

Editor's Note: Langhoff available for interviews.

Note the "editor's note" at the end. Here you can offer additional materials, like pre-written articles, or mention the availability of people for interviews. All editors have an expanding network of contacts they can call upon for expert information on hundreds of topics. You might as well be included.

A news release that gets published is much like editorial copy. It is more believable than any advertisement can possibly hope to be, and much more likely to be read. The news release is a powerful, no-cost tool which should be used extensively at every possible opportunity.

There's another type of news release that can be quite effective. Its basic purpose is to land an interview, and not necessarily get published as is. After all, the broadcast media — radio and TV — can't really do much with your news release by itself. But they do like to interview interesting people or experts on the air. Even with the print media, a feature article about you or your company is better than simply publishing a brief news release.

The rules for this kind of news release are a little looser. Your primary purpose is to get attention. Titillate or tease the editor to get her attention. Make a bold statement (that you can later back up!).

Paul Hartunian, who has written several books, including *How to Be Outrageously Successful With the Opposite Sex*, has been able to get millions of dollars of publicity on shows such as *Donahue, The Jenny Jones Show, To Tell the Truth, Regis & Kathy Lee,* and *Oprah.* One of his more successful headlines reads:

**I Can Help Anyone Find the Love
of Their Life in 90 Days or Less**

Hartunian stresses making an irresistible claim that's difficult to ignore. The media contact will need to call to get more information or even to disprove the claim! Either reason is fine, because you got a response.

According to Hartunian, "The one and only purpose of a press release is to get the media person to read it and contact you for more information." Good advice from someone who has generated well over $6 million worth of free publicity.

The Campaign

I have sold tens of thousands of books through the use of free publicity. In fact, I spend very little on paid advertising. Why should I when I can get free exposure? I have an aggressive, ongoing publicity program for every book I publish. I'm always on the lookout for special events or other reasons to communicate with the media. The techniques I use for promoting books will also work for promoting anything, including a 900-number service.

One of the most effective things for generating publicity for books is to send out lots of free review copies to people in positions to say good things about the book or to recommend it to lots of other people. Usually the media, but this could also include the movers and shakers in the industry. No matter what I say about the book, there is no substitute for reading the real thing. Few people are going to say nice things about something they haven't seen. They have their credibility to protect. It is therefore impossible to get any coverage about a book without first sending a review copy.

How does this relate to a 900-number service? The media will not write about your program without ever calling it first. And they will not want to pay for the privilege of promoting your business! Even if they were willing to pay, which is highly doubtful, they would be calling from an office where 900 calling is probably blocked anyway. It is absolutely essential that you offer the media free access to your program in some manner.

This can be accomplished in several ways. The simplest way is to offer access via a toll-free 800 line to your service. Your service bureau can set this up for you very easily. Obviously, this number would be for the exclusive use of the media only, and you need to be quite explicit about this. Clearly state, "Confidential media access only, DO NOT PUBLISH" next to the phone number. Do not put this number in the body of your news release, because you *want* that information published. You could include this number in an "editor's note" after the news release, in a cover letter or on a separate piece of paper.

You could also assign a special PIN (Personal Identification Number) number for media access, just in case the 800 number got out somehow. You could change PIN numbers without having to change the 800 number, and assign different ones to different media or media categories.

It would be a good strategy to place a time limit for access, which could be tied into the release date. For example, offer access for 30 days prior to the release date: "This PIN number is effective from June 1-30 only." This reinforces the time-sensitive urgency of your message and may actually help generate more media calls to your program.

Another way to offer the media free access is with a prepaid calling card, providing five or ten minutes of free calling to the program. This would be an unusual addition to the press kit, and will get more attention than simply providing a telephone number.

Now that we've nailed down what should go into your press kit, what it should say, and the types of media to contact, who do we send it to?

It should be mailed first-class to all logical mass media, including news directors at radio and television stations, editors at daily newspapers, or to specialty editors at magazines or trade publications.

Some advocate saving time and money by faxing the release. It's fast. But what happens if an editor is desperately waiting to receive some material before deadline and then the only fax machine gets tied up receiving your news release? He's not going to be happy. Indeed, the *Miami Herald* installed a 900 number on its fax for that very reason! You now have to pay to send an unsolicited fax, and I'm sure they have another less-publicized fax number for important information that they ask for. Bottom line: Ask before you fax.

Whenever possible, mail the news release to a name, not just a title. Call first to find out who to send it to. Then follow up with that person by telephone only if you have some additional news to add to the story. Don't call just to see if they got it and don't pester them or ask if the release will be published.

Where do you get actual names and addresses? Fortunately, because publicity is so important to virtually every business, there are specialized companies that offer numerous publicity-related services. Media contact directories and mailing lists are offered by the following:

Gebbie Press
P.O. Box 1000, New Paltz, NY, 12561
914-255-7560

Bacon's Information, Inc.
332 S. Michigan Ave., Chicago, IL, 60604
800-621-0561

Burrelle's Media Directories
75 E. Northfield Ave., Livingston, NJ, 07039
201-992-6600

BPI Communications, Inc.
1515 Broadway, 37th Fl., New York, NY, 10036
212-536-5266

Oxbridge Communications, Inc.
150 Fifth Ave., New York, NY, 10011
212-741-0231

You will be able to find some of the media directories published by these companies in the reference section of a larger library. Check the publication date, however, because libraries have tight budgets and their copies may not be current. Many of these directories are updated quarterly.

I prefer to purchase mailing lists, either on pressure-sensitive labels or on disc. These lists are kept more up-to-date than the directories, usually updated daily. Some of these companies will even do the mailing for you, distributing your news release to any number of media contacts as you wish. You simply provide an original of the news release and the selection criteria (i.e., for a business service, the business editors at major daily newspapers with circulations above 100,000; plus all business and trade magazines). This company will then print and send your release to its list of contacts, which will usually include the name and title of the current cognizant editor.

Because I usually send more than just a news release, I purchase mailing lists from Bacon's Information and do the mailing myself. Bacon's (and most likely the others) will also provide the list on disc, which can be transferred to your database or contact management program. I have transferred all media contacts into my ACT! contact management program so I can keep track of all mailings and other contact with them. Because I mail fairly frequently, it's not too difficult to keep the addresses current. However, unless I periodically purchase a new list from Bacon's I don't get new contacts or new editors when positions are changed, which is frequent in the media. I will periodically purge all contacts I have never heard from and replace them with those from a new disc from Bacon's. I keep the contacts that have given me coverage because those are obviously my prime contact list, and I want to keep a record of the history with those contacts.

Some of these same companies will offer a variety of other related services to help you manage your publicity program. Some offer clipping services, for example. How do you know when the media actually publishes something about you? You can't possibly read every newspaper in the country looking for your news release! This is where a clipping service is helpful. A clipping service will search all the media you designate for any mention of the subjects or even key words you select. Then it "clips" the item from the publication and sends you a copy.

MAT Services

"MAT" stands for "Mechanical Art Transfer," which is typesetting lingo for reproducible paste-ups or proofs. These services are targeted primarily at smaller daily and weekly newspapers, providing the ultimate in easy-to-use materials. The newspaper gets the news item — usually accompanied by a photograph — in a form that is immediately ready to be used by simply "pasting" it in. The piece is sized to fit most standard column widths, in a brief length that makes it ideal filler for a newspaper page that needs some additional material to fill it out.

Editors do indeed use these stories, which are nothing more than your news release in a different format. Although a MAT service will typically not guarantee how many newspapers will pick up your story (after all, they have no control over this), the results can be quite good, particularly with an interesting, timely story accompanied by a good photo or graphic. The visual element is usually important here, so the photo should get your serious attention. Instead of a head shot of the person, an action shot of the person doing something related to the story would be much better. Like using or benefitting from the product or service.

MAT services are not cheap, but they often offer clipping services too, so you will be able to track the results. Smaller newspapers in particular rely on these services to help fill out their papers, and the results are usually good. It is probably worth a try because you can measure your results, and even modest success is usually very cost-effective. I am more inclined to pay for this type of exposure than to go out and buy straight advertising. The following are some of the leading MAT services:

Associated Release Service, Inc.
43 North Canal St., Chicago, IL, 60606
312-726-8693

Derus Media Service, Inc.
500 N. Dearborn St., Suite 516, Chicago, IL
312-644-4360

Metro Creative Graphics, Inc.
33 W. 34th St., New York, NY, 10001
212-947-5100

North American Precis Syndicate, Inc.
201 E. 42nd St., New York, NY, 10017, 212-867-9000
1101 14th St., NW, Washington, DC, 20005, 202-347-5000
500 N. Michigan Ave., Chicago, IL, 60611, 312-558-1200
1901 Ave. of the Stars, Los Angeles, CA, 90067, 818-761-8400
235 Montgomery St., San Francisco, CA, 94104, 415-837-5000
1447 Peachtree St., Ste. 607, Atlanta, GA, 30309, 404-888-0400

MAT services are a cost-effective means for distributing your story to the media, and should be considered seriously for any marketing program. Advertising agencies and public relations firms use such services extensively, which should tell you something about their effectiveness.

PR Newswire

PR Newswire is an electronic version of a MAT service, distributing electronic news to the media worldwide. Several geographic packages are available, including national, regional, state & local, Canada, Latin America, Europe, Japan and global. The PR Newswire itself is for disseminating time-sensitive news. Also available is a Feature News Service for features that are not time sensitive.

The electronic news release is transmitted to media subscribers in all major markets, including newspapers, wire services, magazines and industry-specific trade publications. As part of each package, the newswire is also automatically placed on America Online, CompuServe, Dow Jones News/Retrieval, Nexis and Bloomberg Financial News.

This is a very cost-effective way to get your news release out to a wide media audience, not to mention the potential exposure from the online access. For example, the most recent price for the Feature News Service, which goes to 1,500 nationwide newspoints plus pertinent trade publications, is $275.00 for a release of up to 400 words. That's only 18 cents each (not even counting trade publications), about half the price of a postage stamp. Contact PR Newswire for its latest price list:

PR Newswire
810 Seventh Ave., 35th Floor, New York, NY 10019
212-596-1500 or 800-832-5522 fax: 800-793-9313

Needless to say, I'm a firm believer in the power of publicity. Remember, there are tens of thousands of media companies that must regularly fill up millions of pages of print and minutes of airtime. They all actively want to hear about interesting or newsworthy topics or events. The only reason they exist is to tell us about these things. All you have to do is to give them what they want and need. It really is that simple.

Although it takes more time and effort to get exposure with free publicity, as opposed to simply choosing the media and paying for the ad, the payoff can be quite handsome. Done properly, with the right news release, you could get lucky and generate the equivalent of tens of thousands of dollars in advertising — for free!

It will pay to become proficient with generating publicity. Two books that have helped me tremendously are listed below. They got me started in the right direction, and you should read them both before planning your publicity campaign.

The Publicity Handbook
by David Yale (NTC, 1991). Call NTC at 800-323-4900 or order the book at your local bookstore. The resource section of this book is alone worth the cover price, with listings of all kinds of specialized media directories and other helpful resources.

The Unabashed Self-Promoter's Guide
by Jeffrey Lant (JLA Associates, 617-547-6372). Jeffrey Lant has written several books and is quite successful practicing what he preaches. His no-nonsense advice is priceless.

Chapter 7
Processing the Calls

One of the most important decisions you will have to make is whether to purchase your own call-processing equipment or to use a service bureau. There is no right or wrong decision here, because it depends upon the type of service you are providing, your budget, your technical capabilities, your growth objectives and the degree of control you want to maintain over your operation.

If you're offering a live program, for example, with all your operators located in one place, you don't necessarily need a service bureau. You can use AT&T's Express 900 service, for example, and have the calls come directly into your facility. Unless you can program a greeting on your phone system that repeats the required preamble message, you will have to instruct each operator to verbally recite this message for every call. On the other hand, if you want to place some sophisticated audiotext options in front of the live operator option you may need the voice-processing capabilities offered by a service bureau. The calls would simply be routed through the service bureau before being forwarded to your facility.

Nonetheless, simple live programs rarely require the sophisticated voice-processing capabilities of a service bureau. Interactive programs, on the other hand, can be quite complex, requiring robust computer systems that must operate reliably 24 hours a day, with backup power systems and the technicians and programmers to make it all work. The issue of whether or not to use a service bureau, therefore, applies primarily to interactive programs.

Voice Processing Primer

Only a few years ago it would have been out of the question for a small start-up IP to even consider purchasing his own equipment. The investment required would have easily been $20 or $30 thousand dollars for even a modest call-processing system. Voice processing and computer telephony equipment, however, are going the same route as the basic personal computers that preceded them: they're getting a lot more sophisticated, user-friendly and less expensive — fast. There are dozens of manufacturers producing PC-based voice processing components and systems that are within the reach of budget-constrained entrepreneurs.

Before you can make an informed decision about which route will be best for your specific circumstances you should have a good understanding of what voice-processing technology is all about. I am not the person, however, to expound on this technical subject. I have enlisted Marc Robins, president of Robins Press, a leading New York-based publishing, market intelligence and consulting firm specializing in voice- and fax-processing technology, to help me out. The information on the following pages is adapted from material written by Marc Robins. See Appendix C for publications offered by Robins Press.

Introduction

As voice- and fax-processing technology continues to mature, the opportunities for enterprising companies and intrepid information providers to offer innovative, customer-pleasing services and programs are exploding. The last few years witnessed the beginning of a "golden age" for voice- and fax-processing technology. The fresh ingredients mixed into the smorgasbord include new user- and developer-friendly sophistication and welcome affordability.

We will examine some of the new trends in voice and fax processing technology, while also taking an in-depth look at the "building blocks" of the technology. We'll also explore the choices available to the prospective information provider in setting up a service — whether to use a service bureau, buy a turnkey system, or build a PC-based system. But first, before dissecting the technology, let's go back to the basics and explore the types of functions and features offered by voice- and fax-processing technology.

Back to the Basics

The term "Voice Processing" is being used by many suppliers to denote the full functional range of their systems. But what exactly does this term stand for? Voice Processing is basically a collection of functions that rely on the same or similar system components to work. All these functions revolve around the idea of the telephone as an information terminal, and voice "data" as the information that is conveyed via that terminal.

Since analog voice information is digitized and stored on a computer-based voice-processing system, this digital voice data can be manipulated and processed in the same ways as digital text data. Voice information can thus be stored, sorted, indexed, copied, converted and retrieved — hence the similarity to the term "Data Processing."

Leading Voice-Processing Functions

Call Processing/Automated Attendant. "Call Processing" technology specializes in automating the reception of incoming phone calls and the handling of the call once it's answered. "Automated attendants" are stand-alone (dedicated) systems, or the software function on a voice mail or voice-processing system that provides various call-processing capabilities. Typical automated attendant applications allow a company to answer an incoming call on the first or second ring, greet the caller with a recorded greeting, and then allow the caller to automatically reach the desired extension by simply pressing the extension number on the caller's touch-tone phone.

Audiotext. Sometimes spelled without the final "t," audiotext applications involve the delivery of pre-recorded, digitally stored voice information over the phone. "Dial-it" information services, such as 900-number services, are the leading source of audiotext applications.

Voice Mail or Voice Messaging. Voice mail systems allow users to record, store and retrieve voice messages. Two types of voice mail systems are available today — "stand-alone" and "integrated." Stand-alones are sometimes referred to as "turbocharged" answering machines, with several attractive and important features. This type of system permits forwarding messages to any other phone in the world at a predetermined time, appends and redirects them to another person, sends one message to all users of a system or a subset, and marks messages "urgent" for priority. The range of voice mail features, as with all voice- and fax-processing technology, varies among suppliers. Integrated systems provide additional capabilities through a special connection to the telephone system, such as message-waiting notification and return to an operator or another telephone extension.

Interactive Voice Response. Interactive voice response (also referred to as "IVR" and "automated transaction processing") has become a very popular voice-processing function. Voice-response applications allow callers to reach host computers to access databases and carry out transactions, using the keypad of a touch-tone phone in place of a computer keyboard. Applications of 900 numbers have made extensive use of voice-response technology. Pre-recorded voice or text-to-speech (see below) is used to communicate with the caller, providing instructions, confirming touch-tone entries and translating data from the computer into speech. It's called voice response because the system responds to touch-tone commands with voice responses. Present-day applications of voice response include ordering a product, verifying airline flight departure times, or requesting a bank account balance.

Speech Recognition. Speech recognition technology is designed to respond to spoken voice commands, rather than a telephone's keypad or computer's keyboard input. Speech recognition systems have been in use for several years in special military-security applications. Popular commercial applications include appliance control systems for the handicapped, data and text entry for spreadsheets and word processors (hands-free "typing"), and hands-free voice-controlled operation of voice processing system applications. Speech recognition is especially useful for serving rotary phone callers who want to use interactive voice-processing applications that normally require a touch-tone phone.

Text-to-Speech/Speech-to-Text. Text-to-speech, or "speech synthesis," involves the conversion of text or printed information into spoken form. Speech-to-text involves the reverse process.

Fax Processing. Fax-processing technology helps automate the sending and receiving of fax messages and documents. Fax servers are dedicated systems designed to automate the "broadcasting" of fax messages to a designated number of receivers as well as store incoming messages for later retrieval. Fax-processing capabilities are increasingly found integrated or combined with voice response and voice mail systems. In some ways, this creates a perfect match. The three most popular types of fax processing functions are "Fax Store and Forward (Fax mail)," "Fax Response (or Fax-on-Demand)" and "Fax Broadcasting."

Fax broadcasting (sending one document to several locations), and fax mail (similar to voice mail, except fax messages rather than voice messages are stored by the system) are both important capabilities of fax messaging. Fax-response applications let users access database and other information for delivery via fax hardcopy by using touch-tone phones.

Fax mail helps ensure the security and privacy of faxed documents, allows a caller to redirect a fax when away from the fax machine, and provides another depository for messages in case the main fax machine is unable to receive them.

Fax broadcasting eliminates the long waits and lines at a machine by automating delivery of a fax to a distribution list. Fax response makes it possible to receive a price list, brochure, promotional offer, diagram, map, or any other faxable document on demand using the keypad of a touch-tone phone.

Voice Processing System Building Blocks

The core hardware elements of a basic PC-based voice-processing system are the host computer — with its keyboard, monitor, RAM memory, floppy and hard disk drives, power supply and I/O cards — and internally installed voice-processing cards. To an extent, the telephone network can be considered a system element since it is the primary input and output path of most voice-processing systems.

There are a number of other voice-processing "building blocks," as well as a number of software programs necessary for configuring and controlling the system and creating user-ready applications. We'll take a look at each of these components below, how they work, and what role they play in system design.

Hardware Components

The System Platform. A voice-processing system needs a hardware platform on which to assemble all the necessary components and provide system functionality. PCs, minicomputers or mainframes are all used as platforms. Intel-processor-based 80486 and Pentium PCs have become the platform of choice among most new system developers due to the low cost and impressive computing power.

Voice Boards. Sometimes referred to as the audioboard, voice card, or voice board, these hardware components are the voice "engines" of voice-processing systems. They provide the circuitry for processing voice and other analog signals into a digital format and the essential interfaces for connecting to the telephone network and other peripheral devices. Voice boards are printed circuit cards that install in an empty slot in an "off-the-shelf" personal computer (or custom designed computer "platform"). Generally, the sub-components or elements that make up a voice board include a CPU (central processing unit); tone detection circuitry for detecting DTMF signals generated by touch-tone phones; specialized chips for converting analog voice to digital form and back again (for recording and playback); memory chips for storing firmware programs and data; FCC-approved telephone line interfaces for connecting to phone lines; and a host computer interface for connecting to the PC's bus. Popular voice boards are available from companies such as Dialogic Corporation (Parsippany, NJ), Natural MicroSystems (Natick, MA) and Rhetorex (Campbell, CA).

Loop Start Interface. Telephone interfaces connect the voice card to the telephone lines, as well as provide buffering and protection for audio voice signals. Loop start interfaces seize (get dial tone) a phone line or trunk by giving it a supervisory signal. This signal is typically generated by taking a phone "off-hook." If a loop start interface is not built into a voice card, and one is needed, a compatible loop start interface board for the system must be purchased from a voice board vendor (usually the same vendor you bought your voice boards from).

Ground Start Interface. Ground Start is the other way to signal to get dial tone. Ground starts involve one side of the two-wire trunk (typically, the ring conductor of the "tip and ring") being momentarily grounded. PBX systems work best on ground start trunks, so if you want a voice-processing system to be in front of or behind a PBX, it must be equipped with ground start. Ground start interfaces are generally built-in to voice cards, but again, make sure this is true or a special add-on board will need to be purchased.

DID Interface. DID stands for Direct Inward Dialing and lets a caller from outside a company call an internal extension without having to pass through an operator or attendant. If you want to provide this feature via a voice-processing system (DID voice mail for example), then a special interface is needed. Keep in mind that automated attendant functions provide a similar service and can eliminate the need for DID.

T-1 Digital Interface. T-1 is a standard North American digital transmission link with a capacity of 1.544 Mbps (megabytes per second). T-1 can handle 24 simultaneous voice conversations with each conversation being digitized at 64 Kbps. A few voice cards are available with built-in T-1 interfaces providing direct T-1 connection. Most, however, will need a special add-on T-1 interface board.

FAX Board. If you want to provide fax processing capabilities on your system, such as fax mail, fax-on-demand, and fax broadcasting, the system needs to have a fax board (as well as the necessary device drivers and application generation software) installed. If you are building your own system, make sure the fax board product is compatible with the voice card, and take into account that this will occupy an additional slot in the computer platform. A number of voice card manufacturers have established co-marketing and technology-sharing agreements with fax board suppliers, so ask first what they recommend. In addition, a few manufacturers have also introduced integrated voice/fax boards — eliminating the need to purchase separate components.

Speech Recognition Technology. Likewise with speech recognition, your system will need an add-on board and specialized software to supply this capability. Co-marketing agreements exist with card vendors and speech recognition board suppliers, so they would be a good place to start looking if you're build a system.

Audio Multiplexers. Audio multiplexers are analog switches designed to integrate analog devices into digital T-1- based voice-processing configurations. They are generally designed as add-on board components, and are useful in certain telemarketing, operator services, voice mail and voice-response applications.

Station Adapters. Station (or phone) adapters provide for the connection of local telephones or subscriber telephone lines to audio multiplexers or loop start interfaces. They are generally designed as external devices.

Audio Interface Adapters. Audio interface adapters are external devices that provide connection for typical consumer audio equipment (tape decks, radios, etc.) to voice cards. Applications for these interfaces include music-on-hold, text-to-speech synthesis interface, speech recognition interface, and public address system interface.

Audio Couplers. Audio couplers provide a clean and direct audio path to the telephone interface in order to record high-quality voice prompts. Inputs for tape decks and standard 2500-type telephones are generally standard. High-end couplers add equalizers, DTMF pads, ring generators, and digitization loops as features.

Software Components

Application Generators/Development Toolkits. Application generators are basically pre-packaged voice-processing programs that let users customize applications. Many are highly structured, with a multiple-choice or fill-in-the-blanks format. Many are also menu-driven, with help menus, pull-down windows, a mouse and other aids. Development toolkits are collections of software programs and hardware components for VARs (Value Added Resellers) and systems developers who design, program and configure voice-processing systems.

Device Drivers. Device drivers are software programs, running in the PC, that handle all communication between the voice board and the application program. Every task that must be performed by the voice board needs to be scheduled, initiated and monitored by the device driver. Device drivers are generally operating system specific (MS-DOS, UNIX or OS/2).

Speech Library. A speech library is generally included with most development toolkits. Many IVR applications require spoken responses that include dates (day, month and year), time (minute, hour, AM or PM), and numerical responses (zero through nine, etc.). You could record each of these in the same way customized greetings and messages are recorded using the Voice Prompt software (see below), but this would be time-consuming, so speech libraries provide a prerecorded set of these speech files that can be called up by the Device Driver when needed.

Compilers. Compilers are programs that convert "source code" (the string of characters that you type onto the screen) into "object code," or machine code, which the PC can read and act on. This program usually includes a "linking" program that "strings" together the compiled code into a single program. Compilers are also included in development toolkits.

Debugging Program. A debugging program is also sometimes included in development toolkits. This program allows the user to test the compiled and linked program for programming errors that might cause the system to crash or fail to run.

Call Progress Customization Programs. There are some programs designed to allow system owners and developers to customize the call analysis parameters available on certain voice board products. This software comes in handy when working with PBXs with proprietary call progress tones or old central office exchanges with unique or obsolete call progress signals.

Diagnostic Software. Some voice board vendors offer special diagnostic software programs that test the performance of the hardware. The software can be used for incoming call tests, design debug, system self-diagnosis, trouble-shooting and field service.

Voice Prompt Editors. These programs are software tools that provide the user and developer with all the tools necessary for creating voice prompts. Features of voice prompt editors include menu-driven design, voice-prompt database creation and maintenance, and voice-prompt silence trimming.

Graphical Speech Analyzers. These programs aid in voice prompt creation by graphically representing recorded voice prompts. Many are mouse-driven and use a point, sweep and click method to edit the prompts.

Turnkey System or Service Bureau?

The explosive growth of the audiotext industry has created a virtual army of new and "would-be" information providers, many with little or no familiarity with the necessary technology, intent on setting up their own 900 numbers. Luckily, there are places these novices can turn to help get advice and assistance in setting up a system and launching a new 900-number program or service.

Some turn to turnkey system vendors who specialize in audiotext and voice response systems, and cater to the needs of IPs. A more common, and somewhat more attractive, alternative for a new IP are voice-processing service bureaus — companies that have installed high-capacity voice-processing systems on their own premises, leased a number of 900-number telephone lines from a carrier, and then rent service on these systems and provide applications development and implementation expertise to clients.

A major factor fueling service bureau growth is the growing realization that many interactive voice-processing applications require an extremely high level of expertise to ensure a successful implementation.

Before deciding whether to sign with a service bureau for your voice-processing needs or buy a turnkey system, it's important to compare the benefits and/or drawbacks of each alternative. As prices for voice-processing hardware become more and more competitive, especially in the PC-based category, price has become less of a key decision factor. Therefore, consider other important advantages (or disadvantages) of service bureau use before making a final decision.

10 Key Advantages
of Voice-Processing Service Bureaus

1. No Financing Needed. As opposed to buying a turnkey system, you don't need to establish any special financing to clinch the service, and won't need to tap into any lines of credit or cash reserves.

2. No Commitment. There is little or no commitment expected from a client company. Since service bureau services are leased on a monthly basis, you won't be stuck with the service longer than you want. If you discover that your application or program turns out to be a dud, you can walk away with minimal capital loss.

3. Enormous Call-Handling Capabilities. Programs that are media-driven, such as a sweepstakes contest number that is promoted on television, can generate thousands of calls in a very short period of time. Many service bureaus have high-ported systems designed to handle these peak loads.

4. Constant Upgrading of Technology. Leading-edge technology is a tool of the trade for a service bureau, and they are quick to embrace any new promising software or hardware component, assuring you the latest application the technology can offer.

5. Low Carrier Rates. Since service bureaus buy in bulk, they can get extremely favorable rates from the carriers. These discounts generally mean lower rates to a client when compared to the rates carriers offer to a new customer.

6. On-site Expertise. An in-house voice-processing system requires a full-time staff person trained to maintain the system and program new applications. Service bureaus already have highly trained technicians and programmers on staff who are familiar with a variety of applications. By leaving all the nitty-gritty technical details up to the experts, an end user can focus on the marketing of the program or providing the service.

7. Access to Software Libraries. Many service bureaus have developed extensive software application libraries. The cost of using these available applications is typically much less than the cost of programming one from scratch.

8. Great for Application Trials. Service bureaus are great resources for testing the effectiveness of certain programs or applications before investing in a turnkey system.

9. Great for Seasonal Programs. For programs that only run three or four times a year, a service bureau is the perfect resource. For programs that run daily or on a more regular basis, it may be more cost-effective to look into acquiring a turnkey system.

10. No Hidden Inventory Costs. There's no need to store extra circuit cards, power supplies, hard disks and the like. All equipment, including backup hardware and software, resides in the service bureau.

A Third Option: Building a PC-Based Voice-Processing System

There is a growing number of intrepid, computer-literate techies who can't resist the attraction of building their own systems. Indeed, the incredible sophistication and quality of new voice-processing components is allowing technically adept users to quickly build systems from the ground up: For the price of a 486 or Pentium PC, a double or four-ported voice board, and a software development toolkit and/or application generator, a fairly robust voice-processing system can be built for around $5,000.

If you are swayed in this direction, you will have a number of important factors to consider in order to determine which components are best for your needs. They involve the type of PC platform used, the operating system used, the type of telephone network interface required, the type of application generator software to use, as well as voice card-specific features.

Important system-specific features

What Buses Are Supported? It's important to know which bus your current PC uses, or what bus you will use if you are purchasing a new PC. Some board vendors have a selection of boards for both the 8-bit buses as well as 16-bit buses, but others make boards for only one type of bus. A few vendors also have cards for the MicroChannel and 32-bit EISA bus. The benefit of using a 16 or 32-bit bus, as opposed to an 8-bit bus, is greater system throughput and resulting higher system capacity and performance.

What is the PC's Processor Type and Speed? When it comes to the processing demands of voice applications, the more powerful the PC's processor, the better overall system performance.

What is the Operating System Used? If you want to use the operating system currently installed on an existing PC, then make sure the voice card in question has the appropriate drivers to support the OS. If you are building a system from the ground up, then choose the OS that works best for your intended system application(s). UNIX and OS/2 is usually the operating systems of choice for high-capacity (16 ports or more) systems due to their true multi-tasking performance. Multi-tasking operating systems are also ideal for multi-media platforms.

Amount and Type of Hard Disk Storage. Voice- and fax-processing applications are hard-disk intensive, in that the system is constantly reading and writing data to and from the hard disk to deliver and store voice information. When choosing a hard disk, look for a fast IDE- or ESDI-type drive that has an access time of 28 milliseconds or less (17 or 18 milliseconds is even better). To determine how much storage is needed, take several things into account: how many minutes of voice storage per megabyte of disk space is supported (this depends on the efficiency of the algorithm used by a voice card to digitize voice signals), how many ports will be supported by the drive, how many applications you are providing, and how many callers will be supported.

Number of Available Slots. The number of available (free) slots in a PC will determine how many voice cards can be installed in the system and hence, what the system port capacity will be. Remember to take into account other add-on cards you might need, such as a video card, network interface cards, fax cards, speech recognition cards, etc. These will occupy empty spots and reduce the overall system capacity.

Those who wish to further investigate the option of building a voice-processing system will find help in some of the books listed in Appendix C. Vendors of hardware and software components advertise in the periodicals listed in Appendix A. Request a free copy of the Voice/Fax Processing Library catalog for more information:

Robins Press
2675 Henry Hudson Parkway, Suite 6J
Riverdale, NY 10463
718-548-7245; fax: 718-548-7237

The Voice Response Unit (VRU)

You will also see the term "voice response unit" or "VRU" when discussing voice-processing equipment. Nowadays a VRU often consists of a PC platform with some installed voice cards such as those discussed earlier. Nevertheless, a VRU can also be a proprietary system that doesn't look anything like a PC. A VRU can have anywhere from one to 96 (or more) ports, which means it is capable of handling that number of telephone calls at any given time. Some common service bureau-sized VRUs have 24 or 48 ports. A VRU can be configured with its own T-1 interface with the telephone network, also capable of handling 24 lines. A voice-processing system can consist of one VRU or many VRUs. Multiple VRUs are all connected via a dedicated network to a network server, where all the programs and voice storage resides (often with double or triple redundancy). The server can be another PC or a mainframe computer.

A nice feature of this arrangement is that if one VRU fails, it doesn't effect the operation of the others, and service continues uninterrupted. Any size service bureau can easily expand its volume capabilities by simply adding VRUs. It's a nice, neat modular technology.

The Service Bureau

We already discussed the advantages of using a service bureau in the last section. Although you can purchase your own equipment and build a small PC-based system for a few thousand dollars, is that the best utilization of your time and resources? Starting any kind of business is expensive, and it is usually a good idea to farm out as much of the work as possible, at least until the business is well-established and generating a solid positive cash flow.

You also have to decide what you do best and what your business is all about. Are you an information provider or an equipment technician? Are you technically capable of programming, operating and troubleshooting your own system? Have you factored in the cost of installing the telephone lines and related equipment? A service bureau can provide all the equipment and services you need for a very reasonable monthly and/or per-minute charge. Keep in mind that most Fortune 500 companies use service bureaus, so why should you be any different?

Smart businesses are outsourcing more and more work so they can concentrate more on their core business functions — the things only they can do well. Graphic design, advertising, printing, payroll services, training, and a whole host of functions can be just as well — or better — performed by outsiders. Such jobs are being outsourced in order to trim overhead and to stay competitive. It is invariably cheaper to pay-as-you-go instead of taking on a bunch of fixed costs and overhead.

A major service bureau has the capability of processing hundreds, even thousands, of incoming calls simultaneously. It may have hundreds of thousands of dollars invested in state-of-the-art equipment and facilities, including backup generators for uninterrupted service during power failures, and professional sound studios for voice recording.

A good service bureau will be extremely helpful in designing and setting up your program. It has probably already dealt with just about every conceivable kind of interactive program, and will have excellent suggestions for your program — perhaps ideas you never even considered feasible. Its programmers are likely a talented and creative bunch who enjoy new challenges.

Besides helping with your program design, some service bureaus can also help with other useful services:

- Voice talent for professional-quality recording of your program.
- Marketing help. Some service bureaus have in-house advertising capabilities to help with media placement or planning advertising strategies.
- Television or radio production facilities.
- Live operators for simple messages or order-taking.
- Voice-capture capabilities for order-taking or contest entry, and transcription services as required.
- Turnkey information or entertainment programs which are offered on a program-sharing basis.

Of course, you may not require the services of a large service bureau if your program is targeted to a relatively small niche market. A smaller company may be able to offer you more personalized services. Another reason for not allowing call-handling capabilities to be an overriding concern is the fact that the smaller service bureaus can enter into call allocation arrangements with the long-distance carrier and another service bureau. For example, a smaller service bureau, with equipment capable of handling only 48 simultaneous calls, can contract with a larger service bureau to accept a predetermined percentage of the incoming calls for a specific period of time corresponding with a television promotional campaign. The long-distance carrier is simply instructed to route this percentage of calls to the larger service bureau.

900 Number Ownership

You may get some confusing information regarding the ownership of a 900 telephone number. First of all, the only entity that comes close to "owning" a 900 number is Bellcore, and to a lesser extent, the long-distance carrier. The IXCs are allocated the rights to a certain number of three-digit NXX prefixes by Bellcore, the cooperative research branch of the Regional Bell Operating Companies (RBOCs). Any long-distance carrier may apply to Bellcore for the rights to additional NXXs at any time. It should be noted that NXXs currently cannot be transferred from one long-distance carrier to another, and once you have committed to a carrier and a specific 900 number, you are essentially married to that carrier unless you are willing to change your 900 number. There are efforts currently underway to make the numbers transferable from one carrier to another, but this may still be years away.

Either the IP or the service bureau may contract with the long-distance carrier for the use of a 900 number, becoming the "client of record" with the carrier. The client of record deals directly with the carrier, receiving monthly call summary reports and net call revenues directly from the carrier. This may sound like a real advantage for the IP. Not necessarily. It can be quite expensive for an IP to be the client of record, because there are no price breaks for doing a volume business with the carrier. A small IP, even with a couple of 900 programs, will pay full price for start-up fees and monthly charges. AT&T, for example, charges $1200 for a start-up fee, plus $500 per month for an individual client of record. The service bureau, on the other hand, will be amortizing this same cost over hundreds of telephone lines.

As long as you're dealing with a reputable, financially sound service bureau, there is really little benefit for you to be the client of record. Besides being more expensive, your relationship with the service bureau is not quite as advantageous. When the IP is client of record, he is essentially leasing equipment and services from the service bureau. The service bureau is less a partner in profit, and might be less vigilant about making sure the program is always functioning properly. Complex interactive programs invariably have lots of bugs, at least initially, and need lots of attention by the programmers and technical people. The service bureau doesn't have quite the same vested interest in the viability of the program.

Not being responsible for the program content, the service bureau has no reason to defend the program with the carrier should a legal conformance problem arise. The client of record is responsible to the carrier for all aspects of program content, and a service bureau is simply in a better position to make sure the program doesn't violate any new rules or regulations that may pop up from time to time.

Now for the other side of the coin. Not being the client of record can be dangerous to your financial health. Notice that I qualified the above statement, "As long as you're dealing with a *reputable, financially sound* service bureau, there is really little benefit for you to be the client of record." This statement needs to be expanded upon to some extent.

A smaller service bureau, lacking sufficient financial resources, can suffer seriously if one of its major IP clients gets hit with a huge retroactive chargeback covering a period of several months. If the service bureau is the client of record with the long-distance carrier, it will be responsible for covering the bill. A huge unanticipated expense such as this can completely dry up its cash flow, and guess who ends up holding the bag? The rest of the service bureau's client IPs, who have no control over the situation, and whose chargeback records might be impeccable. They could wait for months to receive their money from the service bureau, or worse, lose it all if the service bureau can never recover and goes out of business.

And I'm not just talking about a hypothetical possibility here. It has happened, and some of the service bureaus have been fairly large and well-known. Over the past few years dozens of service bureaus have gone under, pulling many IPs down with them. Had the IP been client of record, it would have been relatively simple to transfer the 900 number and program to another service bureau. And any funds due would come from the long-distance carrier, paid directly to the IP, so there would be no interruption in the IP's incoming cash flow.

It should be noted, however, that the only major long-distance carrier that will currently accept IPs as clients of record is AT&T. MCI generally contracts only with service bureaus or companies in whose name the trunk group is registered, but it will deal directly with IPs who own their own equipment on a case-by-case basis. Check with your service bureau for the current policies of its carriers.

An established, successful IP who can easily afford the higher monthly costs as client of record is generally well advised to deal directly with the long-distance carrier. Clearly, the alternative is to make sure that the service bureau is financially sound. And many of them are quite sound. Some service bureaus offer either option, so you can save money by starting out with the service bureau as client of record and then change over if and when your program becomes successful. This would be the best of both worlds.

What to Look For in a Service Bureau

The specific capabilities and services to look for in a service bureau will be a function of your unique program needs. Some of the following features will be critically important to the success of your program, and others will be of little value. You will be the only one to judge the relative importance of these criteria:

❒ *Call volume capabilities.* We have already discussed call allocation arrangements, which allow smaller service bureaus to handle higher call volume. Nevertheless, if you anticipate large call volume surges resulting from TV advertising, you might as well start with a service bureau that can handle the volume.

❒ *Long-distance carriers.* Sprint has reduced the scope of its 900 services, leaving two major U.S. players, AT&T and MCI, plus some of the smaller carriers that have recently entered the market. It may boil down to what three-digit prefix, or NXX, is available for spelling a distinctive word. The long-distance carrier may also allocate certain NXXs to different service bureaus, so if these numbers are important, ask the prospective service bureau for a list of NXXs available. See Appendix F for more information about the major long-distance carriers and their current pricing.

❒ *Types of programs and clients.* Does the service bureau currently serve programs such as yours? Having a lot of experience in a certain type of application, which is similar to yours, will mean a shorter learning curve for the service bureau, and fewer program glitches.

❒ *Call count access and verification.* It is very useful, indeed, almost indispensable, to have 24-hour automated access to call counts. This is usually accomplished by calling an interactive program at the service bureau, often using a toll-tree 800 number, entering an exclusive access code and/or password, and then receiving recorded call count and/or call-minute information for your program. A good system will feature a menu of selections so that call counts can be determined by the day or by the hour for the preceding week.

❒ *Written reports.* In addition to telephone access to call counts, this information should be confirmed weekly and/or monthly with written reports. The written reports should summarize interactive menu selections by callers, average hold times, and time of day for calls. The monthly reports should include a copy of the long-distance carrier report as a further independent verification of call count numbers. A service bureau is often able to customize the written reports to meet any specific needs or requirements.

It is extremely important to be able to independently verify call count information. A reputable service bureau recognizes this need, and provides this service without being asked. It is very easy for a dishonest service bureau to fudge the numbers when there is no way of checking their accuracy.

❐ *Rotary capabilities.* It is now possible to offer interactive audiotex services to rotary callers by using speech recognition, a technology with the capability of recognizing the caller's spoken word, eliminating the need to use the touch-tone keypad.

Although rotary callers may not be the best target market for most 900 programs, there are always notable exceptions to every rule. According to AT&T, 38.5% of all households were still on rotary telephones in 1991, with the heaviest concentration in older urban areas.

❐ *Turnkey programs.* As I stated earlier, some service bureaus offer their own 900 programs for program-sharing arrangements. Many of these service bureaus typically started as IPs, and purchased their own call-handling equipment. Because they have unused call-handling capacity, they can offer these services to other IPs. Tapping into someone else's successful program can be a very economical way of starting in the 900 business. On the other hand, if you are launching a new program that would compete with a turnkey program by the same service bureau, you will be in the uncomfortable position of competing with a company that is providing you with very important services, and with ready access to information about your business and its level of success.

❐ *Prices.* Service bureaus generally require a one-time start-up fee to get your program on-line. This charge will often include the long-distance carrier one-time charge, account set-up, and a certain amount of programming services. This fee can vary widely, from $1000 for a simple program to as much as $20,000 for a complex program requiring lots of programming and voice storage. The service bureau may waive the start-up fee altogether if the IP happens to be CBS and plans to market the program extensively on TV.

Of more importance for an ongoing successful program are the monthly service fees and per-minute charges. The monthly fees can range from zero to several hundred dollars, depending upon call volume, programming, and voice storage needs for the program. Many service bureaus will waive the monthly fee if call volume exceeds a certain level. The per-minute charges can range from 10 cents to 20 cents per minute, with 10 cents being closer to the norm for programs that generate some good volume. Most service bureaus will adjust the per-minute charge downward as call volume increases.

When comparing prices, make sure you get all relevant costs that will be required for your specific program, and then compare them at several different call volumes. A service bureau with very low monthly charges but high per-minute charges will look good at low call volumes, but will be expensive once you start achieving the higher volumes.

Also, check out prices for other services such as transcription, custom reports, or voice storage. The relative importance of these costs will obviously depend upon the nature of your program needs. Beware of unusually low prices. There may be hidden charges, or the service bureau may be grasping for business because it's on the verge of going under.

❑ *Power interruption protection.* Does the service bureau have a back-up generator or a UPS (Uninterruptible Power Supply) to assure unbroken service during a power failure? This may not seem very important until you have invested lots of money in a heavy television promotion, only to lose thousands of calls because a violent thunderstorm knocked out power to your service bureau while your best TV spots were airing nationwide.

❑ *Remote program updating.* Say you have some kind of recorded interactive program that must be updated frequently. You should be able to accomplish this by calling the service bureau on a dedicated "editing line," which allows you to update the program using your touch-tone telephone along with an interactive menu designed specifically for updating your program.

Choosing the Service Bureau

First of all, carefully outline all of your program needs. Do you need live operators? Professional voice talent? Are rotary callers a potential part of your target market? Do you require a lot of voice storage? Then, plan ahead and try to anticipate future needs. Will you add additional telephone lines to the program? Will you launch new programs? Will you eventually try your hand at television advertising?

Once you have a good handle on current and future program needs, plus all the relevant price information from several prospective service bureaus, you should be able to narrow down your choices to a few leading candidates. At this point it is imperative to ask for references, and then follow through and contact each one.

In the final analysis, the service bureau will be your partner in profit. Like any other partnership, there must be two-way trust and respect. Even the largest service bureau should recognize that you're just starting, and that it will take time for call counts to grow. It should be willing to help even the smallest IP in every way it can. After all, the service bureau makes most of its money on the per-minute call revenue, so it's in its best interest to help you be as successful as possible.

See Appendix D for a comprehensive listing of service bureaus. Although there are obvious benefits to working with a company that is located nearby, like seeing how your money is spent, keep in mind that geographic proximity is not critically important. The service bureau's integrity, capabilities, services, prices and financial stability are much more important.

Chapter 8
Financial Planning

Now for the $64,000 question: How do you know whether your program will be financially successful? This is probably the most important question you have, and frankly, you really won't know the answer for sure until after you have actually launched your program. This industry simply hasn't been around long enough to accumulate a lot of good historical data about the level of success that can be expected for any given category of program.

Nevertheless, realistic financial projections will serve as a helpful road map on your journey to success. The heart of any business plan are the financial projections and the assumptions behind them. This is the final step before making the decision to launch your program. A realistic evaluation of the numbers may indicate that the program may not succeed as expected, allowing you to pull the plug before spending any more money. On the other hand, unrealistic, overly optimistic revenue expectations may result in losing a considerable investment with an unsuccessful program.

This part of the process is called number crunching. Many people are afraid of numbers and avoid them like the plague. But virtually every successful businessman or entrepreneur is very good at number crunching. Cash is the lifeblood of any business.

Only when it's coming in faster than it goes out does the business stay healthy. Any new business must be prepared for a net outflow of cash for the first few months of operation, and if you don't budget enough for cash transfusions, you won't last long enough to eventually become successful. It's called undercapitalization, and many potentially successful companies have failed for lack of sufficient start-up capital.

Start-up Costs

You are now in a position to calculate all one-time start-up costs associated with launching your program. The following is a fairly comprehensive list of typical start-up costs, but there may be other costs unique to your program or situation, so don't forget to include them as well:

❏ **Research and education.** This includes purchasing this book and others, subscribing to trade publications, calling other 900 numbers to see how potential competitors operate, enrolling in a marketing class, travelling to visit a service bureau, or attending a pay-per-call trade show.

❏ **Service bureau start-up fee.** We discussed this earlier, but make sure you haven't overlooked the initial programming costs or voice talent charges.

❏ **Advertising development.** This includes creative graphics work for print advertising copy or production costs for TV or radio commercials. Although classified as start-up costs, these expenses will become recurring costs as ads are changed or new ones are tested.

❏ **Source Information.** There may be a one-time fee for access to the information or entertainment featured on your program, such as a licensing fee for an interactive telephone game.

❏ *Equipment.* You may need to purchase a computer, a fax machine, or office furniture.

❏ *Legal and accounting.* As a new business, you may wish to incorporate. You may want your attorney to review your contract with your service bureau. If you offer a contest feature, you will need expert legal help setting up the contest rules and procedures. You may want an accountant to set up your bookkeeping system.

After you have assigned realistic numbers to these categories, plus any others unique to your program, you will have a good estimate of how much it will cost to get your business off the ground. This figure will not include, however, the reserve capital you will need to cover any monthly operating deficits in the first few months.

Recurring Monthly Costs

These are essentially fixed monthly expenses that are incurred regardless of the level of volume or revenue achieved. What makes or breaks a business is being able to regularly cover these fixed expenses with sufficient revenue. Needless to say, the monthly profit is the amount by which revenue exceeds these expenses:

❏ *Service bureau fee.* As stated before, the service bureau will usually charge a minimum monthly fee unless a certain minimum call volume is exceeded.

❏ *Communications.* Dedicated business telephone lines for voice, fax, and modem; long-distance services; phone company services such as Call Forwarding; cellular and pager charges; e-mail service; Internet access.

❏ *Space.* Office rent, if applicable, plus utilities.

❏ *Payroll.* This includes not only salaries, but also payroll taxes, benefits, and any other costs associated with having employees.

❏ *Insurance.* This will normally be limited to office contents, tenant betterments, or business interruption and hazard type coverages. Professional liability insurance, if necessary, can be quite costly.

❏ *Office supplies.* From staples to stationary, even the smallest home business can spend $100 or more a month on such supplies.

❏ *Interest.* This applies if you took out a loan to finance the start-up of your business.

❏ *Program source information.* Any applicable costs associated with getting your program information on a regular basis.

❏ *Miscellaneous.* There are always numerous costs which don't fit nicely into any given category, or there may be unique cost elements associated with your program.

❏ *Advertising.* Advertising is not really a fixed monthly cost. You could elect to spend nothing and quickly go out of business. Nonetheless, you should establish a monthly advertising budget and stick to it. And this should be the largest expense category in your budget.

Variable Costs

Variable costs are tied to the volume of business activity. In a pay-per-call business, the variable costs are the per-minute charges that go to the long-distance carrier and the service bureau. For example, using a simple $1 per-minute call charge, the variable costs would be broken down as shown in Table 8-1.

These variable costs will change for different long-distance carriers and service bureaus. Furthermore, the variable costs will likely be reduced for higher call volumes, so your revenue projections should be based upon a realistic range of several levels of call volume.

VARIABLE COSTS		
Gross revenue (per minute)		$1.00
Less variable costs:		
IXC transport fee	0.30	
IXC billing & collection fee (10%)	0.10	
Service Bureau fee	0.10	
Total variable costs		(0.50)
Net revenue		$0.50

Table 8-1

The typical transport fee for long-distance 900 services ranges from low 20s to 32 cents per minute, but can go as high as 44 cents a minute (see Appendix F). It should be noted here, however, that LEC transport fees for regional 976 services are much lower — usually 10 cents or less per minute. A 976 pay-per-call program would obviously be more cost-effective for any kind of limited regional program application. The same variable cost models can be used as shown — simply substitute the appropriate LEC fees for the corresponding IXC fees.

A flat rate call charge for a program with a set call hold time would be calculated in a similar manner as the per-minute example in Table 8-1, except that volumes would be based upon the number of calls, not the number of minutes. A program featuring a dual price structure, for example, $2 the first minute and then $1 each additional minute, would be treated as shown in Table 8-2. Notice that the extra dollar earned for the first minute is subject only to the 10% billing and collection fee. In order to be able to properly project revenue, assumptions must be made concerning both number of calls and the average duration of each call.

For example, assuming the average hold time for each call is five minutes, monthly net call revenue would be calculated as shown in Table 8-3. Notice that every minute earns 50 cents in net revenue, while every *first* minute earns an extra 90 cents.

VARIABLE COSTS - DUAL PRICE STRUCTURE		
	First minute	Each minute
Gross revenue	$1.00	$1.00
Less variable costs:		
IXC transport fee		0.30
IXC B & C (10%)	0.10	0.10
Service Bureau fee		0.10
Total variable costs	(0.10)	(0.50)
Net revenue	$0.90	$0.50

Table 8-2

DUAL PRICING REVENUE	
Number of calls	1000
Call minutes	5000
1st. minute revenue (1000 X $0.90)	$ 900
Per minute revenue (5000 X $0.50)	$2,500
Total net revenue	$3,400

Table 8-3

Projecting Revenue

Costs can be fairly accurately identified. Potential revenue, on the other hand, is far more difficult to pin down. Statistics on response rates and call volumes for different kinds of 900 programs just aren't yet readily available. The industry is still too new, and this kind of information is often jealously guarded by the IPs.

Nonetheless, you have to start somewhere. The key to projecting revenue is determining a realistic response rate to your advertising. If you have targeted 500,000 readers-viewers-listeners, how many of them are likely to call your program? One out of 100? More? A lot less?

If you're offering a specialized service that permits precise rifle shot marketing, the response rates will be higher than with a program targeted to a more general market. However, there are no ready formulas to help you predict what rate of response you might achieve, not until you launch your program and conduct some actual market testing.

What kind of numbers should you begin with? Well, a 5% response rate, even for the most precise rifle shot marketing, would be wildly optimistic. A new program, in its early stages of market exposure, will probably pull in less than 1% in overall response. To be conservative you should start with a number well under 1%.

REVENUE PROJECTIONS			
Response rates	Low: 0.25%	Medium: 0.50%	High: 0.75%
Calls per month/issue (500 K circulation x response rate)	1,250	2,500	3,750
Total call minutes (calls x 5 min./call)	6,250	12,500	18,750
Net call revenue per month (# calls x $2.50)	$ 3,125	$ 6,250	$ 9,375
Cost of ad	($5,000)	($5,000)	($5,000)
Net revenue after ad cost	($1,875)	$1,250	$4,375

Table 8-4

Say you're advertising a specialized service in a well-targeted monthly magazine with a circulation of 500,000 readers. You decide that an initial response rate in the range of 0.25% to 0.75% would be realistic. By the way, response rates should be based upon circulation, not readership, and the response rate is applied to each issue in which your ad is published.

Let's further assume that your call charge is $1 per minute, and the average hold time is five minutes, which, using the previous variable cost example in Table 8-1, results in a net revenue per call of $2.50 ($0.50 x 5 minutes). Also, let's assume that a decent size display ad costs $5000 per issue. Table 8-4 summarizes the projected revenue at response rates ranging from 0.25% to 0.75%.

The net call revenue must cover all of the recurring monthly costs, including the $5000 per month advertising budget.

Now let's make some further assumptions regarding your monthly expenses and variable costs. We'll assume that you're working from home, with very low overhead and no payroll costs. The total monthly expenses are summarized in Table 8-5.

MONTHLY EXPENSES	
Service bureau fee	$ 300.00*
Advertising (budgeted)	5,000.00
Other/miscellaneous	700.00
Total monthly expenses	$6,000.00

* The service bureau fee is zero if a total of 7,500 call-minutes are achieved per month, and if call volume exceeds 15,000 minutes per month, the service bureau per-minute charge is reduced from $0.10 to $0.07.

Table 8-5

Using these assumptions, the revenue projections will be somewhat different, as outlined in Table 8-6, which takes into account different service bureau charges at various volume levels in arriving at the bottom line net income.

Table 8-6 demonstrates how both variable costs (the service bureau per-minute charge) and fixed monthly costs (the service bureau monthly charge for call volume less than 7500 minutes) will be different at various projected levels of anticipated call volume. It's a good idea to project call volumes at several levels within the expected range.

NET INCOME PROJECTIONS			
Response rate	low: 0.25%	med: 0.50%	high: 0.75%
Calls per month	1250	2500	3750
Total call minutes	6250	12500	18750
Net revenue:			
a. $0.50/min.(10¢ SB fee)	$3,125.00	$6,250.00	
b. $0.53/min.(7¢ SB fee)			$9,938.00
Less monthly expenses:			
Service bureau	$ 300.00	-0-	-0-
Advertising	$5,000.00	$5,000.00	$5,000.00
Other	$ 700.00	$ 700.00	$ 700.00
Total expenses	($6,000.00)	($5,700.00)	($5,700.00)
Net income (loss)	($2,875.00)	$550.00	$4,238.00

Table 8-6

In this example, the lower response rate may be realistic for the first few months, and the higher rates would be achieved after the program benefits from longer media exposure and repeat calls from satisfied customers. Obviously, the initial capitalization costs must be sufficient to cover both start-up as well as any anticipated operating deficits for the first few months of operation. Further, once you start earning positive revenues, you must account for the time delay in receiving your first check from the service bureau, which will be a function of both the IXC and the service bureau collection and accounting policies. A delay of 90 days is not uncommon, so check for the timing of call revenue payments.

Before projecting revenue, you must first establish the charge for your program. And it had better be realistic. A charge of $5 per minute might work for live technical advice, but if yours is an interactive game, your revenue projections might look quite impressive, but in reality it's doubtful anyone will call.

In researching your competitor's programs you will find out what they are charging. Your charges had better be in line with these numbers, or even lower, or you will be headed for real trouble. My other book, *Money-Making 900 Numbers*, lists nearly

400 different kinds of programs, along with the call charges in effect, and will give you an overview of what IPs are charging for various programs.

Breakeven Analysis

A useful financial tool is calculating the revenue or volume that must be achieved in order to cover fixed costs, also known as breakeven analysis. At levels below this number, operating deficits result, and above this number, surplus or profit is earned.

Using the previous example, we know that the net call revenue per minute is $0.50, and that the fixed monthly expenses are $6000. The breakeven volume level is calculated as follows:

$6000 / $0.50 = 12,000 minutes

This demonstrates that we must generate 12,000 call minutes per month in order to break even on expenses, or 2400 calls (12,000 / 5 minutes per call) per month. We can also work backwards to determine what advertising response rate we must achieve in order to break even:

2400 calls / 500,000 circulation = 0.48%

Breakeven analysis gives us a concrete number that serves as a target or goal to exceed as quickly as possible. Profit is the amount by which the breakeven point is exceeded.

For example, if a volume of 20,000 call-minutes is achieved in a given month, the net profit for that month can be quickly computed:

20,000 - 12,000 = 8,000 minutes over breakeven point

8,000 x $0.50 = $4,000 profit for month

Knowing your breakeven point allows you to quickly compute your profit or loss, so you will know at a glance how well you did for the past month.

Please keep in mind that the preceding example should in no way imply that you will generate a similar response rate to your advertising. A response rate to carefully-targeted direct mail marketing in the range of 1% to 3% is often considered quite good, and may be achieved only after extensive testing. And remember, direct mail is the most precisely focused rifle shot marketing available, allowing for a lengthy and compelling sales message. Be careful, therefore, about being too optimistic about anticipated response rates. Better to be prepared for the worst-case scenario, only to be pleasantly surprised later by better results.

Larry Werner of CommVox (a service bureau) put it quite well: "I've never met a pessimistic entrepreneur. There isn't enough equipment capacity to handle all the projected call volume expected by optimistic entrepreneurs."

Chapter 9
The 900 Roundtable

The following industry experts have generously contributed their time and experience in addressing some of the most commonly asked questions by start-up IPs. The 900 industry is widely represented here — by IPs, service bureaus, telephone companies and supporting companies and organizations. The format is structured much like a live roundtable discussion, with the participants answering a series of topical questions.

A lot of knowledge and experience is represented here. Instead of relying solely on my advice, you can compare the opinions of other experts on the subjects of concern to you.

What follows is the equivalent of hundreds of dollars in first-rate consulting services from a talented group of people with decades of combined experience.

I had a hard time trying to cut down the length of this chapter. The participants provided so much good information that the most difficult part was deciding what to leave out. On the one hand, I didn't want too much repetition, with many similar answers to the same question. On the other hand, some of the similar answers have important nuances that give a different perspective on the issue. And in some cases the issue is so important that a little repetition is appropriate in emphasizing the point.

Because so many readers justifiably consider this chapter to be the most valuable in the book, I chose to err on the side of leaving material in whenever there was any doubt. It should also be noted that participants were asked to answer only those questions they wanted to address. Some answered most and others handled only a few.

Finally, the order of appearance of the participants, and the order of their answers, is completely arbitrary. No particular meaning should be ascribed to the relative order, as none was intended.

The Participants

Bob Bentz. Director of Marketing, Advanced Telecom Services, Inc., a service bureau with offices in suburban Philadelphia, London and Toronto. He also wrote the other major book on the 900 industry, *Opportunity is Calling* (Appendix C).

Peter J. Brennan. Director of Voice Information Services for the Phoenix Media/Communications Group, Publishers of the *Boston Phoenix, Providence Phoenix* and *Worcester Phoenix*. He is Director of Development for Tele-Publishing, Inc. of Boston, a leading voice information service bureau. Brennan is a past Chair of the Voice Information Services Division of the Information Industry Association, and is a frequent public speaker and published expert in the field of voice services, technology, legislation and applications. He has offered testimony before both houses of Congress, various Attorneys General and public utility commissions, and has been published in *InfoText Magazine, Telemarketing Magazine* and *Information Times*.

Michael Cane. President & CEO, Tele-Lawyer, Inc. Recipient of the American Bar Association Award for Legal Access as well as five audiotext industry awards, Tele-Lawyer is the longest-running professional/consulting program in the pay-per-call industry (and may be its longest-running program). Cane, besides being the founder and sometime consultant on the Tele-Lawyer lines, is author of four books (*The Five Minute Lawyer* series), a frequent consultant to IXCs, service bureaus and other IPs, and a past chairman of the National Association of Interactive Services (since merged with ISA).

Gene Chamson. Founder and President, Intermedia Resources, Inc., an IP, consulting firm and reseller of 900 services, based in Oakland, California. Prior to launching Intermedia Resources, Chamson worked as a planning engineer with AT&T; then as the Product Development Manager for *California 900* at Pacific Bell; and capped his experience as the manager of new product development for Automated Call Processing (ACP), a leading 900 IP and service bureau, where he helped develop interactive voice applications for such well-known clients as *Fortune*, Reuters, Charles Schwab, *Consumer Reports*, and *Sports Illustrated*.

Robert L. Doyle. General Manager of AT&T MultiQuest Services, which entails all product management, strategy and operations functions for AT&T Pay-Per-Call Services, including 900 services, premium billing services and promotional/pay-per-call prepaid card offer sets. Serves as Co-Chair of AT&T MultiQuest executive customer council for pay-per-call services and as a member of the board of directors for the Interactive Services Association (ISA).

Carol Morse Ginsburg. Editor and publisher of *Audiotex News*, the leading industry newsletter, entering its eighth year of publication. She is also co-author of *Money-Making 900 Numbers* and is the publisher of the *Audiotex News Resource Guide* (Appendix C). Morse Ginsburg is an industry veteran who has been featured on CNBC's *Steals & Deals* as well as numerous radio programs. Widely quoted in the media, she has been featured in such publications as *Small Business Opportunity Magazine, Audiotex Briefings, Advance Magazine, Cable & Broadcast, Newsday* and the *Los Angeles Times*.

Phyllis Grant-Parker. Director, business solutions management, Stentor, the association of the major Canadian telecommunications companies. Grant-Parker has over 15 years of marketing experience in telecommunications in a variety of disciplines. She is responsible for the market development of Advantage 900 pay-per-call service in Canada, developing new 900 applications for Phone Power, Stentor's business consulting team.

Bruce Kennedy. Heads a diversified group of companies offering numerous services — advertising, creative consulting, design, production, media buying, direct marketing, multimedia and Internet services to a wide-ranging clientele. Kennedy has been instrumental in the success of some of the largest IPs in the audiotext industry. He specializes in confidential, results-oriented, creative solutions.

Donald C. Klug. Senior Manager, MCI 900 Services. Klug is responsible for development, operations, and marketing of MCI's interactive audiotext product line. He has been an active member of the Interactive Services Association (ISA) since assuming responsibility for MCI's 900 service in 1994. Klug is an active member of the ISA Voice SIG and public policy committees and is also a member of an ISA working group to develop an industry database. Klug's previous experience at MCI included product management responsibility for MCI's customer network management and billing products.

Antoinette (Toni) Moore. President, Moore Telecommunication Consultants, San Diego, California. Moore has been training and consulting in the audiotext business since 1987. She wrote *Dialing For Dollars* (Appendix C), publishes the monthly newsletter *900 NewsReport* (Appendix A), and is a frequent guest on radio and TV talk shows.

Donald Young. President, New Tech Telemedia, a service bureau based in Chicago. In business for 34 years, Young developed the second voice messaging system after VMX, Voice & Data

Systems. He has operated a service bureau since 1982. He is president of Mid America Information Services Association (MISA), a five-state organization serving as a forum for carriers, information providers, related services, and as a stimulus to doing business within the "fraternity" of telephone-related companies.

The Roundtable

In one sentence, how would you define 900 pay-per-call services?

Bruce Kennedy: Taken as a whole, including fax on demand, recorded services and live information, the 900 pay-per-call "model" represents the most convenient and universal means currently available to transmit and receive information on demand.

Robert Doyle: Pay-per-call services provide for the telecommunications delivery and associated payment mechanism for goods or services provided to end users. Notice the word 900 was not used. I add this comment because alternative means such as prepaid cards, on-line service and other technologies are also merging in addition to traditional 900 access means.

Phyllis Grant-Parker: Pay-Per-Call is a telecommunications solution providing an organization an efficient method to market their service at a price they set, benefiting from both universal market access through the telephone and a cost-effective method of billing and collecting their revenues through the telephone bill.

Michael Cane: Services delivered over the phone and billed by a telephone company (nothing more or less).

Peter Brennan: 900 services provide a billing mechanism for a telephonic information transaction.

When should a 900 number be considered the medium of choice, instead of, for example, a newsletter?

Robert Doyle: A 900 number should be the medium of choice, over a newsletter, when the information being provided is time-sensitive, and printed updates become too costly — or when your audience is constantly changing, so a mailing list becomes outdated. In addition to time sensitivity, immediate consumer convenience is another driver for such applications.

Bob Bentz: 900 works better than a newsletter when the information requested is interactive. It also allows information to be provided to the casual user who may not require the information as often and may not wish to subscribe to the newsletter.

Michael Cane: Whenever the following elements come together:
(1) The service can be substantially provided completely over the phone.
(2) There is a need for the client to access the service quickly and conveniently.
(3) The service requires up-front or automatic billing and credit cards are not always available.

Phyllis Grant-Parker: Any time that one is looking for an easy and cost-effective way to bill for service, its a natural. In Canada, the Stentor Owner Companies issue bills monthly to almost every household, so the reach is virtually universal. In fact, companies that are offering service through other mediums today are actually incorporating 900 service purely for its billing capability.

900 works as a complementary tool in a company's overall marketing plan. 900 and a newsletter can work well together. You can use 900 for a potential subscriber to call and order (and pay for) the newsletter. Or you can offer news updates and flash reports between issues. Or perhaps you can use 900 as an alternate distribution method for your newsletter. The caller dials the 900

number and has it faxed back to him. Or you use the newsletter to advertise other services available through a 900 service.

Gene Chamson: A 900 number should be considered the medium of choice for delivering information that is timely, changes rapidly, is concise, and is not otherwise easily available from other sources. Often, newsletters and 900 numbers can work together, and shouldn't be viewed as substitutes. For example, many publishers of stock market newsletters have discovered that 900 numbers provide an effective way of getting out their latest buy/sell recommendations, but they don't take the place of the printed newsletter which can go into more depth, provide a larger volume of information, and present graphs and pictures. Usually a newsletter is a good way to promote a 900 number and vice versa.

Bruce Kennedy: The most unique and powerful quality of the 900 paradigm is its flexibility. One of the most defining features of our contemporary society is the rate at which things become obsolete or dull. This is particularly true of information. Information is power, yes. But it must constantly be updated or be fresh and personal. The information in newsletters is locked into a specific time frame to a specific target audience. It begins to grow stale the moment it goes to press. In the fax on demand and recorded information arena your media is digital. The ultimate in flexibility. Therefore, it can be updated and/or personalized like very few other forms of information. In the live environment everyone can be treated like an individual and receive personalized attention. Very powerful stuff.

What types of services have been successful in the past, and why?

Phyllis Grant-Parker: In Canada we have seen the most success in entertainment programs, which I believe is consistent with the U.S. experience. Because these are mainly entrepreneurial in nature, meaning that they are stand-alone programs developed as revenue generators or profit sources, they are most successful when they have a large market. 900 offers a new and easy access to entertainment and information services.

Bruce Kennedy: Successful services that I am aware of have one thing in common: passion. The content must be of great, emotional interest to the consumers. That is what will drive the primarily impulsive nature of this product. Given the way we are all wired, this passion is often directed by our libido. Therefore, although embarrassing to many associated with the audiotext business, the adult chat concept has been the driving force in opening up the frontiers. There are, however, some other promising areas. Tele-Lawyer is a good example. Preliminary consultations with lawyers which address some pressing need have shown some promise. Psychic services which attend to the emotional needs and questions of many have also been lucrative. Even services such as the results of a lottery drawing for a limited number of hunting licenses have shown steady strength. (talk about basic passions). By way of contrast, I would be very skeptical of any services which simply supplied interesting information. Some day these types of services may find their place at a very low cost. Currently, there is such a widespread distrust or lack of understanding regarding pay-per-call that there must be a very strong motivating factor to get the consumer to "make the call."

Robert Doyle: The success of 900 applications largely follow two paths: traditional entertainment and business and government-sponsored applications.

On the entertainment side: Lottery results have been successful because of the timeliness of the lottery information versus alternative print media results. Psychic applications are also popular, heavily impacted by advertising and marketing. In the last 18 months, voice personals in daily/weekly newspapers have seen extensive growth. Another increasing application set is media-stimulated promotion using pay-per-call technologies.

On the business and government side, the types of services that have been successful include technical or product support, customer service, product promotions, professional information lines (medical, legal, financial), product promotions, and government information (program requirements, eligibility, registration).

Bob Bentz: Media partnerships have been the most common success story. Most entrepreneurs, however, will not be successful in obtaining such a joint venture opportunity with media. Therefore, I recommend niche — as opposed to general — applications since the average IP cannot compete with media-sponsored services.

Donald Klug: The most successful 900 applications have three common attributes: low cost ($2/minute or less), high perceived customer value, and ease of use. One of the most successful applications within the past several years has been the evolution of the voice personals market. Currently, most major daily newspapers provide 900 voice personals in their classified sections. This "virtual bar scene" is relatively inexpensive, fills an unmet market need, and is relatively easy to use. It is also economically attractive for newspapers since there is no initial investment.

Michael Cane: Adult chat and gab, psychic, and sports picks.

Toni Moore: Personal services such as date lines and psychic lines proved to be very lucrative, although the market is now experiencing an oversaturation in these areas. There are many IPs currently vying for the same market share. The curiosity factor that created a percentage of the calls has also lessened.

Gene Chamson: I believe the types of services which have been successful have had one or more of the following characteristics: 1) They take advantage of the convenience and timeliness of providing a service by phone. Examples would include sports and lottery results, sports picks, and stock market recommendations. 2) They have a well-known sponsor, whose name and reputation provides credibility and appeal to the service. Examples would include the *Wall Street Journal's* Journal Phone, Jeane Dixon's horoscopes, *Consumer Reports'* Car Pricing Service — each of these has been successful while "generic" versions of similar services have come and gone. 3) They take advantage of a sponsor's ability to advertise a service inexpensively in their own media. For example, newspapers, magazines and cable TV stations have been successful promoting such 900 numbers as stock quotes and sports scores which never would have survived had they been required to pay regular advertising rates to promote them. And, 4) They appeal to people's basic needs in an impulsive way, providing an "instant fix." In this category I would include sex lines, date lines, chat lines, horoscopes, psychics, games and jokes. The truth is people are often lonely, bored, or depressed, and these 900 numbers provide some short-term relief.

What kinds of services will be successful in the future, and why?

Donald Klug: I expect services that will be most successful in the future will be those where 1) the end user is currently not paying for the call content; and, 2) there is high customer demand. Applications that fit these criteria include government services (local, state, and federal) as well as customer-service oriented applications. In both of these business and government agencies can easily migrate from an 800 to 900 call environment and transform a cost center into a profit center.

Robert Doyle: In general, the kinds of services that will be successful are programs that provide a quick and efficient way to get valuable information or applications which benefit from an alternate payment method in lieu of credit cards. In addition to the programs previously mentioned, applications in the area of fundraising, mass calling, premium customer service, and travel-related services will also flourish. For instance, television networks will utilize 900 services and incorporate them into their promotions and programming to drive ratings, increase market share, and attract new audiences.

Bruce Kennedy: If and when the general "900-services suspicion and ignorance" begin to become less of a factor, the possibilities for convenient, timely, hard-to-find or entertaining information does seem nearly limitless. I am, however, probably being somewhat skeptical when I say it remains to be seen how the future timelines will play out. It's not clear to me that by the time that pay-per-call successfully remakes its public image, new technology or combinations of technology might have already superseded a "telephone only" based pay-per-call model. Might we not see pay-per-Internet-connection services become more powerful and even more convenient? Or some combination of computer and cable information transfer? Who knows? I don't necessarily think these uncertainties should keep people on the sidelines now, however. That would be like waiting for the final and perfect version of the computer to come to market before you buy your first machine. Anyone with rich content and wherewithal to start a 900-based information service should get on the merry-go-round now. Once you have succeeded in today's paradigm you can then begin addressing the future.

Phyllis Grant-Parker: We see real growth in 900 from established companies, governments and non profit organizations as they use 900 and its benefits to address the challenges of change. We believe there are real opportunities for these organizations to cost-effectively disseminate valuable real-time information to their customers, to provide priority service to their select customers, to enhance after-sales support and to fund services that their customers want, but which they can no longer afford to provide for free. I also believe that applications will capitalize on the 900 billing mechanism more than they have in the past. For example loyalty program registration will be successful. And fundraising that combines the ease of 900, offered with an incentive (e.g., a sweepstakes) to encourage participation, will grow significantly over the next year.

Michael Cane: Technical services and information, professional services, and informational services in general.

Carol Morse Ginsburg: Entertainment has its place and always will. The public is accustomed to paying for entertainment, be it movies or miniature golf. Consumers want information, and they want it fast. Applications, business or otherwise, can utilize that concept and have it work for them.

When people look for help, they want it immediately. So lines that provide aid for your computer, your finances, your kid's problems — and legal, medical and marital predicaments — will have their place. Look for the advent of the home fax to play a part in the future of 900. Let's face it, some information is better suited to the printed page than audiotext.

Bob Bentz: Joint ventures with niche media sources will remain successful. Voice personals continue to grow in public acceptance and will continue to be good producers. Sports handicapping is a solid investment because it permits a high-priced call. Interactive fax-on-demand has tremendous potential that will be fully realized when the fax machine becomes as common in homes as the VCR.

Toni Moore: The services that will prosper and survive into the next decade will be those that offer such timely and valuable services as consulting, technical assistance, access to current and detailed data-bases, and possibly order-entry capabilities. It is my opinion that once the industry has stabilized, and the public sees the true value, fulfillment of approved products will be billable via phone bills.

Gene Chamson: Mass-market 900 services will become the domain of large firms, media companies, and well-known brand sponsors. The future of 900 services for the entrepreneur who doesn't have access to any of these is in specialized or niche market applications. For example, I expect we'll see more live professional advice services where the caller can get expert advice in a variety of specialized areas on demand. I also think we'll see more use of 900 numbers with targeted media like newsletters and cable TV. And as the technology for retrieving information by fax becomes more widespread, I think there will be a flock of new applications combining fax-on-demand with 900 numbers.

Donald Young: In the future of 900 will most likely trend to consumer services unless the newly-discovered "business-only" 900 exchanges take off. Most businesses block 900, and the probability of consumers using the 900 line for anything but receiving important information, or that for which they are reimbursed in coupons, has a low likelihood of surviving. Until the FCC mandates disconnects for those who do not pay their 900 bill, the industry will spend too much time and money concerning itself with this critical no-pay issue. Legal, medical, therapeutic, and financial services should rise in popularity with this home group.

What, if any, has been the common denominator found in most successful 900 applications?

Bruce Kennedy: I have already addressed that issue. Instead, let me suggest what I consider to be an even more important question, if we are really trying to get to the heart of successful applications: What are the common elements found in most successful 900 *companies*? As in most entrepreneurial enterprises, the common element I have observed in successful 900 companies is the strength of the people running them. Although we are all in love with the idea of striking out on our own and being captains of our own destiny, sadly, we are simply not all cut out for it. Energy, decisiveness, the confidence to push forward against all odds and, possibly most important, a precise marketing intuition which can "feel" what consumers really want: these are the essential, personal elements I have observed to be common among all the most successful people behind the successful companies in the audiotext industry.

Phyllis Grant-Parker: I believe that the common element is a well-developed marketing plan. 900 programs, whether they are stand-alone offerings or part of an overall organizational marketing initiative, don't just happen because a 900 number is installed. I think the other common denominator is program design. And by that I mean the effective design and implementation of the IVR system behind the program.

Robert Doyle: The keys for a successful 900 application include the following:

1. Useful information or services as viewed by the customer.

2. Awareness that the information or service is available, i.e. advertising and promotion are necessary.

3. Reasonable certainty of cost by the consumer (helps ensure high collection rate for the application).

Our experience and market research shows that, if there is value in the information being provided, people are willing to pay for it.

Bob Bentz: In my book *Opportunity is Calling*, I outline the four requirements for a successful 900 program. I call it "PUFE."

PROMOTION—Supply cost-effective promotion
URGENCY—Audience must have a sense of urgency
FOLLOWING—Significant following of audience
ESTABLISHED— Pre-established audience

Most media partnerships bring the key elements listed above that nearly guarantee success.

Michael Cane: Easy marketability, meaning a service which can be easily explained in advertisements and has immediate appeal to the consumer.

Carol Morse Ginsburg: A line is considered successful when it is a money-maker. There are three elements that most successful lines have in common.

1. They fulfill a need or a want. Will people call your number? Yes, if it fulfills a need. Does anyone want the information you are providing? Is the information you are providing easily obtained — free or at a low cost — from other sources? Of course, there is competition; but the question is, do you have a different spin than the competition? Do you know how to reach that market?

2. They generate repeat callers. Advertising is expensive; therefore repeat callers are the backbone of a successful program.

3. They give value — real and perceived. Callers who hang up feeling they have gotten good value are the callers who will keep the number and call back another day.

Toni Moore: The common element is offering the callers the promised value, and ensuring the advertisements give a clear picture of what the caller will receive. There are some 900 lines that are financially successful for short periods of time due to their appeal to a gullible public; they are, however, short-lived, and the public will eventually become more aware of such scams.

Peter Brennan: The most successful services are those that combine the following ingredients in a variety of proportions: (1) time-critical information; i.e., the latest sports score or business report; and, (2) value to the caller; i.e., novelty, convenience, and content of specific interest. Furthermore, services have succeeded when they have capitalized on a buyer's impulse and when they have been enhanced by the imprimatur of a recognizable provider of content in other forms — newspapers, TV stations or radio, for example.

What has been the major cause of failure for most new 900 programs?

Donald Klug: Most programs don't succeed because call volumes don't meet expected levels. While there may be many reasons why an application doesn't reach projected call volumes, I feel that the two primary reasons are lack of effective advertising and an unrealistic sense of the value of the call content. The market is saturated with Elvis sighting, recipe, and joke lines. The best way to test the value of an application is to ask your mother-in-law if she would call it.

Bruce Kennedy: I have not been personally involved in many unsuccessful programs. However I am aware that poor marketing and advertising decisions, inadequate financing, lack of attention to the vital details and the inability to take risks are among the greatest contributors to failure in this, as with most entrepreneurial undertakings.

Robert Doyle: The major cause of failure for many 900 programs is an inadequate or nonexistent business plan. This can lead to low call volumes caused by a lack of proper advertising or lack of value to the consumer.

Bob Bentz: Unrealistic expectations through inflated call-count projections. Don't just ask your friends if they would call; do some bona fide marketing research before beginning an application. And, if you don't get anywhere near the volume you expected during the test market, drop the idea and look for the next application.

Michael Cane: An insufficient marketing budget and inappropriate product.

Carol Morse Ginsburg: Not selecting the right service bureau. After deciding to go into the 900 business, the most important decision an IP will make is the selection of a service bureau. The service bureau is your link to the long-distance carrier. The right one will hold your hand, and hopefully, send you checks. Service bureaus are responsible for the record-keeping, programming and equipment maintenance. In addition, they can help plan your budget, give advice about advertising and marketing, and on program viability and design. IPs need to spend time checking out the service bureau.

Not knowing where or how to advertise and not having sufficient funds to do so is another major cause of failure, as are unrealistic expectations about the industry. A novice IP once complained to me he had paid $54 for advertising and hadn't gotten any calls.

Phyllis Grant-Parker: Underfunding. Advertising is one of the major costs in 900 marketing. We tell people who want to launch a new program that the key to success is advertise, advertise and advertise.

Toni Moore: The major cause of failure is lack of idea analysis, or feasibility, and undercapitalization of a marketing plan. Many novice IPs are buying into the idea that they can advertise a simplistic line for $200 per month and make a profit. This is highly unlikely.

Gene Chamson: In my experience, most new 900 programs fail for one or more of the following reasons: 1) They have a poor idea; 2) They aren't marketed well; and 3) The sponsor is underfunded and doesn't have enough money to do the job right. Unfortunately, usually it's a combination of all three. As far as having a good idea goes, most 900 entrepreneurs never ask themselves these three questions:

1. Who would use this service, and how large is this potential market?

2. How valuable would this service be to people, and what would they be willing to pay for it?

3. What are the alternatives or substitutes for this service, and what advantages and disadvantages would the 900 service have over them?

Objective, informed answers to these questions would save many fledgling entrepreneurs a lot of time and money. My favorite example of this is the "garage sale line," an idea for a 900 service that would provide a listing of garage sales. This seemed like a good idea until its promoters recognized that newspapers already do a very good job of providing this information for free. What's more, you can carry around a newspaper as you drive through a neighborhood, but you'd have to copy down all the information you hear on a 900 number in order for it to be useful.

Even with a good idea, if it isn't well marketed, no one will find out about it. Many 900 entrepreneurs don't know much about marketing or advertising, and they don't have the good sense to hire a professional. Even worse, many don't have enough money to do much advertising anyway! The typical 900 entrepreneur spends a wad of time and money developing his or her program, and then has hardly any money left for advertising.

There's this widespread myth that with a 900 number all you have to do is place one ad and then the money will keep coming in, with profits available to reinvest in more ads which will bring in more money, and so on. The reality is that most 900 numbers don't make money in their first few months, and you should have enough money to keep going for at least three months.

I recall one client who spent $5000 and four months setting up his 900 number. He placed one small ad in a national daily for $400 and then sat back expecting to become rich overnight. The next day when his ad appeared, he received five calls for a total of $34 in gross revenue. He was so discouraged that he immediately pulled the plug on his number. It's too bad, because he had a good idea and a good program, and with a little persistence, and some better advertising, he
might have had a successful service.

Donald Young: Major cause of failure for 900 programs: undercapitalization and lack of understanding of advertising.

Where are the opportunities, if any, for the entrepreneurial start-up IP with a limited budget?

Bruce Kennedy: In contrast to some of the outrageous hype being pedaled nowadays, I am not a big believer in the potential for "limited budget" launches. The exception might be an idea so new, so exciting that it can overcome all the obstacles. It just doesn't happen. I believe it was Newton who attributed his appearance of great stature in the arena of ideas to the fact that he "stood on the shoulders of giants." Remember, even Bill Gates did very little original creation in the start-up of Microsoft. The launch of that spectacularly successful company was a combination of timing, reworking readily available code and a tremendous amount of chutzpa. The notion of a genius pulling some absolutely new and unique idea out of thin air is almost entirely myth. Nearly all new science, art, business — whatever — are recombinations of successful ideas. Timing, tenacity, luck and a deep knowledge of the field are more likely ingredients for success in any area of endeavor. Deep pockets simply increases your odds of bringing all the necessary elements together and having the time required to promote your new variation.

Robert Doyle: Entrepreneurs can work with a service bureau to minimize their start-up costs, but they need to realize that without a good business plan (which includes an adequate advertising budget to drive and sustain call volumes) they may not be successful. Applications that are marketed as profitable 900 programs as seen in newspapers and infomercials rarely deliver the financial rewards that they claim.

Bob Bentz: I recommend that such IPs approach niche magazines and offer to operate a 900 service reporting on the subject of the magazine. The IP does all the daily updating; the magazine provides the advertising space. The two parties split the profits evenly. Barring this, there are still opportunities for entrepreneurial IPs in sports handicapping and in producing their own specialized singles dating magazine.

Donald Klug: I would recommend teaming up with a business that can provide the advertising support for the application. Potential applications include using 900 for charitable contributions, government agencies, and customer service applications.

Toni Moore: The highest potential for a feasible idea on a low budget is to begin a joint venture with an existing business that already advertises. Most IPs don't go that route because they lack the know-how to arrange a joint venture.

Donald Young: There are few if any opportunities for an IP without an adequate budget in 900 to survive. The only possible approach is to test-market a number in a small area which provides modest advertising rates, and to then graduate to larger markets as the payoff comes along. This will take months, and the IP will probably lose interest and money.

Peter Brennan: The wining entrepreneurs will be those who are able to add value to raw content — by dint of a particular access methodology or a good spin on content or some other "hook." I would advise any entrepreneur on a shoestring not to waste time and money unless he or she can afford to effectively market the service.

Where is 900 headed in the next decade?

Robert Doyle: Rapid changes in technology will transform 900 service as we know it today. Technology development will provide many new and exciting opportunities as the 900 pay-per-call industry is transformed into a pay-per-transaction industry and becomes a reliable and accepted alternative method of payment. Prepaid cards, electronic commerce and on-line services will be the first of these technologies to manifest themselves along these lines.

Bob Bentz: 900 will continue to grow at a moderate pace, but not at the breakneck speed of the early 90s. Its reputation will continue to improve as more legitimate programs proliferate. Added competition and improved collection efforts from the carriers will encourage more Fortune 500 companies to enter the business.

Peter Brennan: I have no reason to think that 900 will not continue as it is for many years to come, but there may be new entrants in the marketplace — alternative billing mechanisms such as 500, 700, and 10XXX services. 900 will continue to be thought of as the most widespread pay-per-call mechanism, and the other services will most likely develop to meet the needs of "boutique" services for specialized niches.

Donald Klug: In a word — cyberspace. The Internet will become the new frontier for pay-per-call, migrating applications from voice media to text and video.

Phyllis Grant-Parker: We see tremendous growth opportunity for 900 in the next decade. We think that the opportunity will be in the areas of government, business and non-profit. As these organizations face the economic realities and need to find ways to do business differently, 900 will offer an effective alternative.

User Fees are becoming a way of life and 900 is a vehicle to collect such fees. And at the same time, I believe that as organizations realize that they can provide extra value in providing chargeable services over 900 — and that the market accepts that value — there will be a real increase in demand. If, for example, I need to pay for my license renewal, and you can save me from standing in a line or traveling across town, I will see the 900 alternative as valuable.

Organizations are being asked to deliver more, but with less. Consumers have never been more demanding. Creative use of 900 pay-per-call programs can allow companies to create new revenue streams to offset costs, and to continue to provide valuable information and services that they might otherwise need to curtail.

And I think that you will see 900 accepted as a valuable fundraising tool. As these applications grow, the image of 900 in the marketplace will improve, and I envision that over the next decade it will take its place alongside 800 service as a valuable marketing tool.

Michael Cane: More sophisticated, mainstream services. Plus integration with other mediums (computers, interactive TV).

Toni Moore: There are applications for database access, Fax-on-demand, and with the future of interactive television, a possible marriage of some of those services. Few people will seek simple, recorded information. Many businesses, small and large, will see the value of offering their customers access, 24 hours a day, to a lot of information. The benefits will be fewer man-hours, and better customer service.

Gene Chamson: I think 900 services are just a first step in the area of premium billing services to be offered by the phone companies. In the next 10 years you'll see other third-party billing options, where an IP will be able to bill for a service on the telephone company bill without having to use a 900 number to deliver it. I think you'll also see some standardization of laws and regulations governing pay-per-call services, similar to what happened in the credit-card industry when it first started. Both these developments will restore some legitimacy and credibility to the pay-per-call business, as well as lowering the cost. And as a result, I think you'll see a whole new birth of applications from large and small businesses for relatively small volume pay-per-call services.

Donald Young: 900 is another optional vehicle for enabling response from callers. Until the companies stop blocking and the FCC mandates payment, it will grow at a reduced rate.

Bruce Kennedy: I would suspect that when some of today's consumers' suspicions and biases against pay-per-call fade away (as it seems they probably will) more niche-type opportunities should open up. Timely, difficult-to-gather information seems promising. A quicker way to accomplish time-intensive interactions with government and industry have already shown merit. But even if the threshold to general acceptance of pay-per-call is lowered in time, I would think new IPs would ignore my concept of "driving passion" at their own peril.

What should a prospective IP do to learn more about the business?

Carol Morse Ginsburg: After reading this book and attending my seminars and subscribing to my newsletter, IPs should consider attending industry conferences and talking to as many service bureaus and other IPs as possible. Sending away to the various Telcos for their packages helps, and visiting their local service bureaus can be a good source of information.

Bruce Kennedy: I'm a great believer in becoming immersed in a subject. If you want to do any really original work I believe that is required. A successful transition from novice to initiate might go something like this: initial interest and some uninformed inspiration; immersion in the subject; "It's-all-been-done-already-and-a-lot-harder-than-I-thought"-type discouragement; further immersion; informed inspiration and renewed interest. I would suggest trade shows, seeking out experts that you can trust, and even libraries. What I would not recommend are the plethora of get-rich-quick hucksters and high-priced turnkey programs. Sorry folks. It's not that easy.

Robert Doyle: In addition to the areas noted in my previous comments, research the marketplace and talk to other successful providers. AT&T also has consultation available by dialing 900-555-0900 should aspiring entrepreneurs be interested (Appendix F).

Bob Bentz: Read this publication and mine, *Opportunity is Calling.* Attend the annual R.j. (sic) Gordon audiotext trade show (Appendix B).

Phyllis Grant-Parker: Reputable service bureaus involved in 900 program development are a great source of information. *Audiotex News* and trade shows are valuable sources. In Canada we have our business consulting organization, called Phone Power, in all our owner companies, that will work with a potential IP to evaluate an opportunity and help to develop and implement a pay-per-call program.

Michael Cane: Meet and talk with several different service bureau reps and existing IPs. Attend conferences. Read books.

Gene Chamson: Read a book such as this one, by someone who isn't trying to sell you something. Call several service bureaus and discuss your application with them. Ask lots of questions. Many of the larger bureaus will send you information packets with much useful information. Go to the library and do a search for articles about 900 numbers. But whatever you do, please avoid "free" seminars or anything sold through a late-night infomercial. These people will give you biased information because they're trying to sell you something. Finally, contact a consultant. This will cost you some money, but it can save you a lot more in the long run. Of course, I recommend that you call me first. For a telephone consultation, call me directly at 1-900-446-6075, ext. 800 ($2.95/minute).

Donald Young: Nascent IPs should read voraciously every publication they can find that serves the audience they are attempting to reach. They should also analyze cable shows and commercials from the standpoint of content, and the types of commercials. They should familiarize themselves with the editorial and program content, and the type of advertisers and the advertising rates so they can understand the scope of what they have to do to become a success. Without an understanding of the media the program does not stand a chance.

Peter Brennan: A prospective IP would do well to read the trades, attend trade shows and ask questions. He or she should explore all carrier and service bureau options. And realize that this business is like most other retail businesses — it requires hard work, and daily attention. Ours is not an ivory-tower industry.

Should a prospective IP attend any of the trade shows, and if so, which ones?

Bruce Kennedy: Trade shows would be an excellent part of an immersion process.

Robert Doyle: One of the best industry associations that I know of is the Interactive Services Association (ISA), which can be reached at 301-495-4955. The ISA has special interest groups for interactive telephone services including pay-per-call applications, which may be of value.

Bob Bentz: The R.j. (sic) Gordon Audiotext Forum show is the premiere event in the industry today. It attracts both domestic and international attendees.

Peter Brennan: Mt advice is to participate in the Interactive Telephone Council of the Interactive Services Association. In addition to two major industry conferences each year, the monthly meetings and the various chapter meetings provide excellent networking and educational opportunities. *Audiotex News* (Appendix A) does a good job of acquainting the beginner with the industry. Stay away from shows or meetings which seem to guarantee that you'll be a millionaire within the next 20 minutes.

Donald Klug: Yes, trade shows are an excellent place to learn and to network. I recommend joining the Interactive Services Association and participating in its annual conference.

Toni Moore: I don't feel the novice will gain much more than info-overload by attending most of the audiotext trade shows. For less than $100 they would have access to better information via books, magazines, etc.

Gene Chamson: Trade shows are great if you work for a big company that is paying for it, or if you have money to burn. If you're a start-up entrepreneur with limited capital, I think your money would be better spent elsewhere. One exception: Trade shows are a unique opportunity to network with key players in the industry. If this is important to what you are doing — if you are searching for a high powered sponsor or media partner for your unique program — then a trade show is a good place to go.

What are the most common mistakes made by start-up IPs?

Michael Cane: Not having a viable product or having one that has been overdone. Not having sufficient marketing power.

Bruce Kennedy: Believing the hype about audiotext being a "fast and easy way to riches," and just being generally uninformed. Being under-funded and ill-prepared for the truly nerve-racking level of risk. Trusting the wrong people. Not finding an experienced "mentor."

Donald Klug: Lack of a comprehensive business plan and a thorough understanding of who your major competitors are. Many IPs attempt to compete on price but would be more successful finding a niche market or differentiating themselves based on customer service or some other attribute.

Carol Morse Ginsburg: Having insufficient information about the industry. Not having a good business plan or at least a budget and a plan that includes a step-by-step progression into the business. With the last, and not the first step, being buying their lines.

Not understanding the billing and collection issues. Not understanding the elements of advertising and marketing a line. Not understanding that there is a time lag in getting paid.

Thinking of this as a get-rich scheme that needs little information, little expertise and little money. Not having a broad perspective on the industry and not keeping up with the quick changes and understanding how these changes impact what's going on.

Not ever calling a 900-number program. It's astonishing how many IPs have never called a 900 number! It seems to me that just plain common sense would dictate spending $100-$200 on 900 phone calls before going into the business.

Bob Bentz: When most IPs consider starting a 900 service, they ask their friends and business associates if they would call such a service. This is not acceptable marketing research; most people tend to associate with others like them who will respond in the affirmative. Be sure to poll consumers not in your immediate circle. This will prevent you from having unrealistic expectations.

Also, many IPs simply don't know when to throw in the towel. 900 is direct response advertising that gives immediate feedback. Know when to quit and go on to your next idea.

Finally, almost all IPs have unrealistic expectations in terms of call counts. Your first goal should be to break even, not get rich.

Toni Moore: Failure to verify the feasibility of their idea. Failure to target their market. Failure to create an advertising plan based on facts. Lack of enough knowledge of the industry to know what questions to ask when looking for a service bureau. Lack of training.

Phyllis Grant-Parker: Lack of a solid business case and underfunding. A start-up IP has to develop a business case just like he or she would for any other business venture. They need to evaluate the market opportunity, the market size, potential demand, price acceptance, competition (both direct and indirect) and, of course, the best communications vehicles to reach that market. If you don't have a large enough market, or a program that will generate repeat calling and an advertising campaign that will make those phones ring, then there probably is no opportunity for success.

And, of course, having the financial resources to run the program for a period of time without revenues. It takes time to establish market awareness and then time for the billing process to deliver funds.

Gene Chamson: In addition to the mistakes I mentioned before, I'd like to mention three others that are frequently made, and yet easy to avoid:

The first is failure to do any market research. This tends to be an "idea" business, and entrepreneurs fall in love with their ideas. Everyone wants to get rich quick, and no one wants to waste any time doing tedious market research. But if you're going to spend a chunk of your time and money, you'd be wise to get answers to some basic questions before you start. You'll be surprised how easy this can be. For example, if you're thinking of starting an Asian Personals service in your city, you'll probably want to get answers to questions like: How many Asians live in this area? How many of them are single? Are there existing media that directly target this group where you can advertise your service? Are there any competing 900 services? What about Asian dating services? How many are there? How long have they been around? You can answer these questions in a day or two using public information. By doing a little market research in the beginning you can avoid spending your resources on a bad idea, maybe change a bad idea into a good one, or get verification that your idea is a winner.

The second mistake is related to the first, and that is the failure to do market testing. Again, 900 entrepreneurs fall in love with their services, and they don't see any reason not to tell the whole world about them as soon as they can. I've see many IPs spend the bulk of their advertising budget the day after their 900 number is turned on. This is a bad idea for several reasons: First, there are almost always bugs in your program when it's new. This is just Murphy's Law. Better to be totally confident that everything's OK before you turn up the gas on your advertising. Remember: You never get a second chance to make a first impression, and even a small error in a pay-per-call service can turn a caller away forever, or even worse, drive them to call the phone company and ask for a refund! But perhaps even more important, you don't want to spend a lot on advertising in the beginning because despite what you might think, you don't know if your service is a winner, or if your ads will work.

Test marketing is especially important in the 900 business because you can easily measure results, and quickly change things that aren't working. Better to run a few ads that don't work than a whole lot of them. Be methodical: run an ad, measure the response, tweak some things, see if results get better; learn from trial and error. Do this on a small scale until you come up with a formula that works, meaning your advertising produces a respectable profit. Then you're ready to reproduce that formula on a large scale.

Peter Brennan: The three most common mistakes are the lack of enough capital to advertise, overestimating the appeal of your service in the marketplace and being taken in by the 900-number shysters.

What characteristics are shared by the most successful IPs in this business?

Donald Klug: The critical success factors are timely payment, customer service, and flexible management reporting. Successful IPs are also able to benefit from economies of scale associated with large fixed costs, such as VRUs.

Michael Cane: Finding a unique niche and/or having a lot of marketing money.

Carol Morse Ginsburg: A thorough understanding of the business, and careful attention to what is happening on a month-by-month basis. Tenacity in analyzing call counts and which media is working for them. Sufficient capital and knowing where and how to spend it. A willingness to put the time in when needed.

The most successful treat this as a regular business, subscribing to industry publications, joining industry associations, keeping up on what's happening. Letting their congressmen and state legislators know they are interested in how they vote.

Using an ad agency that knows the 900 business; or taking the time to place their advertisements properly, writing the best ads they can, tracking other ads.

Testing ads and spending time in the library reading and researching niche publications, and checking ads there.

Bob Bentz: Knowledge of which advertising to use to generate the first call to the service and consistent and informative updating to keep those calls coming.

Toni Moore: The successful IPs look on this opportunity as a business, not a get-rich-quick scheme, or a hobby. They do their homework, they seek professional advice and take it, and they persevere by creating a plan and sticking to it.

Gene Chamson: Because 900 numbers are an advertising-driven business, I believe the most consistently successful IPs have been those companies already in the media business (newspapers, magazines, cable TV) who have access to virtually free advertising through unsold space or time. Also more likely to be successful are marketing-savvy experts in direct response advertising, or who have enough money and good sense to hire such expertise.

Peter Brennan: Attention to detail, but more importantly, a commitment to build a business and an industry for the long haul.

When should an IP be the client of record with the long-distance carrier?

Phyllis Grant-Parker: Smaller IPs can gain from the volume discounts achieved by a larger service bureau. The advantages of being the client of record is that you have more control over your program, so that if you are not satisfied with the services you are receiving you can change at any time and take your 900 number with you. It's always a challenge from a carrier perspective, since we deal with and answer to the client of record. As long as your bureau is aligned with your needs and expectations, they can represent you well with your carrier. In Canada, as the 900 carrier, the Stentor Owner Companies try to work very closely with our service bureaus, recognizing the value that they bring to the IPs, and together we deliver a total solution to the IP. I would always recommend that an IP who chooses to have his or her bureau be the client of record have a clear contract with that bureau.

Bruce Kennedy: I can't understand why anyone would want to invest in promoting a product that they didn't own. The phone number is what the consumers identify as your product. If you do not own that number you are building up goodwill on a product that could be taken away from you tomorrow.

Robert Doyle: There is no right answer to this question. Frequently, clients with their own equipment and staff with associated technical expertise are their own customer of record with the long-distance carrier and billing entity. Service bureaus as customer of record are also routine within the industry, whereby the bureau serves as a full-service integrator. In such cases, contracts with a service bureau are strengthened by the IP if the rights to the 900 number are maintained for transfer purposes by the IP should changes in service bureau or a direct carrier and billing entity relationship be desired at a later date.

Bob Bentz: Only when the service bureau's financial stability is in question. And, if the bureau is not financially stable, you shouldn't be there in the first place! By being your own customer of record with the carrier, you will be subject to a holdback, large initial fees, and higher monthly fees. The service bureau, through its larger negotiating ability, is able to negate all of these fees. Moreover, if you are the customer of record, then the service bureau will not obtain its own quantity discounts and therefore will need to charge you more to make up the difference.

Michael Cane: When volume is large enough to sustain higher cost (set up; monthly fees). IPs should always have the right to move their 900 number from one service bureau to another as part of their service bureau agreement.

Gene Chamson: IPs with large start-up budgets, many numbers, or ongoing programs with significant call volumes should consider becoming the client of record for their number(s). In return for paying more up front and more per month, the IP is assured of getting paid, and usually getting paid quicker. Think of the extra cost as an insurance policy. If you're not making much money yet, it's probably not worth spending more to protect it. Also consider becoming the client of record if your relationship with your service bureau is deteriorating, or if it has a lot of questionable 900 programs, since uncollectibles from these programs could quickly and suddenly drive a service bureau out of business.

Donald Young: The only time an IP should become the client of record is when he or she has determined the success of the program in advance of its debut and is willing to take what would have been good advertising dollars and put them into the ownership deposit required to become a client of record. Otherwise, a simple letter of understanding with the service bureau will enable the IP at an appropriate time to become the client of record if he or she wishes. Protection would seem to be the only advantage for the IP to relate directly with the carrier.

Peter Brennan: An IP should insist on being the client of record only when there is enough traffic to negotiate a more favorable rate from the carrier. Most reputable service bureaus will allow clients to take a number with them, provided their account is in good standing — and IPs should look for that in their contact. This is often a false issue that trips a lot of people up. Transmission is a commodity.

When should an IP purchase his or her own voice-processing equipment and bypass the service bureau?

Bruce Kennedy: Equipment is expensive and complex. Until an IP is processing tens — probably hundreds — of thousands of minutes a month, he shouldn't even consider going into another new business: becoming a service bureau. Build your business plan with the service bureau expenses as a cost of doing business. In time, with volume, it may make sense to lower your cost of doing business by putting in your own equipment, but it is not a step to be taken lightly or early on.

Michael Cane: Only after they are not only doing extremely high volume but have also demonstrated the long-term viability necessary to justify long-term capital purchases (which is rare).

Phyllis Grant-Parker: IVR is both high-tech and expensive. Unless an IP has in-house expertise to support such a system, purchasing his or her own equipment is probably not a good idea. Service bureaus not only offer state-of-the-art equipment, they also possess the expertise to design and manage such systems, and you gain the cost-efficiencies of sharing these platforms with their other clients. So, in addition to evaluating the costs of the equipment and the associated maintenance, an IP needs to evaluate the lost revenue should his or her program go down, even for a day.

Bob Bentz: If you needed something printed, would you buy a printing press? Leave voice processing to the professionals and hire a service bureau.

Toni Moore: The first consideration would be the cost of the equipment, programming and maintenance (plus expandability). All of this should be covered by existing profits, and not on hoped-for profits. It's important to realize that there are no guarantees of longevity of any program, so take into consideration what you would need to do with said equipment if you no longer kept your program active.

Peter Brennan: An IP should bypass a service bureau when he or she is generating enough traffic to use equipment most efficiently, or when the nature of the program is so unique that dedicated equipment is absolutely the only way to go. Last year's "state-of-the-art" is next year's doorstop.

What is the price range for purchasing a complete in-house voice processing-system, say, from a fairly simple two-port interactive system to a sophisticated 200-port system?

Bob Bentz: The minimal system I would be comfortable with costs $30,000. That cost, however, is only the beginning. You'll need at least four engineers to supply 24-hour, seven-days-per-week coverage of the equipment.

Toni Moore: $6,000- to $100,000-plus

Peter Brennan: $5,000 to $100,000. But the processing equipment is only part of the puzzle. There are many other components: local loop, switching equipment, channel banks, call diverters, back-up power, and so on.

What are the most important capabilities to look for in a service bureau, and why?

Bruce Kennedy: A successful audiotext business is founded on doing two very broad areas of business very well. The first is promotional. Getting the phones to ring. That's what I do. The second is technological. This broadly includes answering your calls, capturing your customer's information, billing and fraud control, program maintenance and hopefully coming up with some inspired content. Imagine being a new IP who has invested his or her life's savings into an advertising campaign. Just as your ads are breaking your service bureau has a failure and the system goes down. Who do you kill first?

Reliability then, in my mind, becomes one of the first things to look for in a service bureau. I would suggest that any new IP interview numerous other IPs regarding service bureaus. You will probably get as many opinions as people questioned. That's normal in an evolving business — there are no really easy answers. But at least you will have some place to start and be able to make an informed guess. More important, you should be on track to becoming savvy enough, in time, to control and manage your vendor. You must be the boss of your business. Remember, the experts are only there to tell you their options and suggest directions. The final decisions are, *and should be*, yours. That's what being an entrepreneur is all about.

Bob Bentz: The most important capability is its ability to pay you what you deserve. Many bureaus are not financially stable. Second, be sure that the "service" in service bureau is emphasized. You should have multiple contacts there, including an account executive, account manager, and sales manager. You'll need to be able to speak with somebody often, and too many bureaus are overloaded with accounts and understaffed. Also, be sure that the service bureau has an effective way to process rotary calls; there are still a lot of them out there! You'll also want to work with a service bureau that is licensed under any patented technology or you may get prosecuted yourself. Finally, if your program is successful in the U.S., you'll want a way to easily expand it to other countries—especially Canada and the United Kingdom. Find a company that offers international expansion opportunities.

Donald Klug: The most important capabilities to look for are length of experience in the industry, customer service, and flexibility. A successful service bureau is also capable of offering the IP a rich mix of service offerings — voice capture, transcription, fax-back, outbound calling. In some cases, it makes sense to seek out a service bureau that specializes in such particular applications as customer service or voice personals.

Phyllis Grant-Parker: No matter what your application, the first thing is to look at is the bureau's track record and its financial stability, as you would in choosing any other partner. Then you need to look at your program; the content requirements, what areas of expertise you possess, and what areas you need to get from an outside expert. Then you know what the important capabilities are relative to your personal needs. For example, if your program will be interactive, then expertise in IVR program design would be important. Or, if you need fulfillment for your program, a bureau with fulfillment capabilities is important.

No matter which of the capabilities you need, one of the evaluating criteria should be its technical capabilities and its disaster recovery plan. You want to be sure that it has survivability and redundancy built into its system, and that it is available from the carrier it selects. As part of our consulting services we provide a brochure on how to select a service bureau, and lists of bureaus that we have selected as our Alliance Partners — outlining their capabilities — allowing an IP to select those with the capabilities that they need.

Michael Cane: Longevity. Satisfied IPs (meaning they have been paid). Flexible service and customer support for new applications.

Toni Moore: It's important that your service bureau can provide detailed menu-driven programs, voice capture, call counts, personal program access (to enable the IP to re-record messages), possibly fax-on-demand capabilities, approval process, flow chart and script assistance. Timely and detailed reports, *PLUS* automatically including a copy of the phone company billing detail with the statement to the IP.

Donald Young: Capabilities in a service bureau should include an ability to relate to the IP in areas of need, such as advertising, packaging and pricing. High grades for dependability and reliability from other clients of some longevity. The carrier recommendation may or may not be enough to assuage concerns among the beginning IP who may have heard stories of how people were burned. Success stories that can be checked are useful.

24-hour service available through calling the company which forwards to a pager after hours or a pager direct that activates an immediate response are requisites for the responsible bureau. On staff counselling or related professionals for advertising media and copy for IPs.

Peter Brennan: The single most important capability to look for in a service bureau is honesty, because it assumes a fiduciary responsibility to the IP. Beyond that commitment to client service, capacity, and the capability for internal programming may be important considerations depending on the nature of the program. The bureau's relationship with the carrier(s) should also be considered.

What are the least important capabilities of a service bureau, and why?

Bob Bentz: Too many IPs worry about simultaneous call capacity. If your primary advertising is print, most service bureaus will have plenty of capacity. Only if the advertising is television, which yields large call bursts, does simultaneous call capacity become important.

Toni Moore: If a service is required by the IP, then it becomes important enough to be considered by the service bureau. In other words, there are no unimportant capabilities.

Donald Young: Least important are the lengthy descriptions of the equipment and staff. The business is really one on one, and the IP deals usually with one or two people at most.

Peter Brennan: The site or physical location is usually not very important unless it impacts cost.

How have the services and functions of service bureaus evolved over the years, and where are they headed in the future?

Bob Bentz: Good service bureaus have become partners with IPs, not simply vendors of services. They are being relied on more for consulting and advice. Service bureaus now realize that their success is dependent on the success of its IPs.

Toni Moore: Service bureaus have evolved from being merely equipment providers to being proactive service providers. In order to stay competitive in the legitimate information services market, they will need to hone their marketing skills, enhance their equipment with state-of-the-art capabilities, and seek sound business applications for audiotext services.

Peter Brennan: Generally, the bureaus have become more consultative — less willing or able to simply provide a service to client specs without altering them based on the bureau's experience. Therefore, experience is an important criteria when shopping for a bureau. The winner is the program provider and, of course the user.

How many service bureaus have gone out of business in the last few years, and what was the main reason?

Bob Bentz: More than half of the service bureaus that were around in 1990 are no longer in the business. Many disappeared with the demise of adult entertainment. Many went bankrupt when the alternate carrier Telesphere went out of business. Still others bought a lot of equipment and could not afford to pay for it. There has been a major shakedown in the industry and the result has been fewer, but stronger, service bureaus.

Donald Klug: My guess is that there are over 350 service bureaus today, ranging in size from several hundred minutes per month to over 100 million. The number of service bureaus has increased faster than the overall market growth, creating an environment where more and more service bureaus are competing to capture fewer customers. Undercapitalization and lack of a well thought-out business plan remain the primary reasons for failure.

Toni Moore: I'm unaware of the actual number, however I would say the main reasons for failure are: undercapitalization, and poor marketing.

Peter Brennan: I don't know how many — but many have. Undercapitalization, lack of a broad product line, the demise of adult services, technological advances — all of which have contributed to a consolidation in the industry — have been main reasons.

How many service bureaus will be around five years from now, and how will they be different?

Bob Bentz: There has definitely been consolidation and strategic partnerships in the service bureau business. Bureaus are finding that there are considerable advantages to consolidating and not duplicating resources. There will be less bureaus around five years from now, but those that remain will be much larger. Many service bureaus will be bought out by major media outlets.

Peter Brennan: I don't know — it depends on what happens with the convergence of other media — TV and on-line, etc. — and what role if any service bureaus will play in the new environment. It also depends on what role the Baby Bells are allowed to play in this mix.

What are some of the best markets, or demographic and psychographic characteristics, for 900 services, and why?

Bruce Kennedy: I'm not aware of any research on this subject, but I suspect the demographics are pretty much middle- to upper-middle class. As with all new stuff, younger people are probably more receptive to this new form of information.

Robert Doyle: The Interactive Services Association is currently profiling the entire pay-per-call industry and would be a good source for this information when it becomes available.

Bob Bentz: To date, the best callers to 900 services have been at opposite ends of the educational spectrum — those without high school degrees and those with master's degrees or above. Minorities, especially African-Americans, are good callers. The single best demographic group is 18- to 34-year-old males.

Toni Moore: The 900 programs that succeed in the future will be those offering legitimate self-help, technical assistance, and detailed database access. The target markets for these lines will be the middle- to upper-income professionals, including the growing ranks of the self-employed, and home-based businesses.

Donald Young: Business-related services stand an excellent chance if the originators can pinpoint media required to reach that segment most interested in the service. The reason: lower ad costs, greater probability of payment of bills.

Peter Brennan: Traditionally, younger people on the lower end of the socioeconomic spectrum have represented the most lucrative market, but that may be because of the products being offered. People outside that traditional market have demonstrated a willingness to use the services, if they are the right services.

Is any particular advertising medium, such as TV, significantly better than others for a broad range of 900 applications, and why?

Peter Brennan: I favor print because it allows the use of a printed menu and unlike television, it rarely creates a surge which the telephone network cannot handle. Ultimately, it depends on the program.

Robert Doyle: Television is usually the strongest medium for a broad range of 900 applications because it offers sight, sound, and the potential to reach a very large audience. Because of the expense however, national television is not always an option for businesses or small IPs with 900 numbers. The advertising medium depends on the market and the audience. No one medium is inherently better than the other. For example, the best advertising for a software support line may be in the packaging of the software itself. The best advertising for a psychic may be print or cable TV.

Bob Bentz: I like magazines the best because of their ability to effectively target a specific market and because of their longer shelf life than newspapers. TV is very effective but also frustrating because 900 is often relegated to late-night and there are no consistent advertising content standards.

Toni Moore: I feel television and magazine advertising are the best mediums. TV has a high impact, and can be targeted to specific time slot programming. Magazine advertising is less expensive and has greater longevity per insertion. Magazines are also a more targeted medium.

Gene Chamson: The best advertising medium for a 900 application is the one that targets the most potential users at the lowest cost per exposure. That said, my preference is almost always print (newspapers, magazines). I think it's easier to target an ad to the right audience using print, and there's some permanence to it, so a caller doesn't have to remember the phone number. With radio or TV, you typically have 30 or 60 seconds to get the person to call. The trouble with radio is that most people listening to it are either waking up, going to sleep, driving somewhere, or doing something; they're not near their home phones ready to make a 900 call. TV is better, especially late-night TV, because the viewer is usually bored or lonely, sitting by the phone, and your commercial can give him something more exciting to do than watch some silly program. Psychic lines and fantasy lines do well on late-night TV. The trouble with TV is it's expensive, and so I wouldn't recommend it for anyone with a budget of under $10,000. If you're doing TV, make sure your service bureau has enough lines to handle the spike in call volume that hopefully comes during your ad. Ask for a report that shows how many lines you used versus how many were available. My favorite way to advertise is classified and in-column display ads because I can target where they go, and I can test the ad and refine it without spending that much, and then run the same ad in many places. Also, it's easier to muscle in on the competition. Just find out where your competition is advertising, then place your ad so that it's bigger, is seen first, or makes your service seem better than the rest.

Bruce Kennedy: Each media has its own strengths and weaknesses. TV spots and cable are relatively high-cost (using cost-per-thousand comparisons) and are fairly inefficient for targeting a niche. Another downside is that there is very little in the way of "residuals." Typically, when an ad breaks there is a spike of calls which then quickly taper off, with few repeat calls. The good news is that you get more immediate results. Tabloids and newspapers are less expensive but have less impact and longer lead times. They have some limited residuals but most people treat these publications as highly expendable and throw them out after a short time. Although national publications are less expensive per person they can be very expensive as a total dollar outlay. They also have long (three to four month) lead times. These publications are typically held onto for a longer period of time so that ads in this media can generate calls for months and, sometimes, even years after they have gone on sale. A good media buyer can help you find the right mix for your product. The most important thing remains having something worth advertising in the first place.

In the absence of a media partner, what should be the minimum monthly advertising budget for a national 900 program?

Toni Moore: Assuming that by "minimum" you mean giving it your best shot at reaching the target market through national publication(s), I would have to say $5,000 to advertise in one or two national publications.

Bob Bentz: For standard programs, I would recommend at least $5,000 per month. For niche programs, it could be less.

Bruce Kennedy: In general, I consider anything less than $10,000 a month in media buys a "test." It cannot generate sufficient amounts of business to reach any kind of "economics of scale." As a result the cost per call will probably always remain too high to turn much of a profit. But this type of limited ad campaign can be very useful, if carefully planned, in finding the right marketing approach to use to go forward with more confidence in spending larger amounts of money in the future.

Peter Brennan: It depends on the program and the marketing objectives. Sometimes the program is purely a direct-response mechanism — then you need to advertise for every call. Other programs — a medical information service for example — call for the generation of top-of-mind awareness, which is a different marketing task and would require a different approach.

Is it possible to grow a 900 information business slowly, starting with a fairly modest budget, and using imaginative, low-cost marketing strategies?

Michael Cane: Yes — I think I did it. Start locally, with media partners (per-inquiry deals) and other guerrilla marketing strategies.

Bob Bentz: Yes, but you'd better not make too many mistakes early on or you may be out of the business before you find the winning formula.

Toni Moore: This is a difficult question. There are so many variables. I'd venture to say yes it's possible, but riskier. This is often where the novice needs a feasibility study.

Gene Chamson: Yes. The more unique your 900 service, the more you can (and should) take advantage of low-cost promotion using publicity. I recall some years ago, the Potato Board of America sponsored a 900 number giving out potato recipes. I thought it was a sure loser, but then it got written up in *USA Today,* and the lines were humming for weeks. If you're doing a "me-too" service such as a date line or joke line, don't bother with press releases, unless you can come up with a unique angle. But there are other low-cost advertising strategies you can use. For example, if you can find media partners who are willing to advertise your service for a share of the profits, you'll eliminate your advertising risk and gain greater exposure. There are many books about "guerrilla marketing" that can give you other good ideas.

Peter Brennan: It is certainly possible, but not at all easy (How modest is modest?).

Under what circumstances, if any, would a 900 information business be a good choice for a home-based or part-time entrepreneur?

Carol Morse Ginsburg: This is an excellent home-based business, and over the years I've spoken to many retirees, as well as parents, who are running 900 businesses from their homes while raising their families.

Phyllis Grant-Parker: When a home-based business has information to offer, the billing mechanism of 900 service provides it with an easy accounts-receivable system. I was discussing this recently with a gentleman who plans to offer training consulting services from his home, a kind of semi-retirement venture. He had been advised that his demand would be too low to make a 900 program successful. I pointed out to him that it wasn't the volume that should determine his decision to use 900, but rather his decision on how to administer his receivables. His business isn't 900. It's consulting. But having his clients call him on 900 takes care of the billing element, and he avoids the need to issue bills or to carry merchant accounts for all the major credit cards. 900 is just a vehicle to take calls and bill for his services.

Bruce Kennedy: Home-based is very doable. I don't believe part-time is. If you accept my argument that total immersion is required to overcome the learning curve and succeed in this fast-paced, ever- changing business, it will be obvious why I take this position. As far as place of business is concerned, I really don't think it has to make a lot of difference. However, if you are in some remote part of the world and wish to truly meet and learn from others, only so much can be done over the phone. That translates, particularly in the early going, into a certain amount of travel.

Bob Bentz: If the entrepreneur has a media partner, has specialized information not readily available anywhere else, or has experience in advertising.

Toni Moore: If that person had a source of valuable information, such as his or her own database, or expertise in a specific field. In such cases, 900 numbers may be a good way to create additional revenue. It would be assumed that the entrepreneur had a marketing plan!

Gene Chamson: Starting a new 900 service can be a time-consuming, expensive, and ultimately risky endeavor. But there are some proven ways that a 900 number can work for a home office or part-time entrepreneur. First, if you're already in some form of advice or information business, you can use a 900 number as a tool. Prepare a recorded message with some type of specialized information related to your field. For example, one of our clients, a small-business consultant, has a line with a recorded message that gives 12 tips on how to increase your business without spending money on advertising. The 900 number establishes his credibility as an expert, promotes his consulting business, and earns money 24 hours a day! Or use a 900 number to offer telephone consultations and let the telephone company do your billing and collection. We recently set up a service called The Professional Network, which lets professionals share a 900 number for live consultations through the use of extensions. This way the cost of the 900 number is affordable, and practical for low call volumes.

Donald Young: The majority of individuals who bring programs to our service bureau — upwards of 95% — are presently employed. They see this business as a possible add-on to their existing income. Only if they have retired or have a chunk of cash "in between assignments" do they vary from that profile. The business of 900 is perceived as one they would *like* to grow into full time. But rather than risk everything, they stick their foot in the water. Without adequate risk capital the foot will be bitten off by the alligator of undercapitalization.

Peter Brennan: The key to a successful service is a source of information to sell. If that information can be generated by an entrepreneur at home, fine.

What new legislation or restrictions do you see on the horizon?

Robert Doyle: The most powerful piece of legislation in the pay-per-call industry is by far the Telephone Dispute and Disclosure Resolution Act (TDDRA) of 1992. It was a landmark piece of legislation for the industry. The FTC and FCC are charged with administering the provisions of the Act and we should look for their continued focus on violations which may be occurring within the industry to avoid these regulations. Congressional actions as a result of the 1995 Telecommunications Act may also produce further clarifications and consumer safeguards. Finally, 900 portability is an open issue in front of the FCC which may see action in the future.

Bruce Kennedy: I'm by no means a legislative expert. It is my belief, however, that the guidelines for the 900 business have been very clearly laid down for some time. If you remain within those guidelines you should have no significant legislative problems on the immediate horizon.

Bob Bentz: Hopefully, we've seen the end of the legislation. It has gone from nonexistent in 1989 to being overly obtrusive. Campaigning against 900 is politically correct and many attorneys general have benefited politically by attacking the industry. I believe that we've seen most of the legislation concerning 900, but there will certainly be increased efforts in controlling international audiotex providers who are not subject to the same legislation as domestic 900 providers.

Peter Brennan: TDDRA is the law that governs the national 900 industry. Some states have also developed specific laws pertaining to consumer information services using the telephone. Going forward, look for increased attention to be paid to our industry by state taxation agencies, and also for an effort on the part of the federal government to regulate international pay-per-call services.

Donald Klug: I expect that Congress or the FCC will mandate 900 number portability in the 1996-1997 time frame. 900 portability will be driven by demand for number portability in general, particularly as PCS-type services emerge. I also anticipate that the FCC will require all pay-per-call services to be restricted to 900 instead of 800, 700, and 500.

What is the most interesting or imaginative pay-per-call program you have seen?

Robert Doyle: Two particularly interesting applications include the following:

Product Promotion — In 1992 Maxwell House Coffee ran a promotion and sweepstakes for the Winter Olympics. Part of the promotion included a 900 number for people to call in and leave a good luck message for the athlete of their choice. Every night tapes would be delivered to the athletes at the Olympics for them to hear the messages from home.

Law Enforcement — Low-risk parolees call into a 900 number sponsored by BI Inc. for monthly monitoring. The 900 number offsets the cost of the county or state criminal justice monitoring program and the ANI (automatic number identification) information confirms the parolee is where he or she should be.

Bob Bentz: My favorite application is still the old tried and true crossword puzzle answer line. This is a perfect 900 application because it a win-win situation for everybody involved. To think that people will pay money to cheat on a crossword puzzle still amazes me. You can get the solution the following day, but people don't want to wait and will call to get help. On one of our crossword puzzle answer lines, we allow callers to leave a message for us. This helps us to create a better service. One day, we were checking the messages and one man said: "Ah ha, today I did the entire crossword puzzle and didn't even have to call you!"

Peter Brennan: I must push modesty aside and tell you that the most interesting and imaginative 900 program I am acquainted with is our own Personal Call program. Callers use the service to respond to personal ads which appear in the newspaper. In addition to leaving a response to a particular ad, callers can establish a profile in the system, describing the type of person they would like to meet. The program then matches them with other individuals in the database.

The Roundtable participants were asked to add their own question and answer, or to comment on any topic of their choice:

Bruce Kennedy: Running an advertising agency, I am very interested in efficient advertising. One particularly clever approach is to "piggy-back" your promotions on top of some larger wave of public interest. A good example of this was the 1995 Miss America pageant hyping the "swimsuit/no swimsuit" controversy to get literally millions of people to call during the program. They managed to link up their main product — the pageant — with some larger issues in our culture, and as a result created an nice little million-dollar plus "side business." And if they hadn't busied out (overloaded the circuits) it could have been two or three times that much. Pretty smart.

Bob Bentz: When should an IP avoid the 900 business altogether? If you really have no idea of what to do, have no promotional background, and are undercapitalized, then you should save your money rather than buy a "turnkey" 900 product from a hotel seminar. Save your money and buy lottery tickets instead; you'll have a greater chance of success.

Donald Klug: What criteria should a service bureau consider in selecting a carrier? Selecting a carrier for audiotext programs is often a difficult decision. Should you select one of the big three — MCI, AT&T, or Sprint — or one of the second tier of smaller carriers? The decision really depends on each service bureau or IP's unique strategy. Some of the criteria that may be helpful in the selection process include the following:

❐ Customer and sales support
❐ Industry commitment and position
❐ Product line depth
❐ Information flow and flexibility
❐ Price

Customer and sales support. The carrier should have a well-staffed support group to answer questions and to assist service bureaus in implementing new programs. This staff needs to be knowledgeable not only regarding the technical aspects of the program but should also be able to answer questions related to the state and federal regulatory environments as well. For example, an in depth understanding of the TDDRA is crucial in avoiding costly mistakes related to preambles and program content.

Industry commitment and position. In selecting a carrier, the service bureau should view the decision as a long-term commitment. The carrier should have a successful track record in the audiotext industry and should be able to provide references of current customers. Active participation in key industry associations like the Interactive Services Association (ISA) also demonstrates commitment to the industry.

Product line depth. Many service bureaus have a full range of offerings — both inbound and outbound. A carrier should be selected that can provide a range of services in order to provide one-stop shopping for the service bureau. The carrier should also provide a rich set of 900 features. This is particularly important for smaller service bureaus that do not have the capability to provide these features themselves. For example, MCI's Tailored Call Coverage feature allows selective blocking of calls by originating state or area code or prefix. This allows a service bureau to select specific service areas to maximize the effectiveness of a program.

Information flow and flexibility. Service bureaus, particularly smaller ones, are dependent on carriers for providing timely and accurate management reports. The minimum set of reports should include call detail (originating telephone number, date and time, call duration, and the price of the call). The information should be available in a variety of media — paper, disk, magnetic tape — and should be sortable based on service bureau defined attributes. Call credit detail, or chargebacks, is an additional area where accurate and timely information is critical to the success of a service bureau.

Price. Price is an important decision criteria but should not be the only factor nor the most important. Most carriers are willing to provide volume discounts for large customers and are flexible regarding billing and collection fees and monthly charges. Carrier discounts are determined by the size and length of the commitment made by the service bureau. In some situations, carriers may be willing to provide favorable terms in order to provide the service bureau with payment sooner.

Toni Moore: What would you consider to be the most negative aspect of the 900 industry now? I feel the multitudes of resellers who are offering "cheap" lines to an ignorant public is degrading the business. There may need to be some truth in advertising regulations required, or a concerted effort by those of us in the industry to educate the public.

Phyllis Grant-Parker: How does the Canadian market differ from that in the U.S.? What changes can we expect to see to 900 service in Canada?

We all know that from a market size, Canada is about one-tenth the size of the U.S. market. The challenge for American companies or IPs deciding to do business in Canada is that we Canadians can trick them. Canadians generally look like

Americans, we eat the same kinds of food, dress the same, and are exposed to much the same media. But in fact the Canadian culture is unique in terms of its attitudes and marketing practices. For example, a program that may be very well accepted in the U.S. may receive negative market reaction in Canada — or vice versa. That's one of the services that our Phone Power consultants can offer to an IP interested in the Canadian market. We can help him or her to evaluate how a program might work and what adjustments could be considered to make it more successful. We can help him or her understand the Canadian pay-per-call market, what similar programs ar charging, what the average chargeback rate is in a particular segment , and so on.

As I have identified, we see a very important market in what we call the traditional market applications. We believe that this market will continue to grow with new innovative programs. Our major service bureaus have identified needs that are required to help encourage new applications in the market, and we are addressing these needs throughout 1996. You will see enhancements that will provide service bureaus with easier billing and collections, and enhanced service management and control capability.

The other market segment is that of emerging applications which provide government, business and non-profit organizations with solutions that can help them address the challenges they face. These applications require new product enhancements such as new routing and management features, new call-handling capabilities, increased universality of access and marketing features such as directory listings. We will focus on addressing these needs and expanding the ways in which the unique features of 900 service can address new business challenges.

Gene Chamson: How can a new IP protect his or her idea? You really can't, so it's better to assume your idea will be copied, and get ready to deal with the competition. In the long run, it's how you execute the idea, and not the idea itself, that will determine your success.

Over the years, I've talked to hundreds of prospective IPs. They'll say, "I've got the greatest idea for a 900 number and I need you to help me set it up." When I ask what the idea is, they usually say something like, "Oh, I can't tell you yet. It's a secret, and I don't want anyone to steal my idea." That's when I know that their idea isn't really great. A good idea can be easily copied and improved upon. A great idea preempts the competition. Here's an example: a recorded horoscope on a 900 number is a good idea. But once the idea is out, there will be lots of competitors with similar services eating into your business. But a recorded horoscope from Jeane Dixon, America's best-known astrologer, now that's a great idea! Because every competitor who enters the market just reinforces your position as the premiere horoscope service. And indeed, while hundreds of horoscope lines have come and gone, Jeane Dixon is still around after a decade.

So when you come up with that next great idea for a 900 number, don't think about how you can keep others from stealing or copying it. Think about what you're going to do that will make your service better than all those who will copy it when it turns out to be a success.

Donald Young: The 900 business attracts idealists who dream of success and money without the necessary underpinning of understanding about the business. Most typical is the individual (and sometimes a company) that produces a 5 to 10 minute voice program that intends to "educate" a caller.

The best thing that can be done for these aspirants is to counsel them on either reducing the text to 90 seconds, tops, or converting to fax delivery if this information is required to understand whatever the theme. There is a tolerance level among callers that seldom exceeds 90 seconds on a listen-only basis. The ability to follow a complicated set of instructions (they all sound complicated after 90 seconds) is limited to a very small, select group.

A bureau is serving its own interests only — a short-term business-building philosophy — by taking the start-up money and first-month deposit. Usually the same minds that conceived that program will advertise in a very limited fashion with incorrect media. The bureau should offer advertising services either through staff counselling, or through related professionals with whom the IP may deal directly, totally unrelated to the cash flow of the bureau.

A successful advertising program will benefit the IP — and ultimately the bureau — through longevity of relationship.

Peter Brennan: It is difficult to address this industry as a whole. When people say they are in the 900 industry, it is like a restaurant owner saying he's in the credit-card industry. It is just a payment mechanism — one of many. Therefore, be careful what conclusions are drawn from anecdotal experience, and remember that in more ways than one ours is like other businesses which require constant attention and commitment.

Chapter 10
Parting Thoughts

What types of programs have been successful in the 900 industry? Your review of current media advertising will give you some indication. Repeat advertising for any generic type of 900 program is a good indication that this kind of program has been successful. Voice personal classified (or dating) lines are very successful, and you will find them advertised in just about every alternative weekly newspaper, as well as in quite a few mainstream newspapers.

Adult programs still appear to be quite popular, although most of the steamy, indecent programs have migrated over to 800 lines. The more tame "romance" or "chat" programs, however, can still be found on 900 numbers, usually with third-party billing.

Horoscope, tarot card, and psychic lines are doing well. Sports lines can be successful, particularly the specialized ones that deal in information which is not readily available elsewhere, such as Penn State's *Blue White Hotline* or the Lacrosse Foundation's 900 line.

Except for the sports lines, what do these programs have in common? They appeal to lonely people or to people trying to improve their social lives or conditions. This is a common thread that is worth remembering. However, although these types of programs are successful, the playing field is getting somewhat crowded, and the market may already be saturated with too many of them. Or you may be in direct competition with a major media company that owns the best vehicle for reaching the target audience — a company that will likely not want to feature *your* advertising touting a similar program that would compete with its own. You might have to invent an even better mousetrap that still appeals to the basic human motivations that drive these successful 900 programs.

Folio magazine's 1-900-PROFIT survey			
Magazine	**Service**	**Cost**	**Rating**
Newsweek	"Voice your comments" to the editor.	$1.95 1st 95¢ ea. add.	5
Ladies' Home Journal	Monthly poll asking readers' opinions on various issues	75¢/call	7-10
New Woman	Horoscope forecast	95¢/min.	NC
Mirabella	Weekly horoscope	95¢/min.	8
Harper's Bazaar	Astrological Hotline	$1.50/min.	10
Elle	Weekly numerology line	$1.25/min.	10
Sassy	Music hotline	95¢/min.	9
Spin	Sample music release	95¢/min.	NC
New York	Respond to personal ad	$1.50/min.	8
Playboy	Talk to a Playmate Vote for Playmate of the Year	$3/min. $1/call	7+ 7+
Penthouse	Talk to a Penthouse Pet Penthouse Dateline Talk to Two Girls	$5/1st, $3/ad. $5/1st, $3/ad. $5/min.	10 10 10
Source: Folio Magazine, 2/15/93 issue		NC: Declined comment	

Table 10-1

Folio, a trade magazine for magazine publishers, presented some interesting results from a survey of some of its subscribers who offer 900 number services. The participating magazines offer a variety of 900 services to their readers, and they were asked to rate their success on a scale of 1 to 10 based on reader response and profitability. The results, displayed in table 10-1, seem to indicate that these 900 programs are doing quite well for the most part. It is safe to assume that many more media companies will add 900 information or entertainment programs to their mix of services. After all, 900 services dovetail nicely with a publisher's or a broadcaster's primary function: delivering information. Such pay-per-call services allow the media company to better serve its customers in a manner that is complementary to its main function, while at the same time earning a new source of revenue.

The current and projected industrywide revenue for 900 services are shown in Table 10-2. It should be noted that revenues shot up to nearly $1 billion in 1992, but then dropped quickly back down to around $540 million in 1993.

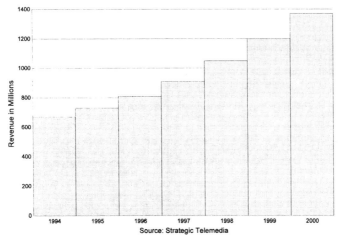

900 Services Revenue Forecast

Source: Strategic Telemedia

Table 10-2

The spurt in growth was caused primarily by the immense popularity of adult services, and the quick drop-off was caused by many adult IPs migrating over to other payment vehicles (such as

800 credit card), due to excessive regulation and chargebacks associated with 900 services. Henceforth 900 revenues should increase at a steady, more predictable pace. According to Strategic Telemedia, the total 1994 revenue number can be broken down into the following percentages:

Messages (Voice Personals): 27%
Entertainment: 26% (85% of this was psychic)
Information: 14% (steady share)
Telepromotions: 14%
Media Programs: 9%
Customer Service: 4% (25% over prior year, and growing fast)
Fundraising: 3%
Order Capture: 2%
Other: 1%

Be careful how you interpret these numbers. The fact that there are numerous 900 psychic programs doesn't mean that they are all profitable — it simply means that there are lots of psychic programs. Many of them may in fact be quite short-lived. The market could be oversaturated with such programs, and fierce competition for a limited pool of potential callers may result in a high percentage of failures.

Targeting a Market

As I mentioned in Chapter 4, the best approach for a smaller start-up IP with limited capital is to identify a precise target market first, before coming up with a specific 900 application. The best opportunities will be in specialized niche markets. According to Bob Bentz, director of marketing at Advanced Telecom Services, "Most people start with the idea, and then look for the right advertising medium. My recommendation is to look to the medium first, and then design the application to fit that medium."

Remember, advertising drives this business and represents the greatest ongoing expense. It makes sense to seek out a precise target market capable of being reached with rifle shot advertising, and to then design a 900 application which will appeal to this market, hopefully resulting in many repeat callers. This will keep advertising expenses cost-effective, and will bring you the lowest cost-per-response possible.

How do you find such a target market? Back in Chapter 4 several reference publications were listed — most of which can be found in larger libraries — that list thousands of periodicals and organizations that serve specific, well-defined markets. Think about collectors of all stripes, sports enthusiasts, professional or business associations, hobbyists, or any organization with a special interest. Consider minority groups or foreign language applications. Any specialized grouping of people or businesses will generally be served by a specific magazine, periodical, or mailing list, so they will be easy to reach. They also have specialized information needs that can possibly be delivered through a 900 program.

The perfect example of a successful niche program is one operated by Keith Mueller (see The 900 Advertising Club in Chapter 5, and *TeleLetter* in Appendix A). Mueller tapped his experience and contacts as a producer for NBC-TV in New York City to start a 900-number program that provides specialized information for the TV and radio broadcast industry. He advertises in a couple of the trade magazines, such as *Electronic Media* and *Broadcasting*, and he updates his program daily. This program was launched in 1989 and was profitable from the very beginning. Mueller lives comfortably in Newport Beach, California from the income generated by this one 900-number program.

Many start-up entrepreneurs overlook business-to-business services when evaluating their market options. Businesses will spend money on valuable information that helps get the job done in a cost-effective way. A 900 number can be much more economical than other alternatives, such as on-line computer databases that would be accessible via a PC and a modem, along with the pertinent software and monthly subscription fees. A 900 number allows the business user to get only that specific information she needs right when she needs it, without the hassle and expense of on-line services or printed directories. It's a direct, simple, inexpensive way to get highly focused information from any telephone.

Up to now, however, many businesses have blocked all access to 900 numbers to prevent employees from running up the phone bill with unauthorized calls to horoscope lines or Dial-an-Insult. Some of the long-distance carriers have recognized this problem and have introduced a solution. AT&T launched a new Business Exchange with a dedicated prefix, 900-555, which can be selectively unblocked by businesses wishing to have access to business-related information services. AT&T also uses a dedicated business-to-consumer exchange, 900-225, which is used for customer service and technical support. Similarly, MCI uses the 900-733 exchange for business use. The standards for getting these prefixes are quite stringent, and only irreproachable applicants providing valuable business-related services are accepted.

New Developments

As you now know, 900 is simply one billing mechanism in the pay-per-call arena. It may or may not be around in five years. It doesn't matter, except for the fact that I may have to change the title of this book for future editions.

In the meantime, we will probably see increasing use of 900 for product fulfillment (paying for merchandise). We will see other creative uses as well. Michael Lindsay of Galaxy-Net Telecommunications (he is also owner of 900 Numbers Unlimited, a service bureau listed in Appendix D) in Campbell, California (408-364-7900), is pioneering the use of 900 to pay for access to specialized information on the Internet. World Wide Web surfers who visit a home page that offers specialized information, for a fee, are invited to call a 900 number to get a pass code in order to get access into the Web site. Information providers can now charge for information provided on their Web site, and don't have to wait for the financial security issues to be resolved regarding transferring money and account information over the Internet.

In this case 900 numbers happen to be an established billing mechanism that is already in place and ready to use. Lindsay hopes to provide this service to many Internet-based IPs who currently don't have any easier alternatives for collecting money from their clients.

Although the Internet has been a freewheeling frontier where much of the information has heretofore been free, this cannot continue indefinitely. After all, you do indeed ultimately get what you pay for, and free information by its very nature cannot be worth much. The creators of Internet information and content — scientists, researchers, writers, artists, composers, editors, musicians, illustrators, and so on — cannot exist without food and shelter. They deserve payment for their talent. It costs money to conceive, produce, package and deliver the final product. Consumers recognize this and are willing to pay commensurate with the perceived value received.

Realistic Planning

If you are starting a 900-number business from scratch, and you've never started a business before, you need to learn everything you can about what it takes to start any kind of business. You need to write a thorough business plan, the most important elements of which are a well-conceived marketing plan and realistic financial projections. Buy a book or computer software on business plans and do sufficient preliminary planning to give your new business a fair chance for success.

Be realistic. You probably won't get a fraction of the call volume you think you will. At least initially. You are very close to your program, having lived with it and nurtured it over several months. Don't be surprised and disappointed if no one else feels the same degree of interest in it. The benefits of calling your program might be very real and compelling to you, but don't expect everyone to recognize this automatically without a lot of prodding and constant reminders. Sometimes you have to beat people over the head with a two-by-four several times before the light goes on. To put it more delicately, be prepared to pay for enough advertising repetition for your message to sink in.

Remember that successful entrepreneurs rarely become successful overnight. It simply doesn't happen that way. Virtually every success story is preceded by years of effort, sacrifice and perseverance. Many don't find success with their first venture, and finally get it right the second or third time around.

My publishing company is my fourth business, and it took a good three years to turn the corner and become successful. If there is one trait that virtually all entrepreneurs share, it's tenacity. Despite years of sweat and toil with little reward, they stick with it long enough and eventually succeed. You don't have to be particularly smart, just unrelentingly stubborn. I sincerely believe that 80% of being successful is just hanging in there long enough to turn the corner.

I often use a freight-train analogy to demonstrate my point. You will expend a tremendous amount of effort trying to physically push a train down the tracks. You push and push with all your might and it doesn't budge. At first. Eventually, assuming you haven't given up in frustration, it starts to inch along the tracks. You keep up the effort and it slowly builds up speed. Eventually the train builds up a momentum of its own, and you can finally start slacking off a little. If you're lucky, you hit a downward incline and the train takes off away from you, and you end up having to chase after it!

It always takes at least three times longer to reach your goal than you originally think. At least it always seems to work out that way. Be patient, be tenacious, and don't give up too early.

Do More Research

What the common thread that pervades this book? Marketing. Success in this business is not possible unless advertising costs are shared, cut to the bone, or optimally cost-effective. I've said it before and it bears repeating. This business is very easy to get into. Maybe too easy. But it is not necessarily easy to succeed. Not if you don't have a good handle on how to get lots of people to call your program without spending a fortune on ineffective advertising.

Get as much advice as you can from the experts before launching your idea. Seek them out at the next pay-per-call trade show and pick their brains. Contact advertising agencies and consultants who specialize in the 900 industry. Talk to people at prospective service bureaus. They have worked with all kinds of programs and their advice is free. Ask lots of questions and listen very carefully to their answers. However, don't pay too much attention to anyone who claims you will get rich quickly in this business. Or anyone who is wildly enthusiastic about all of your 900 application ideas, no matter how flaky they might be.

The chapters on marketing and publicity are the most important chapters in this book, but they really only represent the tip of the iceberg. If you're planning to go it alone, without the help of marketing professionals, you need to collect more books on this subject. And there are literally hundreds of them about marketing and advertising, from direct mail to print to television. Check them out of the library or purchase them for ongoing reference. Find books that specialize in the media you will be using for your program, and become an expert in advertising. The easy part is learning the 900 business and launching a program. The hard part is learning the marketing — what works and what doesn't work. Avoid too much hands-on education — it can become a pretty expensive lesson! Prepare yourself as thoroughly as possible before you start marketing your program. This is the only way to succeed in this business.

Pay very close attention to the advice from the industry veterans in *The 900 Roundtable* and those you seek out yourself. These people know what it takes to succeed in the 900 business. They are working with a lot of successful programs, and they have also seen just as many fail.

Yes, it is possible to succeed. Heed the advice in this book and your chances will be quite good. I'm not trying to scare you away — on the contrary, I'm trying to offer solid guidance so you can maximize your chances for success.

The future of the 900 industry is quite exciting. The public's perception is gradually but inexorably improving. Electronically literate young adults are becoming an ever-increasing force in the marketplace. There are plenty of novel 900 applications that have yet to be attempted. Pay-per-call will always be an ideal home-based business for a start-up entrepreneur with a good workable idea, and the drive to make it succeed.

The advantages to operating a successful 900 business are quite impressive. Even unique. In what other business can you earn money 24 hours a day, even while out on the golf course or while vacationing in Hawaii?

There's no reason you can't be a successful 90Q IP. Equipped with the right knowledge, and a realistic business plan, you will be able to succeed in this business.

Please stay in touch. Put me on your mailing list for your news releases and marketing materials. I am always interested in hearing from my readers, and I'm always looking for interesting pay-per-call applications to profile in later editions of this book or my other book, *Money-Making 900 Numbers*. You might even win an award.

The first Alex Awards were held in 1996 at the Audiotex Forum (Appendix B). Sponsored by *Audiotex News* (Appendix A), the awards are named after Alexander Graham Bell. According to *Audiotex News* publisher Carol Morse Ginsburg, "We hope that just as the Tonys, Emmys, and Hollywood Oscars recognize the leaders in their fields, the Alex Awards will recognize outstanding pay-per-call applications and the service bureaus and carriers that support them." Submissions are judged in six categories: Best Consumer & Business Communications; Best Classifieds & Voice Personals; Best Sports & Gaming; Best Entertainment; Best Overall Marketing Strategy; and Most Innovative Pay-Per-Call Application.

Again, stay in touch, and good luck!

Appendix A
Magazines & Newsletters

Audiotex News
Published monthly by Audiotex News, Inc.,
2362 Hempstead Turnpike, 2nd Floor, East Meadow, NY 11554
Telephone: 516-735-3398
Subscription: Annual: $249 Six-month: $179

This is the leading newsletter for the audiotex industry, published without interruption every month since 1989 in a format which allows it to respond quickly to fast-breaking information and news about the industry. *Audiotex News* is dedicated to circulating independent, unbiased information for and about the pay-per-call industry, setting the standard for clear, concise presentation of information, and analysis of the competitive elements of the 800/900 pay-per-call market. Be sure you call to check before subscribing because the newsletter normally runs promotions that include free books for new subscribers.

InfoText
Published bimonthly by Gordon Publishing, Inc.,
9200 Sunset Blvd., Suite 710, Los Angeles, CA 90069
Telephone: 310-724-6783
Annual subscription: $64

This magazine has gone through some changes over the years, starting as a monthly, then being incorporated into *Voice*

Processing magazine (which itself changed to *Enterprise Communications* for awhile, and is now defunct), and is now published bimonthly by Gordon Publishing, its third publisher. This magazine is recognized as one of the major trade publications for the pay-per-call and interactive telephone industries. Its new tag line reads: "Integrating Electronic Commerce and Communications."

InfoText contains current topical information relating to all facets of the audiotex industry, including new applications, legal updates, marketing information, and many newsworthy articles. It remains one of the best sources for information in the industry.

900 NewsReport
Published monthly by Moore Telecommunications,
6046 Cornerstone Court, West, #126, San Diego, CA 92121
Telephone: 619-587-8126
Annual Subscription: $45

Published by Toni Moore, a respected industry consultant and author of *Dialing For Dollars,* this newsletter offers helpful nuts-and-bolts advice aimed at the start-up IP, at an affordable price.

Outside the Envelope
edited by Warren E. Miller, Jr.
Published monthly by Hattrick Publishing Group, Inc.,
1220 L Street, N.W., Suite 330, Washington, DC 20005
Telephone: 800-953-1700
Fax-on-Demand Directory: 800-872-1899
Annual Subscription: $24 for print version, free by fax

This newsletter features analysis and comments on developments in the 800, 900, Online, Fax, IVDS and long-distance markets with illustrations and examples of how regulatory policy and carrier actions impact upon information providers. The editor, Warren Miller, is also president of Telecompute Corporation, a leading service bureau, and has been an active industry leader for many years. The primary emphasis is on pay-per-call, telemarketing, and information delivery applications in the U.S. and Canada.

The fax-on-demand system offers numerous brief papers and article reprints on a variety of topical subjects. The materials are offered for free or for only a nominal charge. An excellent source of current information about industry issues.

The Audiofax

Transmitted weekly by Gordon Production Group, Inc.,
9200 Sunset Blvd., Suite 710, Los Angeles, CA 90069
Telephone: 310-724-6781 or Fax: 310-786-2781
Subscription: Annual: $215.46 Six-month: $119.70 (U.S.A.)

This weekly fax service keeps IPs updated on fast-breaking industry developments. Covers pending legislation, new companies, new promotions, new products & services, and the latest industry happenings. Also includes a unique classified advertising section called "The Fax-Ifieds."

Telemedia News and Views

Published monthly by OPUS Research, INC.,
345 Chenery Street, San Francisco, CA 94131
Telephone: 800-428-OPUS
Annual Subscription: $295

This newsletter was launched in May 1993 as the successor to *Audiotex Now* and *800/900 Review,* both of which were published by Strategic Telemedia. OPUS Research is closely allied with Strategic Telemedia, and this newsletter is a vehicle for publishing some of its research results. This newsletter is a good source for in-depth analysis and behind-the-scenes coverage of telemedia markets and trends, including new developments in the evolution of the information superhighway. An important source of timely information and intelligence for the serious players in this industry.

TeleLetter

Published by Keith Mueller, The 900 Advertising Club,
P.O. Box 5048, Newport Beach, CA 92662
Telephone: 714-721-9280
Subscription: Included with club membership.

This quarterly newsletter is for the membership of The 900 Advertising Club, which uses bulk purchasing to get better advertising rates for its members. The newsletter describes ad programs and deals that are available, offers tips on how to advertise effectively, profiles actual marketing programs and covers demographic profiles of 900 callers.

Teleconnect Magazine
Published monthly by Telecom Library, Inc.,
12 West 21st Street, New York, NY 10010
Telephone: 215-355-2886 (subscriptions)
                 800-LIBRARY (publications and catalog)
Subscription: $15

This is one of the major trade magazines covering the overall telecommunications industry. According to its tag line, it is "the independent guide to choosing, using and installing telecommunications equipment and services." This magazine will keep you up-to-date on all facets of the telecom industry, of which audiotex is only a small part.

The Telecom Library also publishes *Call Center* magazine and several telecommunications books that may be of interest to you. Call or write for its catalog.

Computer Telephony
Published monthly by Telecom Library, Inc.,
12 West 21st St., New York, NY 10010
Telephone: 215-355-2886 (subscriptions)
Subscription: $25

Tag-lined "The Magazine for Computer and Telephone Integration," this magazine is targeted at computer professionals — users, software and hardware developers, ISVs, systems integrators, VARs, network resellers, distributors, consultants, OEM integrators and carriers. Despite its technical focus, this magazine is a good way to keep up with the inexorable trend towards the merging of computer and telecommunications technologies.

Phone+

Published monthly by Taurus Publishing, Inc.,
4141 North Scottsdale Road, Suite 316, Scottsdale AZ 85251
Telephone: 602-990-1101
Annual subscription: $50

This magazine is tag-lined, "The Monthly Journal for the Public Communications Industry," and is targeted at equipment and service providers, with an emphasis on long-distance services and issues.

InformationWeek

Published weekly by CMP Publications, Inc.,
P.O. Box 1093, Skokie, IL 60076-8093
Telephone: 800-292-3642 ext. 40
Annual subscription: $63.95

This weekly magazine is written for information and technology managers and businesses — or anyone who needs to stay up-to-date on what is going on on the information superhighway. CMP also publishes *CommunicationsWeek*, a sister magazine with more emphasis on equipment, technology and networks.

Interactive Age

Published biweekly by CMP Publications, Inc.,
(see above)
Annual subscription: $79

This newspaper covers the entire interactive industry, including the telecommunications, computer, entertainment-media and information industries, and how they are converging. Timely news and information for those who need to stay on top of developments in this fast-changing environment.

Telephony

Published weekly by Intertec Publishing,
P.O. Box 12901, Overland Park, KS 66282-2901
Telephone: 800-441-0294
Annual Subscription: $45

This magazine serves the public telephone network market, and its readers are primarily telecom professionals at the various local, regional and national telephone companies. Although the subject matter is targeted to these people, this is a good magazine for keeping current on what is happening with the carriers. *Telephony* lists *CommunicationsWeek* (see above) as one of its main competitors.

Voice International (Incorporating World Telemedia)
Published bimonthly by Europe Media Ltd.,
41-47 Kings Terrace, London NW1 0JR, United Kingdom
Telephone: 011 44 171 911 6002 Fax: 011 44 171 911 6020

This used to be two separate magazines, which have since merged into this combined publication. Pay-per-call has been international in scope for quite some time, and this resource will help you keep on top of what's going on globally, primarily in Europe and Asia.

Appendix B
Trade Shows, Seminars & Associations

Trade Shows & Seminars

900 Business Seminars
Conducted by Carol Morse Ginsburg, editor and publisher of *Audiotex News*, 2362 Hempstead Turnpike, 2nd Floor, East Meadow, NY 11554
Telephone: 800-735-3398   Fax: 516-735-3682

Need some help exploring the possibilities in 900? Meet Carol Morse Ginsburg and attend her acclaimed 900 business seminar. Call the *Audiotex News* office for a copy of the year-round seminar schedule. Ginsburg has been giving this seminar for more than five years to grateful participants. It's a no-nonsense, factual, inside look at the 900 business. Find out if 900 pay-per-call is for you, how to be successful and how to avoid the pitfalls. Seminars are offered regularly throughout the year in Washington, DC and New York City. If you cannot find the time to attend a seminar, cassette audio tapes of the full seminar are available for $49.95.

Audiotext Forum
R.j. Gordon & Company, Inc.
9200 Sunset Blvd., Suite 515, Los Angeles, CA 90069

Telephone: 310-278-8080   Fax: 310-274-8686

With the demise of *InfoText's* annual conference in Las Vegas dedicated to the audiotext/pay-per-call industry, R.j. Gordon & Company has filled the void with an event that specifically targets the information providers in this industry. Although the entertainment side of the industry is heavily represented, this conference will be quite helpful for IPs offering any kind of information services. Like its *InfoText* predecessor, this event is held annually in January in Las Vegas. It is currently the largest trade show devoted to the audiotext and pay-per-call industries.

Interactive 2000

Arch Communications,
3700 South Las Vegas Blvd., Las Vegas, NV 89109
Telephone: 702-597-1829

This is a new entrant in the audiotext trade show business, with the first show in January 1996, and subsequent shows to be held every January in Las Vegas timed so as not to interfere with the Audiotext Forum. Priced at $250 for a full pass (seminars and exhibits) and $100 for exhibits only, this is an affordable show for start-up IPs.

UMiiX (Unified Messaging & Interactive Information Exchange)

Business Communications Group, Advanstar Expositions,
201 E. Sandpointe Avenue, Suite 600, Santa Ana, CA 92707
Telephone: 714-513-8645

This trade show is an important event for the voice processing/audiotext industry, replacing the *VOICE Exposition & Conference* and the *InfoText*-sponsored exposition that was held each January in Las Vegas up until a few years ago. This trade show is a "forum in which users and suppliers of various means of messaging and information exchange can come together to discuss the issues that will affect enterprise-wide communications." It has a broader focus than the former *InfoText* and *Voice* shows, encompassing voice processing and automation, computer-telephone integration, and interactive information technologies, as

---

well as audiotext and voice information applications.

According to its news release, "As companies continue to search for ways to integrate computer and telephone systems, UMiiX will focus on the convergence of voice, fax, e-mail, wireless and LAN-based communications, pulling all of these areas together into one understandable, solutions-oriented package."

If you can't afford the time or money to attend a trade show, purchasing the cassette tapes (seminar recordings) of the latest one is a good substitute. For more information call Advanstar Communications at 800-598-6008 or 216-243-8100.

Voice Asia/Europe/Mexico.

Advanstar Expositions, a Division of Advanstar Communications, Inc., P.O. Box 42382, Houston, TX 77242
Telephone: 713-974-6637   Fax: 713-974-6272

Advanstar Communications has gone international, with conferences held in London, Mexico City and Hong Kong. These shows are focused on the trends, issues and opportunities for voice processing and audiotext manufacturers, service providers, and information providers in emerging markets.

World Telemedia Asia & Voice International Asia.

Triton Telecom Publishing, Ltd., 41-47 Kings Terrace, London NW1 0JR, United Kingdom
Telephone: 011 +44 171 911 6002 Fax: 011 +44 171 911 6020

The Pacific rim contains half the world's population, with economies that are growing fast. This Hong Kong exposition is for IPs who want to investigate Asia as a viable market. This is a two-track event, with World Telemedia covering audiotext and information services while Voice International covers the equipment side of the business.

Associations

You will likely find numerous associations that can be of help to you in planning and researching your particular pay-per-call information service. Those associations that deal directly with the pay-per-call audiotext industry are listed here. There are many others that can also be of help, depending upon your circumstances, such as the Direct Marketing Association (DMA), the Promotion Marketing Association of America (PMAA), the U.S. Telephone Association (USTA) or the Telecommunications Industry Association (TIA). For a complete listing of associations, consult the *Encyclopedia of Associations* by Gale Research, available in the reference section of larger libraries.

Interactive Services Association (ISA)
8403 Colesville Road, Suite 865
Silver Spring, MD 20910
Telephone: 301-495-4955
Membership dues: Starting at $450

The former National Association for Interactive Services (NAIS), which served the pay-per-call and audiotext industries for several years, was merged into the ISA in May 1994. The ISA is now the major trade association representing the interests of the evolving telecommunications-based personal interactive services industry.

The ISA advocates the business and public policy interests of a wide variety of companies, including computer, consumer electronics, publishing, telephone, software and other multimedia companies. Members include cable television companies, long-distance carriers, RBOCs, audiotext companies, information providers, service bureaus, local exchange carriers, equipment manufacturers and a variety of others.

The ISA offers business development opportunities to its members through networking and cross-industry education. A sponsor of various conferences and member publications, the ISA provides a carefully screened stream of updated information to its members about the rapidly evolving interactive media industry.

Other important functions of the ISA are to advocate industry perspectives, to develop and enforce national industry standards through self-regulation, and to serve as a clearinghouse for industry information and education. Of particular value are the

ISA's efforts in promoting a positive image for the industry and in lobbying with regulatory and legislative authorities with regard to proposed regulations and laws.

TeleServices Industry Association (TIA)
777 Alexander Road, Suite 204
Princeton, NJ 08504
Telephone: 609-243-0066
Membership dues: Starting at $500

This association was established in January 1994 to serve the international audiotext industry. Membership is targeted to IPs, and the association's goal is to promote the welfare of its members by addressing their common goals and issues both locally and globally.

The key roles of the TIA are to provide a forum to increase the dialogue between the telephone companies, carriers, PTTs (foreign Post Telephone & Telegraph organizations), regulatory bodies and the rest of the audiotext industry and to promote a better understanding of the contributions made by all the participants. TIA also strives to develop and monitor a set of guidelines and procedures with the specific intent of comprehensively addressing the business policies from the perspectives of information providers, exchange carriers, and the consumers.

Information Industry Association (IIA)
555 New Jersey Avenue, N.W., Suite 800
Washington, DC 20001
Telephone: 202-639-8262
Membership dues: Starting at $500

IIA's Voice Information Services Division brings together equipment vendors, service bureaus, telecommunications companies, information providers, marketing organizations, consultants, and other businesses involved in the voice information field. Membership benefits are targeted to the larger players in the industry, and membership would be inappropriate for the start-up IP.

An established IP, on the other hand, should seriously consider joining this organization. IIA has been particularly active in pay-per-call consumer education, and has established Standards of Practice for voice information services.

Appendix C
Books & Directories

Money-Making 900 Numbers:
How Entrepreneurs Use the Telephone to Sell Information
By Carol Morse Ginsburg and Robert Mastin
Published by Aegis Publishing Group,
796 Aquidneck Ave., Newport, RI 02842-7202
Telephone: 800-828-6961; fax: 401-849-4231
Price: $19.95

This book consists of nearly 400 profiles of 900-number programs in 12 different categories: Customer Service & Helping Consumers; Government & Non-Profit Organizations; Professional Services & Advice; Investment, Finance & Business Information; Sports; Environmental Information; Lifestyle, Travel & Leisure; Education, Careers & Self-Improvement; Entertainment; Product & Business Promotion & Marketing; Fundraising & Charity; and News, Politics & Opinions.

This book answers the question: What programs are out there, which have been successful and which have failed? The profiles are from one paragraph to several pages in length. An excellent overview of the industry, demonstrating which elements make a successful 900-number program.

Promoting Your 900 Number
By the editors of *Audiotex News*
Published by Audiotex Publishing, Inc.,

2362 Hempstead Turnpike, 2nd Floor, East Meadow, NY 11554
Telephone: 800-735-3398; 516-735-3398   Fax 516-735-3682
Price: $29.95

A one-of-a-kind reference guide packed with specific know-how and advice for marketing a 900 number. Includes a special bonus supplement — *Print Media Placement* — a complete compendium of more than 200 newspapers and magazines that accept pay-per-call advertising. Includes advertising rates, circulation, addresses, telephone numbers and restrictions (if any) for accepting 900 number advertising.

Audiotex News Resource Guide
Published by Audiotex Publishing, Inc. (see above)
Price: $50

This is the only up-to-date comprehensive reference guide for the entire industry, including pay-per-call, automated voice response, computer telephony and voice information services. With more than 200 pages, if there's a telephone involved, this guide gives you the profiles and the detailed listings of the companies you're looking for. Features service bureaus, regulatory agencies, telephone companies, advertising agencies, hardware & software systems and components, publications, industry events and every other source you need. Compiled by the editors of *Audiotex News*, the leading newsletter for the pay-per-call industry, this directory belongs on every player's desk.

Opportunity is Calling:
How to Start Your Own Successful 900 Number
By Bob Bentz
Published by ATS Publishing (1993),
996 Old Eagle School Rd., Suite 1105, Wayne, PA 19087
Telephone: 610-688-6000
Price: $29.95

Written by Bob Bentz, the director of marketing at Advanced Telecom Services, one of the leading 900 service bureaus, this book is quite valuable for serious IPs. In helping establish some 3,000 pay-per-call programs, Bentz has probably seen every conceivable 900 application or idea, from the totally unworkable pie-in-the-sky scheme to the highly imaginative and well-conceived success story.

The Directory of 900 Service Bureaus: How to Select One
By Audiotex Publishing, Inc.,
2362 Hempstead Turnpike, 2nd Floor, East Meadow, NY 11554
Telephone: 800-735-3398; 516-735-3398   Fax: 516-735-3682
Price: $19.95

A listing of service bureaus that offer 900 pay-per-call services. Arranged alphabetically (as well as by states), this frequently updated directory provides the contact persons, addresses, phone and fax numbers for 160 service bureaus throughout the United States. Includes a six-page narrative which lists the 21 crucial questions to ask a service bureau, and a thorough discussion of selection criteria, call volume capacities, customer service, cost, system security, contracts, and tips on how to interview the service bureau representative.

The Power of 900
By Rick Parkhill
Published by Advanstar Communications (1991),
7500 Old Oak Blvd., Cleveland, OH 44130
Telephone: 800-598-6008
Price: $45

This is the original book about the 900 industry. Great section on the history and evolution of the pay-per-call business. Some very useful directories and lists, including a directory of caller-paid services. The original edition was published in 1991 and has become somewhat dated, but a new edition may be forthcoming in the future.

Operating a "900" Number —
Entrepreneur Business Guide No. 1359
Published by Entrepreneur Group (1995),
2392 Morse Avenue, Irvine, CA 92714
Telephone: 800-421-2300

Price: $69.50

Published by the same company that publishes *Entrepreneur Magazine*, this is one of the latest in a long series of helpful business guides designed for the start-up entrepreneur. This comprehensive 200-page guide describes not only the specifics of starting a 900 business, but also the numerous considerations common to launching any new business venture. This guide will be particularly helpful for anyone who has never started a new business.

The Voice Response Reference Manual & Buyer's Guide
By Marc Robins
Published by Robins Press,
2675 Henry Hudson Pkwy., West, Ste. 6J, Riverdale, NY 10463
Price: $85
Telephone: 800-238-7130

This reference book is a complete resource for interactive voice technology, vendors and systems. It provides up-to-date information necessary for purchasing or building a voice response system. Included are comprehensive equipment vendor profiles and surveys on more than 50 vendors and 60 systems. Hardware and software specifications, configurations and pricing, host computer interfaces, user management features, and selection and implementation advice are all included. Updated regularly.

DIALING FOR DOLLARS:
A Guide to the 900 Business
By Antoinette Moore
Published by Moore Telecommunications Consultants (1993),
6046 Cornerstone Court West, Suite 126, San Diego, CA 92121
Telephone: 619-587-8126
Price: $29.95

Written by telecommunications consultant Toni Moore, this is a good introductory book about the 900/976 pay-per-call business, offering immediately useful nuts-and-bolts information for the start-up IP. The step-by-step Activation Guide is both unique and helpful, and this book reflects the author's considerable experience in this business.

Newton's Telecom Dictionary
By Harry Newton
Published by the Telecom Library, Inc.,
12 West 21st St., New York, NY 10010
Telephone: 800-LIBRARY
Price: $24.95

This massive 1,120-page volume was written by Harry Newton, publisher of *Teleconnect, Call Center* and *Imaging* magazines, in an easy-to-read non-technical style. This is an everyday working dictionary for anyone involved in telecommunications. The user-friendly prose reads more like a good tutorial than a technical dictionary, and you'll never be confused again with the arcane language of the telecommunications industry.

The 900 Guide
By Madeline Bodin
Published by the Telecom Library, Inc. (1993) (see above)
Price: $11.95

This helpful 96-page booklet offers sound advice from several experts in the 900 industry; including Brad Magill, Direct Response Broadcasting Network, Philadelphia, PA; Keith Dawson, associate editor of *Call Center* magazine; Deborah Vohasek, a voice response service bureau marketing expert; Gary Maier, president of Dianatel, a maker of PC boards; and Madeline Bodin, editor of *Call Center* magazine, to name only a few.

Telecom Made Easy:
Money-Saving, Profit-Building Solutions for Home Businesses, Telecommuters and Small Organizations
By June Langhoff
Published by Aegis Publishing Group (1996),
796 Aquidneck Ave., Newport, RI 02842

Telephone: 401-849-4200; 800-828-6961   Fax: 401-849-4231
Price: $19.95

This is an easy-to-understand guide to getting the most out of telephone products and services. It is specifically written for small businesses, offices and organizations with fewer than five phone lines, who don't have telecom managers or the resources that large organizations have, but who still want to sound like them. Covers all the latest telecom products and services that are available, in simple, non-technical language, and how to put them together to best serve your specific needs. Available directly from the publisher or in most bookstores.

Service Access Codes (N00) NXX Assignments (500/800/900 List) (Document SR-OPT-001843)

Published quarterly by Bell Communication Research (Bellcore), and available by calling its Document Hotline:
Telephone: 800-521-2673
Price: $40 (subject to change)

This is a compilation of all NXXs assigned within the Service Access Codes (SACs) 500, 800 and 900 by the North American Numbering Plan Administrator. For each of the NXXs assigned, the name of the company to which it is assigned and the telephone number of a contact in that company are given. NXX availability changes regularly, and this publication will give you the latest assignments.

PC-Telephony

By Bob Edgar
Published by The Telecom Library, Inc.
12 West 21st Street, New York, NY 10010
Telephone: 800-LIBRARY
Price: $34.95

Previous editions of this book were titled *PC-Based Voice Processing*. This is the first book written exclusively about voice processing, aimed at the developer of a PC-based voice processing or computer telephony systems.

Appendix D
Service Bureaus

This list of service bureaus was compiled in early 1996, and was accurate at that time. Nonetheless, some of these companies may no longer be in business, or they may no longer serve 900-number information providers.

Neither the author nor the publisher endorses any particular company in this list, and the fact that a company is listed does not imply that the company is recommended in any way. You should follow prudent business practices in checking out any company you plan to do business with, including asking for and speaking with references. The larger, more established service bureaus are often members of relevant trade organizations, particularly the Interactive Services Association (ISA). Contact the ISA (Appendix B) for a list of its service bureau members.

See Appendix A, Magazines & Newsletters, for publications that offer service bureau listings that are updated frequently. The author regrets any omissions or inappropriate inclusions, and invites service bureaus to contact me to make necessary corrections or changes to this list for future editions. Please call 401-849-4200 or write the publisher at the address on the title page of this book.

Alabama

Information Management
Consultants (IMC)
Tim Michael, President
208 Adams St.
Mobile, AL 36633
334-434-6409

Alaska

Alaska Info & Marketing, Inc.
Kevin R. Tubbs
2142 Forest Park Dr.
Anchorage, AK 99517
907-277-9996

Arizona

Kris Kupczyk & Assoc., Inc.
Kris Kupczyk
Suite 201
4839 E. Greenway Rd.
Scottsdale, AZ 85254
602-992-5779

Touch Tone Interactive, Inc.
Andrew Wise, President
650 East Camelback Rd.
Phoenix, AZ 85012
602-254-8250

California

900 Numbers Unlimited
Michael Lindsay
Suite 202
1875 S. Winchester Blvd.
Campbell, CA 95008
408-364-7900

Accelerated Voice
25 Stillman St., Suite 200
San Francisco, CA 94107
415-543-2773

Almarc
Ronald A. Resnick, President
8921 DeSoto, Suite 200
Conoga Park, CA 91306
818-773-2080

American International
Communications
Paul Keever
Suite 110
5595 East 7th St.
Long Beach, CA 90804
310-433-8818

AmTec Audiotex, Inc.
Chris Ewing, Dir. Sales &
Marketing
Suite 200
8670 Wilshire Blvd.
Beverly Hills, CA 90211
310-358-2000

Applied Response Systems
Ron Lee
Suite 255
8885 Rio San Diego Dr.
San Diego, CA 92108
619-491-2900

Bellatrix International
David Kahn, President
4055 Wilshire Blvd., Suite 415
Los Angeles, CA 90010
213-736-5600

Creative Call Management
Bob Kushner, President
316 W. 2nd St., Suite 1110
Los Angeles, CA 90012
800-777-4976

Dialtronix Corporation
Suite 305
5675 Ruffin Rd.
San Diego, CA 92123
800-510-5500

Gigaphone, Inc.
Nancy R. Conger, President
1525 Aviation Blvd., Suite A188
Redondo Beach, CA 90278
310-374-4313

Integrated Data Concepts
Warren Jason, President
P.O. Box 93428
Los Angeles, CA 90093
800-367-4432

Interactive Strategies, Inc.
J. Edward Hastings, Exec. VP
Suite 100
31194 La Baya Dr.
Westlake Village, CA 91362
818-879-9992

Intermedia Resources
Gene Chamson, President
6114 LaSalle Ave., #230
Oakland, CA 94611
510-339-3646

Intertel Systems
Jeff Allen
P.O. Box 4384
Berkeley, CA 94704
510-649-0404

MCE TeleCommunications
Michaelle Ashlock, Account Executive
17911 Sky Park Circle, Suite D
Irvine, CA 92714
714-476-8007

Money by the Minute
Bobby Bosone, President
Suite 621
3419 Via Lido
Newport Beach, CA 92663
800-675-3534

Network Telephone Services, Inc.
Gary Passon, President
6233 Variel Ave.
Woodland Hills, CA 91367
800-727-6874

New Media Telecommunications, Inc.
David Fersten, Sales Manager
4225 Executive Square, Suite 1070
La Jolla, CA 92037
800-900-4968

Speech Solutions
Tim Marentic, CEO
139 Townsend St., Suite 301
San Francisco, CA 94107
415-243-8300

Strauss Communications, Inc.
Lance Strauss, President
P.O. Box 223542
26135 Rancho Blvd., Ste 16
Carmel, CA 93922
408-625-0700

Tel-Ad Communications & Advertising
John Masso
7760 E. Doheny Ct.
Anaheim Hills, CA 92808
714-281-1206

Telemedia Network
Steve Fecske
Suite 800A
15260 Ventura Blvd.
Sherman Oaks, CA 91403
818-382-1300

US Teleconnect
Dana Dunn
Suite B
432 Bonito Ave.
Long Beach, CA 90802
310-436-1326

WorldWide Communications
Services
Jim White
Suite 379
2899 Agoura Rd.
Westlake Village, CA 91361
818-706-1921

Zycom Network Services, Inc.
An ICG Company
Hal Critz, Director of Sales
201 S. Lake Ave., Suite 507
Pasadena, CA 91101-3005
800-880-3061

Colorado

Advanced Communications
Services
Jerry Krenning, CEO
155 N. College Ave., #222
Ft. Collins, CO 80524
970-482-5542

ICG Enhanced Services, Inc.
J.R. Edwards, National
Account Manager
9605 East Maroon Circle
Englewood, CO 80112
800-900-4101

IdealDial
Ronald Kubicki, VP, Sales &
Marketing
910 15th St., Suite 900
Denver, CO 80202
800-582-3425

Delaware

American TelNet, Inc.
Bill Rivell, Vice President Sales
1701 Augustine Cut-Off, Suite
40
Wilmington, DE 19803
302-651-9400

Mega900 Communications
Jeff Platt, President
901 West 24th St.
Wilmington, DE 19802
302-654-0829

District
of Columbia

Telecompute Corp.
Warren Miller, President
Suite G-9
1275 K St., NW
Washington, DC 20005
202-789-1111

Florida

Audio Text Ventures, Inc.
Joni Lawler
Suite 800
200 West Forsythe St.
Jacksonville, FL 32202
904-346-1303

Audiotext Services, Inc.
Roderic van Beuzekom,
President
P.O. Box 2449
Orlando, FL 32802
407-426-8355

Connections USA, Inc.
P.O. Box 030459
Ft. Lauderdale, FL 33303
305-525-4141

ICN
Eric Cherry, Sales Director
Suite 300
1801 South Federal Hwy.
Delray Beach, FL 33483
407-272-5667

Innovative Telemedia Corp.
6278 N. Federal Hwy.
Ft. Lauderdale, FL 33308
305-771-2798

Megatech Services
Jack Potenza
2308 23rd Way
West Palm Beach, FL 33407
407-689-7493

Millennium Marketing Group
Lee Watson, Director of
Marketing
Suite 310
2500 Maitland Center Pkwy.
Maitland, FL 32751
800-432-4347

National Call Center, Inc.
Chris Soechitz, acct. exec.
P.O. Box 9090
Clearwater, FL 34618
813-572-8585

ONE 800/900, Inc.
Tom Ruffin
200 North Laura St., 12th
Floor
Jacksonville, FL 32202
800-821-1819

Saturn Communications
Steve Alan
P.O. Box 848367
Hollywood, FL 33084
305-438-7000

Georgia

Overlook Communications
International
Edward Wolffe
2839 Paces Ferry Rd., Suite
500
Atlanta, GA 30339
770-432-6800

The Intermedia Group
Suite 404
3232 Cobb Pkwy.
Atlanta, GA 30339
770-368-2838

Illinois

Ameritech Audiotex
Services, Inc.
600 South Federal, Suite 122
Chicago, IL 60605
800-451-5283

New Tech Telemedia, Inc.
Donald Young, President
444 North Wells
Chicago, IL 60610
800-376-6654

Northwest Nevada Telco
Michael Dawson, Director of
Sales
1324 Evers Ave.
Westchester, IL 60154
800-279-0909

Stargate Communications, Inc.
G. Gary Chaffin
Floor 2
400 N. Schmidt Rd.
Bolingbrook, IL 60440
800-282-6541

Maryland

AEI TeleSonic
E. Escobar
Suite 102
31 Old Solomon's Island
Annapolis, MD 21401
410-841-6920

Massachusetts

Advanced Voice Fax
Communications
Jim McCormack
P.O. Box 173
Woburn, MA 01801
617-932-9939

Facsimile Services, Inc.
(Fax-on-Demand only)
573 Washington St.
South Easton, MA 02375
508-230-2000

Inpho, Inc.
(976 bureau)
Steve Kropper, President
225 Fifth St.

Cambridge, MA 02142
617-868-7050

Pilgrim Telephone, Inc.
Steve Shinnick
1 Kendall Square
Cambridge, MA 02139
617-225-7000

Tele-Publishing, Inc.
Paul Twitchell, Director of
Marketing
126 Brookline Ave.
Boston, MA 02215
800-874-2340

Michigan

Dobbs Enterprises, Ltd.
John C. Dobbs, President
855 Forest St.
Birmingham, MI 48009
810-540-2149

Minnesota

MicroVoice Applications, Inc.
Michael A. James, Sales
Supervisor
Suite 1800
100 South 5th St.
Minneapolis, MN 55402
612-373-9300

Nebraska

Call Interactive
Steven Kutilek, Director of
Sales
2301 North 117th Ave.
Omaha, NE 68164
402-498-7197

Call Interactive
Rich Nelson, Dir. New Bus.
Dev.
2301 North 117th Ave.
Omaha, NE 68164
402-498-7197

Prairie Systems
Mark Frei, Director of Sales
7200 World Communications
Dr.
Omaha, NE 68122
402-398-4306

West Interactive Corp.
Mike Sturgeon, Executive VP,
Sales & Marketing
9223 Bedford Ave.
Omaha, NE 68134-4725
800-841-9000

Nevada

Arch Communications
Steve Hearne
3700 S. Las Vegas Blvd.,
#1000
Las Vegas, NV 89109
702-597-1829

B.F.D. Productions
Bruce F. Dyer, President
1221 South Casino Terrace
Las Vegas, NV 89104
800-444-4233

MRO Communication
Eric Olsen
Suite 106
5190 S. Valley View Blvd.
Las Vegas, NV 89118
702-736-2242

Northwest Nevada Telco
Brian Hall, Sales Manager
2910 Mill St.
Reno, NV 89502
702-333-3600

Technology Support
Corporation
Ben Greenspan, President
PO Box 6494
Incline Village, NV 89450
702-832-7358

New Jersey

900 Plus Communications
Al Edward
25 Main St., Crt. Plaza N.
Hackensack, NJ 07601
201-489-8909

American Audio Service
Bureau
Betty Fogal
2007 Hoyt Ave., 2nd Floor
Fort Lee, NJ 07024
201-585-8100

International
Teleprograms, Inc.
David Lapidus
Suite 5
10 Dell Glen Ave.
Lodi, NJ 07644
201-624-6020

Userland Communications
Michael Anderson
777 Alexander Rd.
Princeton, NJ 08540
609-987-1000

Voice Communications, Inc.
Frank Giarratano,
Director of
Telecommunications
350 Main Rd.
Montville, NJ 07045
201-299-1200

New York

Audio-Voice, Inc.
Jo-Ann Sickinger
Suite 401
545 8th Ave.
New York, NY 10018
212-868-1121

TRX Corp.
Gary Glicker, President
160 East 56th St.
New York, NY 10022
212-644-0370

VOCALL Telecenter Plus
Laura Pettinato
70 East 55th St., Heron Tower
New York, NY 10022
212-754-2525

Weather Concepts, Inc.
1966 Route 52
Hopewell Junction, NY 12540
914-226-8200

Ohio

900 America, Ltd.
Larry D. Lomaz, CEO
1 Cascade Plaza, Suite 1940
Akron, OH 44308
216-379-9900

Advanced Concepts, Inc.
Tim Stauffer
472 Langford St.
Columbus, OH 43230
614-475-4200

Digital Communications
R.J. Jones, Sales Manager
3031 Market St.
Youngstown, OH 44507
800-769-3238

Prism Telecommunications,
Inc.
Steve Harper
565 Dearborn Park Lane
Columbus, OH 43085
800-200-0806

Scherers Communications, Inc.
575 Scherers Ct.
Worthington, OH 43085
800-356-6161

Pennsylvania

Accu-Weather, Inc.
Sheldon Levine, Director of
Sales
619 W. College Ave.
State College, PA 16801
814-234-9601

Advanced Telecom
Services, Inc.
Bob Bentz, Director of
Marketing
996 Old Eagle School Rd.
Wayne, PA 19087
610-688-6000

General Fax, Inc.
Christopher Stephano,
President
Front & Ford Sts., Suite A103
Bridgeport, PA 19405
610-277-1722

Gralin Associates, Inc.
5525 Swamp Rd.
Fountainville, PA 18923
800-724-0992

Inter#Net, Inc.
Mitch Sheffler, Director of
Sales
1001 East Entry Dr., Suite 110
Pittsburgh, PA 15216
412-571-3350

Sports Network
Ken Zajac
701 Masons Mill Business Park
Huntington Valley, PA 19006
215-947-2400

Tennessee

Hall International
Gary Hall
Suite 4201
5709 Lyons View Pike
Knoxville, TN 37919
423-588-1945

Texas

Celebration Computer Systems
Pete Owens, President
5444 Westheimer, Suite 1850
Houston, TX 77056
713-625-4000

Net Communications
Dave Knapp, President
500 East 50th St.
Lubbock, TX 79404
806-791-0101

Voicetext Interactive
Eileen Williams, President
702 Colorado St., Suite 125
Austin, TX 78701
512-404-2300

WTS Bureau Systems, Inc.
J.L. Summers, President
14850 Venture Dr.
Dallas, TX 75234
214-353-5000

Utah

Teleshare 900
Paul Hickey, Vice President
Suite 3000
1875 South State St.
Orem, UT 84058
801-226-4222

Washington

Automotive Experts
Tom Barrett
P.O. Box 2994
Renton, WA 98056
206-271-7200

Bureau One, Inc.
Chris Schott, Dir. of New
Accounts
921 14th St.
Longview, WA 98632
360-636-2000

MMI-America's Best 900
Numbers
Jay Dietz, President
Suite 704
1400 Hubbell Place
Seattle, WA 98101
800-664-9007

WKP Incorporated
1200 Fifth Ave., #1206
Seattle, WA 98101
800-882-9215

Wisconsin

Internet, Inc.
Bill Luebke
Suite 420
741 N. Milwaukee St.
Milwaukee, WI 53202
414-274-3820

Canada

2 PM Group
Suite 200
822 Richmond St., West
Toronto, ON M6J 1C9
416-703-7300

4th Media
Suite 103
30 East Beaver Creek
Richmond Hill, ON L4B 1J2
905-886-6600

Advanced Telecom
Services, Inc.
Roy Hobbs, sales manager
Suite 523
6-2400 Dundas St., West
Mississauga, ON L5K 2R8
905-615-8415

Audio-Tex Communications
Jules Goldstein
4117 Lawrence Ave.
Scarborough, ON M1E 2S2
416-720-2400

Audiotex Vox-Tel
Francois Lemire
Suite 3
1083 St. Denis
Montreal, PQ H2X 3J3
800-985-2570

BBA Communications Link,
Ltd.
Jeff Brock, President
Suite 911
525 Seymour St.
Vancouver, BC V6B 3H7
604-689-9340

BC TEL Interactive
Ken Redekop
4th Floor
4595 Canada Way
Burnaby, BC V5G 4L9
604-482-2847

C & C Telesys
Tibor Plesko
2200 Grenville Dr.
Oakville, ON L6H 4W9
905-842-6680

Castle Communications, Inc.
69 Yorkville Ave., Suite 301
Toronto, Ontario M5R 1B8
416-515-1254

CCS-Interactive Voice
Response
Jim MacRae
P.O. Box 244 Station A
Toronto, ON M9C 4V3
416-695-8556

Connectel Communication Corp.
Dan Scheunert
2407 Kaladar Ave.
Ottawa, ON   K2C 3N6
613-224-2835

Courtier Royal, Inc.
Claude Verret
6789 Boul. Henri-Bourassa
Charlesbourg, PQ   G1H 3C6
418-623-1215

Digital Call Centres, Inc.
Tony Prinzen
Suite G12
200 Ronson Dr.
Toronto, ON   M9W 5Z9
416-241-7000

DMS Intelecom
1867 Younge St.
Toronto, ON   M4S 1Y5
416-481-2300

Groupe Cerveau, Inc.
Alain Quirion
1213 Sainte-Catherine Est
Montreal, PQ   H2L 2H1
514-525-7776

Infotel 800/900 Service Bureau
Vito Proietti
Suite 100
6433 Jarry Est
Montreal, PQ   H1P 1W1
800-463-6900

ITEL Interactive Media, Inc.
John Calveley
Suite 301
1534 West 2nd Ave.
Vancouver, BC   V6J 1H2
604-654-2200

Messagebank of Calgary
Suite 200
1121 Center St., North
Calgary, Alberta   T2E 7K4
403-531-4000

Multicom
Marie-Andree Lessard
4545 Rue Frontenac
Montreal, PQ   H2H 2R7
514-599-5805

National Inbound Call Centre
5 Kodiak Crescent, Suite 10
Downsview, ON   M3J 3E5
416-635-7393

Phoneworks Canada
Sybelle Srour
905 King St., West
Toronto, Ontario M6K 3G9
416-263-6263

Rosenbrewer Communications
Chris Rose
Suite 300
6080 Young St.
Hafifax, NS   B3K 5L2
902-454-0333

S&P Response Management
Dan Plashkes
Floor 9
1 Concord Gate
Don Mills, ON   M2H 2Z1
416-443-6800

Saturn Telecom
Alan Williams, Marketing Manager
4592 Avenue Verdun
Verdun, PQ   H4G 1M3
800-815-6295

Telesoft Systems
David Filwood
840 Peterson Rd.
P.O. Box 56
Bowen Island, BC   V0N 1G0
604-947-0117

Universal Teleresponse
Susan Farrell
17 Yorkville
Toronto, ON   M4W 1L1
416-927-8434

Videoway Multimedia, Inc.
Francois Goedike
300 Viger East 7 Etage
Montreal, PQ   H2X 3W4
514-985-8462

Voice Courrier
Julia O'Brien
1300 Bay St., Suite 200
Toronto, Ontario   M5R 3K8
416-921-0033

Watts Communication, Ltd.
Colin Taylor
839 Oxford St.
Toronto, ON   M8Z 5Z2
416-255-8000

Zentel, Inc.
Therese Senger
Suite 550
700 4th Ave., SW
Calgary, AB   T2P 3J4
403-531-6100

Appendix E
Federal Laws & Regulations

Federal Communications Commission (FCC) Regulations

The FCC regulations that resulted from passage of the Telephone Disclosure and Dispute Resolution Act (TDDRA), the relevant federal law, are reproduced in full here. The following is a verbatim transcription from Title 47 of the Code of Federal Regulations, Part 64, Sections 64.1501 through 64.1515, which are the complete FCC regulations governing pay-per-call services:

Section 64.1501 Definitions

For the purposes of this subpart, the following definitions shall apply:
(a) Pay-per-call service means any service
    (1) In which any person provides or purports to provide
        (A) Audio information or audio entertainment produced or packaged by such person;
        (B) Access to simultaneous voice conversation services; or
        (C) Any service, including the provision of a product, the charges for which are assessed on the basis of the completion of the call;
    (2) For which the caller pays a per-call or per-time-interval charge that is greater than, or in addition to, the charge for transmission of the call; and
    (3) Which is accessed through use of a 900 telephone number.
(b) Such term does not include directory services provided by a common carrier or its affiliate or by a local exchange carrier or its affiliate, or any service the charge for which is tariffed, or any service for which users are assessed charges

only after entering into a presubscription or comparable arrangement with the provider of such service.

(b)(1)   Presubscription or comparable arrangement means a contractual agreement in which

(i)   The service provider clearly and conspicuously discloses to the consumer all material terms and conditions associated with the use of the service, including the service provider's name and address, a business telephone number which the consumer may use to obtain additional information or to register a complaint, and the rates for the service;

(ii) The service provider agrees to notify the consumer of any future rate changes;

(iii) The consumer agrees to utilize the service on the terms and conditions disclosed by the service provider; and

(iv) The service provider requires the use of an identification number or other means to prevent unauthorized access to the service by nonsubscribers.

(2) Disclosure of a credit- or charge-card number, along with authorization to bill that number, made during the course of a call to an information service shall constitute a presubscription or comparable arrangement if the credit or charge card is subject to the dispute resolution procedures of the Truth in Lending Act and Fair Credit Billing Act, as amended, 15 U.S.C. Section 1601 *et seq.* No other action taken by the consumer during the course of a call to an information service, for which charges are assessed, can be construed as creating a presubscription or comparable arrangement.

64.1502 Limitations on the Provision of Pay-Per-Call Services

Any common carrier assigning a telephone number to a provider of interstate pay-per-call service shall require, by contract or tariff, that such provider comply with the provisions of this subpart and of titles II and III of the Telephone Disclosure and Dispute Resolution Act (Pub. L. No. 102-556) (TDDRA) and the regulations prescribed by the Federal Trade Commission pursuant to those titles.

64.1503 Termination of Pay-Per-Call Programs.

Any common carrier assigning a telephone number to a provider of interstate pay-per-call service shall specify by contract or tariff that pay-per-call programs not in compliance with Section 64.1502 shall be terminated following written notice to the information provider. The information provider shall be afforded a period of no less than seven and no more than 14 days during which a program may be brought into compliance. Programs not in compliance at the expiration of such period shall be terminated immediately.

64.1504 Restrictions on the Use of 800 Numbers.

Common carriers shall prohibit, by tariff or contract, the use of any telephone number beginning with an 800 service access code, or any other telephone number advertised or widely understood to be toll-free, in a manner that would result in

(a) The calling party or the subscriber to the originating line being assessed, by virtue of completing the call, a charge for the call;

(b) The calling party being connected to a pay-per-call service;

(c) The calling party being charged for information conveyed during the call unless the calling party has a presubscription or comparable arrangement; or

(d) The calling party being called back collect for the provision of audio or data information services, simultaneous voice conversation services, or products.

64.1505 Restrictions on Collect Telephone Calls.

(a) No common carrier shall provide interstate transmission or billing and collection services to an entity offering any service within the scope of 64.1501 (a)(1) that is billed to a subscriber on a collect basis at a per-call or per-time-interval charge that is greater than or in addition to, the charge for transmission of the call.

(b) No common carrier shall provide interstate transmission services for any collect information services billed to a subscriber at a tariffed rate unless the called party has taken affirmative action clearly indicating that it accepts the charges for the collect service.

64.1506 Number Designation.

Any interstate service described in 64.1501 (a)(1) - (2) shall be offered only through telephone numbers beginning with a 900-service access code.

64.1507 Prohibition on Disconnection or Interruption of Service for Failure to Remit Pay-Per-Call or Similar Service Charges.

No common carrier shall disconnect or interrupt in any manner, or order the disconnection or interruption of, a telephone subscriber's local exchange or long distance telephone service as a result of that subscriber's failure to pay

(a) Charges for interstate pay-per-call service,

(b) Charges for interstate information services provided pursuant to a presubscription or comparable arrangement or

(c) Charges, which have been disputed by the subscriber, for interstate tariffed collect information services.

64.1508 Blocking Access to 900 Service

(a) Local exchange carriers must offer to their subscribers, where technically feasible, an option to block access to services offered on the 900-service access code. Blocking is to be offered at no charge, on a one-time basis, to

(1) All telephone subscribers during the period from November 1, 1993 through December 31, 1993; and

(2) Any subscriber who subscribes to a new telephone number for a period of 60 days after the new number is effective.

(b) For blocking requests not within the one-time option or outside the time frames specified in paragraph (a) of this section, and for unblocking requests, local exchange carriers may charge a reasonable one-time fee. Requests by subscribers to remove 900-services blocking must be in writing.

(c) The terms and conditions under which subscribers may obtain 900-services blocking are to be included in tariffs filed with this Commission.

64.1509 Disclosure and Dissemination of Pay-Per-Call Information.

(a) Any common carrier assigning a telephone number to a provider of interstate pay-per-call services shall make readily available, at no charge, to Federal and State agencies and all other interested persons:

(1) A list of the telephone numbers for each of the pay-per-call services it carries;

(2) A short description of each such service;

(3) A statement of the total cost or the cost-per-minute and any other fees for each such service; and

(4) A statement of the pay-per-call service provider's name, business address, and business telephone number.

(b) Any common carrier assigning a telephone number to a provider of interstate pay-per-call services and offering billing and collection services to such provider shall

(1) Establish a local or toll-free telephone number to answer questions and provide information on subscribers' rights and obligations with regard to their use of pay-per-call services and to provide to callers the name and mailing address of any provider of pay-per-call services offered by that carrier; and

(2) Provide to all its telephone subscribers, either directly or through contract with any local exchange carrier providing billing and collection services to that carrier, a disclosure statement setting forth all rights and obligations of the subscriber and the carrier with respect to the use and payment of pay-per-call services. Such statement must include the prohibition against disconnection of basic communications services for failure to pay pay-per-call charges established by 64.1507, the right of a subscriber to obtain blocking in accordance with 64.1508, the right of a subscriber not to be billed for pay-per-call services not offered in compliance with federal laws and regulations established by 64.1510 (a) (iv), and the possibility that a subscriber's access to 900 services may be involuntarily blocked pursuant to 64.1512 for failure to pay legitimate pay-per-call charges. Disclosure statements must be forwarded to:

(i) All telephone subscribers no later 60 days after these regulations take effect;

(ii) All new telephone subscribers no later than 60 days after service is established;

(iii) All telephone subscribers requesting service at a new location no later than 60 days after service is established; and

(iv) Thereafter, to all subscribers at least once per calendar year, at intervals of not less than 6 months nor more than 18 months.

64.1510 Billing and Collection of Pay-Per-Call and Similar Service Charges.

(a) Any common carrier assigning a telephone number to a provider of interstate pay-per-call services and offering billing and collection services to such provider shall:

(1) Ensure that a subscriber is not billed for interstate pay-per-call services that such carrier knows or reasonably should know were provided in violation of the regulations set forth in this subpart or prescribed by the Federal Trade Commission pursuant to titles II or III of the TDDRA or any other federal law;

(2) In any billing to telephone subscribers that includes charges for any interstate pay-per-call service

(i) Include a statement indicating that:

(A) Such charges are for non-communications services;

(B) Neither local nor long distances services can be disconnected for non-payment although an information provider may employ private entities to seek to collect such charges;

(C) 900 number blocking is available upon request; and

(D) Access to pay-per-call services may be involuntarily blocked for failure to pay legitimate charges;

(ii) Display any charges for pay-per-call services in a part of the bill that is identified as not being related to local and long distance telephone charges;

(iii) Specify, for each pay-per-call charge made, the type of service, the amount of the charge, and the date, time and, for calls billed on a time-sensitive basis, the duration of the call; and

(iv) Identify the local or toll-free number established in accordance with 64.1509 (b)(1).

(b) Any common carrier offering billing and collection services to an entity providing interstate information services pursuant to a presubscription or comparable arrangement, or for interstate tariffed collect information services, shall, to the extent possible, display the billing information in the manner described in paragraphs (a) (2) (i) - (ii) of this section.

64.1511 Forgiveness of Charges and Refunds.

(a) Any carrier assigning a telephone number to a provider of interstate pay-per-call services or providing transmission for interstate tariffed collect information services or interstate information services offered under a presubscription or comparable arrangement, and providing billing and collection services for such services, shall establish procedures for the handling of subscriber complaints regarding charges for those services. A billing carrier is afforded discretion to set standards for determining when a subscriber's complaint warrants forgiveness, refund or credit of interstate pay-per-call or information services charges provided that such charges must be forgiven, refunded, or credited when a subscriber has complained about such charges and either this Commission, the Federal Trade Commission, or a court of competent jurisdiction has found or the carrier has determined, upon investigation, that the service has been offered in violation of federal law or the regulations that are either set forth in this subpart or prescribed by the Federal Trade Commission pursuant to titles II or III of the TDDRA. Carriers shall observe the record retention requirements set forth in 47 C.F.R. Section 42.6 except that relevant records shall be retained by carriers beyond the requirements of Part 42 of this chapter when a complaint is pending at the time the specified retention period expires.

(b) Any carrier assigning a telephone number to a provider of interstate pay-per-call services but not providing billing and collection services for such services, shall, by tariff or contract, require that the provider and/or its billing and collection agents have in place procedures whereby, upon complaint, pay-per-call charges may be forgiven, refunded, or credited, provided that such charges must be forgiven, refunded, or credited when a subscriber has complained about such charges and either this Commission, the Federal Trade Commission, or a court of competent jurisdiction has found or the carrier has determined, upon investigation, that the service has been offered in violation of federal law or the regulations that are either set forth in this subpart or prescribed by the Federal Trade Commission pursuant to titles II or III of the TDDRA.

64.1512 Involuntary Blocking of Pay-Per-Call Services

Nothing in this subpart shall preclude a common carrier or information provider from blocking or ordering the blocking of its interstate pay-per-call programs from numbers assigned to subscribers who have incurred, but not paid, legitimate pay-per-call charges, except that a subscriber who has filed a complaint regarding a particular pay-per-call program pursuant to procedures established by the Federal Trade Commission under title III of the TDDRA shall not be involuntarily blocked from access to that program while such a complaint is pending. This restriction is not intended to preclude involuntary blocking when a carrier or IP has decided in one instance to sustain charges against a subscriber but that subscriber files additional separate complaints.

64.1513 Verification of Charitable Status.

Any common carrier assigning a telephone number to a provider of interstate pay-per-call services that the carrier knows or reasonably should know is engaged in soliciting charitable contributions shall obtain verification that the entity or individual for whom contributions are solicited has been granted tax exempt status by the Internal Revenue Service.

64.1514 Generation of Signalling Tones.

No common carrier shall assign a telephone number for any pay-per-call service that employs broadcast advertising which generates the audible tones necessary to complete a call to a pay-per-call service.

64.1515 Recovery of Costs.

No common carrier shall recover its cost of complying with the provisions of this subpart from local or long distance ratepayers.

FCC Dial-a-Porn Rules

Because the FCC Dial-a-Porn Rules apply to the use of indecent communications over all telephone lines, not just 900 pay-per-call lines, these rules are distinct from the FCC 900 Rules that were just presented. The following is a verbatim transcription of the FCC Dial-a-Porn Rules:

64.201 Restrictions on Indecent Telephone Message Services

(a) It is a defense to prosecution for the provision of indecent communications under section 223(b)(2) of the Communications Act of 1934, as amended (the Act), 47 U.S.C. 223(B)(2), that the defendant has taken the action set forth in paragraph (a)(1) of this section and, in addition, has complied with the following: Taken one of the actions set forth in paragraphs (a)(2), (3), or (4) of this section to restrict access to prohibited communications to persons eighteen years of age or older, and has additionally complied with paragraph (a)(5) of this section, where applicable:

(1) Has notified the common carrier identified in section 223(c)(1) of the Act, in writing, that he or she is providing the kind of service described in section 223(b)(2) of the Act.

(2) Requires payment by credit card before transmission of the message; or

(3) Requires an authorized access or identification code before transmission of the message, and where the defendant has:

(i) Issued the code by mailing it to the applicant after reasonably ascertaining through receipt of a written application that the applicant is not under eighteen years of age; and

(ii) Established a procedure to cancel immediately the code of any person upon written, telephonic or other notice to the defendant's business office that such code has been lost, stolen, or used by a person or persons under the age of eighteen, or that such code is no longer desired; or

(4) Scrambles the message using any technique that renders the audio unintelligible and incomprehensible to the calling party unless that party uses a descrambler; and,

(5) Where the defendant is a message sponsor subscriber to mass announcement services tariffed at this Commission and such defendant prior to the transmission of the message has requested in writing to the carrier providing the public announcement service that calls to this message service be subject to billing notification as an adult telephone message service.

(b) A common carrier within the District of Columbia or within any State, or in interstate or foreign commerce, shall not, to the extent technically feasible, provide access to a communication described in section 223(b) of the Act from the telephone of any subscriber who has not previously requested in writing the carrier to provide access to such communication if the carrier collects from subscribers an identifiable charge for such communication that the carrier remits, in whole or in part to the provider of such communication.

Federal Trade Commission (FTC) Regulations

Unlike the FCC, whose 900 regulations are relatively brief, the FTC's 900 regulations were published in a 219-page document that is too lengthy to reproduce here. Fortunately, along with the actual rules, the FTC published a concise news release that does a good job of summarizing the highlights of the new regulations. The full text of the FTC rules are available from the FTC's Public Reference Branch, mentioned at the conclusion of the following FTC news release.

FTC News Release
For release: July 27, 1993

FTC ANNOUNCES 900-NUMBER INDUSTRY RULE

New Regulations Will Require Cost and Other Disclosures, and Set Procedures for Consumers to Resolve Billing Disputes

Beginning this November, companies that offer 900-number, or pay-per-call, telephone services will be required to disclose the costs of these services in their advertising, and to begin calls costing more than $2 with a "preamble" stating, among other things, the cost of the call. Consumers will not be charged for the call if they hang up shortly afterward. The requirements are outlined in a new Federal Trade Commission rule announced today. The new rule also established procedures for resolving consumer billing disputes for pay-per call services, and will require certain disclosures to be made in billing statements.

The FTC promulgated its 900-Number Rule pursuant to the Telephone Disclosure and Dispute Resolution Act, which was signed into law in October 1992.

Disclosures

Under the new rule, companies that offer pay-per-call services will have to disclose in any print, radio and television advertisements they run for the services:

—for flat-fee services, the total cost of each call;

—for time-sensitive services, the cost-per-minute and any minimum charges, as well as the maximum charge if it can be determined in advance;

—for services billed at varying rates depending on which options callers select, the cost of the initial portion of the call, any minimum charges, and the range of rates that may be charged;

—all other fees charged for these services; and

—the cost of any other pay-per-call services to which callers may be transferred.

The rule sets out requirements to ensure that these and other mandated disclosures will be clear and conspicuous. The requirements will vary depending on the particular disclosure and on the advertising media. The cost disclosures explained above, for example, generally will have to be made adjacent to the telephone number, and in the same format (visual, oral, or both) as the number. When the 900 number is displayed visually, the cost disclosure will have to be at least half the size of the telephone number.

Other advertising disclosures to be required under the 900-Number Rule include:

—for pay-per-call sweepstakes services, a statement about the odds of winning the sweepstakes prize (or how the odds will be calculated) and the fact that consumers do not have to call to enter the sweepstakes, as well as a description of the free alternative method of entering the sweepstakes (alternatively, these last two statements may be disclosed in the preamble);

—for services that provide information about federal programs but which are not affiliated with the federal government, a statement at the beginning of the advertisement that the service is not authorized, endorsed or approved by any federal entity (this statement also will be required in the preamble);

—for services directed to consumers under the age of 18, a statement that parental permission is required before calling the service (this statement also will be required in the preamble).

The rule also will require billing statements for pay-per-call services to disclose, for each pay-per-call service charge, the type of service, the amount of the charge, the date, time and, for time-sensitive calls, duration of the call. These charges will have to appear apart from local- and long-distance charges on consumers' telephone bills. Finally, each billing statement will have to include a local or toll-free number for consumers to call with questions about their pay-per-call charges.

The Preamble Requirement

The preamble required by the rule will identify the company providing the service, state the cost of the call, and inform the caller that charges will begin three seconds after the tone following the preamble and that they must hang up before that time to avoid charges. Companies will be prohibited from charging consumers for calls if the consumers hang up before the three-second period ends. The rule will allow companies to install a mechanism that would enable frequent callers to bypass the preamble, as long as the companies disable the mechanism for 30 days after each price increase.

Ban on 900-Number Services to Children

Another provision in the FTC rule will implement a provision of the Telephone Disclosure Act banning 900-number services directed to children. The rule will prohibit companies from advertising or directing pay-per-call services to those under 12, unless the services are bona fide educational services dedicated to areas of school study. The rule adopts a two-test approach to the definition of children's advertising. The first test will be whether the ad appears during programming or in publications for which 50 percent of the audience or readership is under 12. These ads are banned. Under the second test, if competent and reliable audience composition data are not available, the Commission will consider a variety of factors in determining whether the ad is directed to children, including the placement of the ad, subject matter, visual content, language, the age of any models, and any characters used in the ad. (Advertisements for services directed to consumers under 18 — which require a parental-permission disclosure — also are defined by the medium in which the ad appears, or the nature of the ad.)

Billing-Dispute Resolution Procedures

The billing-dispute resolution section of the 900-Number Rule will require entities that perform billing for pay-per-call services to give consumers written notice at least annually of their billing rights for telephone-billed purchases, including the procedures for disputing charges. Under the FTC rule, billing errors will include charges for calls not made by the customer or for the wrong amount, and charges for telephone-billed purchases not provided to the customer in accordance with the stated terms of the agreement. Under the procedures set out in the rule for resolving these disputes, a customer will be required to notify the responsible billing entity, using the method described in the billing statement, within 60 days after the first statement containing the error was sent (oral notifications will be permitted under the rule).

Thereafter, the billing entity will be:

—required to acknowledge the customer's notice in writing within 40 days of receiving it (unless the dispute is resolved within that time);

—required either to correct the billing error and to notify the customer of the correction, or to investigate the matter and either correct the error or explain to the customer the reason for not doing so, within 90 days or two billing cycles;

—prohibited from charging for investigating or responding to the alleged billing error; and

—prohibited from trying to collect the disputed charge from the customer, and from reporting the charge to a credit bureau or other third party, until the billing error has been investigated and the resulting action has been completed (this prohibition will apply to billing entities, carriers and vendors).

Finally, under this section of the 900-Number Rule, billing entities that do not comply with their billing-dispute resolution responsibilities forfeit the right to collect up to $50 of the amount of each disputed charge.

Miscellaneous Provisions

Further, the 900-Number Rule will prohibit companies from running ads that emit electronic tones that dial 900 numbers automatically. In addition, the rule generally will prohibit companies from using 800 numbers for pay-per-call services, connecting 800-number callers to 900 numbers, or placing collect return calls to 800-number callers.

The rule also will allow the Commission to hold service bureaus (the entities that process pay-per-call service calls) liable if they know or should know that their clients are violating the FTC rule. Finally, companies that have offered pay-per-call services in violation of the rule or any other federal rule or law will be held liable for refunds or credits to consumers, under the FTC rule.

The Commission vote yesterday to promulgate the 900-Number Rule and to approve the Statement of Basis and Purpose in support of it was 4-0, with Commissioner Roscoe B. Starek, III recused. The final rule is a modified version of a proposed rule announced in March 9 (1993) news release. The Commission received 99 comments on that proposal, and in April held a two-day workshop to obtain additional feedback from the public and a variety of interested parties.

The 900-Number Rule will be published in the Federal Register shortly and will become effective Nov. 1 (1993). Copies of the new rule, the proposed rule and the news release issued when it was announced for public comment, as well as news releases on FTC lawsuits involving deceptive use of 900 numbers, are available from the FTC's Public Reference Branch, Room 130, 6th Street and Pennsylvania Avenue, N.W., Washington, D.C. 20580; 202-326-2222; TTY for the hearing impaired 202-326-2502.

The FTC also publishes a free 21-page business guide titled *Complying with the 900-Number Rule*, which is available at the address above or from any FTC Regional Office.

Appendix F
Long Distance Carriers

The following information is intended to help you in making an informed selection of a long-distance carrier that will meet your specific needs. Price, or any other single criteria, should never be the only factor in choosing a carrier.

All of these carriers have stringent guidelines for doing business with them, particularly with regard to using their premium billing services. For the most part, the individual IXC guidelines are based upon the laws and regulations outlined in Appendix E (Federal Laws and Regulations). The NXXs assigned to these carriers are listed in Appendix G.

IXC prices and guidelines are subject to change, and although this information is accurate as of this writing, you should verify this information with the pertinent IXC.

When this book went to press these were the only long-distance carriers that were providing national long-distance transport services for 900 numbers in the U.S. and Canada. This situation can change at any time. An up-to-date listing of 900 carriers can be found in the *Audiotex News Resource Guide* (Appendix C).

It should be noted that regional telephone companies, including RBOCs and GTE, offer regional 900-number services, and these companies can be quite competitive for 900 applications that don't need full national coverage.

AT&T MultiQuest

MultiQuest Action Center
Tower 3, Floor 2
3701 East Golf Road
Rolling Meadows, IL 60008

AT&T has a helpful information line, 1-900-555-0900, which offers information on its MultiQuest Pay-Per-Call Services, using its Vari-A-Bill℠ calling charge option, including the following information choices:

1. Free. Three-minute recorded message giving an explanation of the 900-number business.
2. Free. Pricing information on AT&T MultiQuest Services.
3. $3 flat fee. To receive information by mail.
4. $3 flat fee. To receive information by fax.
5. $0.50/minute with a maximum fee of $15. To speak to a live operator.

AT&T offers three separate 900 service categories, depending upon the nature of the program:

Interacter. This is the most common service, and virtually all recorded interactive programs would come under this service. Through this service, callers can interact with your sales or service specialists, voice-response equipment or computer databases to obtain value-added services and information. Interacter Services handles up to 1,800 calls per minute.

Express900. This service gives you a low-cost, low-risk way to test the power of 900 service. These 900 numbers piggyback onto your local number, and the IP generally deals directly with AT&T as the client of record because a service bureau is usually not needed. Express900 Service is designed for businesses that expect fewer than 100 hours of 900 usage per month.

HiCap. This service is designed for high volume "burst" applications resulting from national TV advertising, such as polling, voter choice and sweepstakes applications with short hold times between 15 and 60 seconds. Under this service AT&T will coordinate termination of the call at one or as many service bureaus as are necessary in order to allow the completion of as many calls as possible in the shortest period of time.

AT&T MultiQuest 900 Service Prices			
	Interacter	Express900	HiCap
One-time Start-up Fee	$1,200.00	$1,000.00	$1,250.00
Additional Numbers	$125.00 each	$75.00 each	$125.00 each
Monthly Service Charge	$500.00	$75.00	$1,000.00
Interstate Usage: 1st 30 seconds each addl. second	$0.162 $0.0054	$0.219 $0.0073	
Intrastate Usage: 1st 30 seconds ea. addl. sec.	$0.15 $0.005	$0.21 $0.007	
Flat Rate per Call			$0.06
Billings and Collections Fee	10% of caller charge	15% of caller charge	10% of caller charge
Caller Grace Period	$0.12	$0.15	$0.12
Payout Interval	30-90 days	90 days	60-90 days
These prices were effective going to press and are subject to change. Call the AT&T MutiQuest 900 number on the previous page for up-to-date pricing and product information.			

Table F-1

The preceding prices are those charged the client of record, which in many cases will be the service bureau, who will usually pass on these fees to the IP. Nonetheless, the service bureau can charge whatever it wants, which can be more or less than these amounts. The start-up fee applies to each new account, not necessarily each new program, so an IP may have several programs in operation and pays the start-up fee only once.

AT&T offers several options that allow the IP wide flexibility in structuring the charges for the call:

Vari-A-Bill^{SM}. This service allows the IP to charge different amounts based upon the caller's choice of information received. The rate can be usage-based (i.e., per-minute), a flat rate, or free, depending upon the interactive menu choices made by the caller.

Enhanced Rate Sets. This allows the IP to establish a rate period other than one minute, in 60-second increments up to 24 hours. For example, the IP could set the charge at $2 for the first four minutes, then $5 for each additional increment of seven minutes each.

Caller Free Time Option. Normally, there is a 19-second period, for the preamble message, that is free to the caller. With this feature, the IP can determine the length of the free time period ranging from 12 seconds up to 999 seconds (16+ minutes) in one-second increments, allowing for a more detailed message or menu description before the call charges begin (applies to Interacter and Express900).

Time of Day/Day of Week Rating. This allows the IP to set different rates based upon the time (the caller's local time) of the call or the day of the week. For example, this feature could be used to help even out call volume, encouraging customers to call during off-peak hours, reducing the peak call volume to more manageable levels.

Call Prompter Rating. This service is similar to Vari-A-Bill^SM in that it allows the IP to vary the call charge for different menu selections. The significant differences, however, are that the menu prompts are at the network level, instead of at the IP's or the service bureau's equipment; the prompts, or levels, are limited to four branches; and once set up, there is little flexibility in changing the prompts or the price structure. This is a good choice for a static situation where the service and its pricing rarely changes.

MCI

MCI 900 Business Unit
1650 Tysons Blvd.
McLean, VA 22102

Information about MCI 900 pricing and services can be received by calling 1-900-733-MCI9 (6249), for a flat charge of $4 per call. Callers hear a three-minute overview of the industry, including information about start-up costs, regulations and definitions. Callers can leave their address at the end of the call to receive a hard copy of the information, including other resource materials, at the end of the call.

This section highlights the types of programming for which MCI will not provide Billing and Collection Services.
1. Programs that do not contain a preamble.
2. Fundraisers without not-for-profit status.
3. Programs conflicting with LEC billing restrictions.
4. Unlawful applications such as in violation of election laws, laws concerning unfair, deceptive or fraudulent advertising, securities laws and anti-gambling laws, etc.
5. Defamatory applications containing inflammatory or demeaning portrayals on the basis of race, religion, political affiliation, ethnic group, etc.
6. Fraudulent Programs.
7. Children's programming which is usage-sensitive or exceeds the price cap of $4.
8. Adult Programming.
9. Programs using fraudulent sales techniques such as reference to another 900 number for which there is a charge; repetitive, extraneous or drawn-out messages with the purpose of increasing end user charges; programs that utilize

multi-level marketing or pyramid schemes; programs that use a PIN number for the purpose of receiving fulfillment on a subsequent call.

10. Any program using autodialers or computer-generated announcements to induce calls.

11. Programs that do not clearly, concisely and accurately disclose the costs of the call and all costs associated with receiving fulfillment.

12. Programs that generate excessive caller credits or uncollectibles.

13. Programs which relate to or offer information on obtaining credit, loans, or improving credit.

14. Programs which offer travel accommodations or transportation in conjunction with a sweepstakes or contest.

15. GAB lines e.g., group access bridging.

16. Sweepstakes programs.

17. Job line programs.

18. Personal, date lines, voice mailboxes and one-to-one programs that do not comply with MCI's policies.

PRICING AND FEATURES

A. PRICING
1. Transport - $0.31 per minute
2. Billing and Collection Charge — 10% charge based on price charged to the caller.
3. Credit Pass Through — all credits and reported uncollectibles returned from the LEC are passed through to the sponsor.
4. Unbillables — calls passed back to the sponsor that are in violation of the LEC's restrictions and which the LEC will not or can not bill and collect.
5. Deferral — 10% of the monthly amount payable to the sponsor is deferred until four months after the calls appear on the settlement statement. This creates a reserve against which caller credits can be charged should the program no longer generate sufficient revenues to cover caller credits. After five months of history is established, the percentage used to calculate the deferral will change from 10% to the actual caller credit rate that is experienced. For example, if the caller credit experience is less than 10%, the deferral amounts will go down; conversely, if the caller credit experience is greater than 10%, the deferral amount will go up.
6. Access — T1 access facilities cost vary.

MCI's pricing is competitive and volume discounts are available. Our transport charges are among the lowest in the industry. In addition, there are minimum usage fees for each line and a $100 per month line fee.

B. DISCOUNTS
Applied monthly at the following transport thresholds;
$70,000 to $140,000   6%

$140,000 +   12%

Multi Option Discounts (MOD):
5% discount of all traffic over $25,000

C. FEATURES

Tailored Call Coverage — Allows selective blocking of calls by originating state or area code/prefix. This allows you to select your service areas to maximize the efficiency of the program.

Point of Call Routing — Routes calls to different terminating locations based upon the caller's state or area code/prefix. This allows you to balance the traffic between several terminating locations. For example, calls from Florida could be handled by Atlanta, while calls from New Jersey would be handled by New York.

Real Time Automatic Number Identification (RTANI) — Provides originating caller phone number (restrictions apply). This allows you to build a database of callers and to control abuse.

Dialed Number Identification Service (DNIS) — Allows multiple 800/900 numbers to be terminated on one service group and receive pulsed digits to identify the 900 number called. This helps you to maximize the efficiency of your channels and to route calls to the appropriate serving point.

2-Way Access — Inbound and outbound calls may be terminated on the same access trunk group. This reduces the number of access facilities that you need, and thus saves you access costs.

These are just some of the many features MCI 900 Service offers.

Sprint TeleMedia
800-SELL-900
6666 West 110th Street
Overland Park, KS 66211

The following is a verbatim transcription of Sprint TeleMedia's published guidelines as of the date of this writing:

PROGRAM AND ADVERTISING GUIDELINES
FOR SPRINT TELEMEDIA 900 SERVICES

INTRODUCTION

The following program and advertising guidelines ("Guidelines") apply to all programs that use Sprint TeleMedia's billing or collection services in connection with Sprint TeleMedia 900 services. Each program must comply in full (1) with these Guidelines which are incorporated in full and are part of the Information Provider Agreement, and (2) with all other terms of the Information Provider Agreement.

THESE GUIDELINES DO NOT CONSTITUTE LEGAL ADVICE. THEY ARE MINIMUM STANDARDS THAT AN INFORMATION PROVIDER MUST MEET BEFORE SPRINT TELEMEDIA WILL AGREE TO PROVIDE BILLING OR COLLECTION SERVICES FOR ANY PROGRAM. INFORMATION PROVIDERS MUST CONSULT THEIR OWN ATTORNEYS REGARDING THE LEGALITY OF THEIR PROGRAMS.

I.   PROGRAM REQUIREMENTS
    A. GENERAL PROHIBITIONS
       1. CONTENT RESTRICTIONS
          a. SPRINT TELEMEDIA WILL NOT PROVIDE BILLING OR COLLECTION FOR PROGRAMS CONTAINING THE FOLLOWING CONTENT:
             (1)   Romance, Adult, Live One-on-One, GAB, Personals and Dating Bulletin Boards
             (2) Credit Card and Loan Information
             (3) Job Lines
             (4) Sport Pick Lines
             (5) Stand Alone Horoscope
             (6) Giveaways
             (7) Programs directed towards children
          b. SPRINT TELEMEDIA WILL NOT PROVIDE BILLING OR COLLECTION FOR ANY PROGRAM WHOSE MESSAGE CONTENT OR PROMOTIONAL MATERIALS CONTAIN, IN WORDS OR VISUAL IMAGES, THE FOLLOWING:
             (1) Vulgar language, explicit or implicit descriptions of violence or sexual conduct, adult entertainment, or incitement to violence;
             (2) Inflammatory or demeaning portrayals of any individual's or group's race, religion, political affiliation, ethnicity, gender, sexual preference, or handicap;
             (3) Criticism or disparagement of the general use of telecommunications or data communication products and services;
             (4) Material that is unlawful, highly controversial or that may generate widespread adverse publicity;
             (5) Multi-level marketing or "pyramid" schemes (generally defined as programs where purchasers of goods, property or services are

compensated in the form of rebates, commissions or payments when they induce other persons to participate in the program);

(6) False, misleading or deceptive advertising; or

(7) Commentary adverse to the policies or practices of Sprint TeleMedia or its affiliates.

2. SPRINT TELEMEDIA WILL NOT BILL OR COLLECT FOR ANY PROGRAM:

a. That is promoted or advertised by means of recorded or live outbound telemarketing or automatic dialing equipment (autodialers). This includes, but is not limited to, programs that use outbound telemarketing or autodialers to advertise an 800 number that, when dialed, refers callers to a 900 number. Sprint TeleMedia may permit live outbound telemarketing for fundraising programs on a case-by-case basis.

b. Where a caller is required to dial more than one 900 number in order to obtain the service advertised.

c. That uses radio or TV advertising where an electronic tone signal is emitted during the broadcast of the ad and automatically dials the 900 telephone number.

d. Where the total price of the call exceeds fifteen dollars ($15.00). (Exceptions to this policy only occur in extreme rare occasions.) Any program which exceeds $15.00 must be first approved in writing by the Sprint TeleMedia Vice President General Manager and designated representatives of both the Legal and Finance Departments.

e. That violates FCC requirements.

f. That utilizes "minimum pricing" -- for example, "$1.95 per minute, 10-minute minimum."

g. Containing cross-referrals to other 900 programs or similar programs offered through the other media such as television and print, that are prohibited by any of the above.

h. Where the Service Bureau refuses to provide Sprint TeleMedia with the name, address, and customer telephone number of the Information Provider.

i. Found to be in non-compliance with Sprint TeleMedia's Guidelines. Sprint TeleMedia will terminate billing services immediately and may refuse to provide billing services for any new programs submitted by the Information Provider in the same applications category as that of the terminated program.

j. That does not comply with all applicable federal, state and local laws. Information providers must consult their own attorneys to determine what federal, state and local laws apply to their programs.

3. THESE GENERAL PROHIBITIONS APPLY TO BOTH VISUAL IMAGES AND TEXT USED IN ANY 900 SCRIPT OR ADVERTISING OR PROMOTION USED TO ENCOURAGE CALLS TO A 900 PROGRAM.

B. FCC REQUIREMENTS
INFORMATION PROVIDERS MUST COMPLY WITH ALL APPLICABLE FCC RULES GOVERNING PAY-PER-CALL SERVICES, INCLUDING BUT NOT LIMITED TO THOSE RULES WHICH GOVERN "PREAMBLES." THE CURRENT RULES ARE PUBLISHED AT 47 CFR SECTIONS 64.709 THROUGH 64.716, AND 68.383 (C) (2). ANY ADDITIONS OR CHANGES TO THESE RULES WILL AUTOMATICALLY BECOME PART OF THESE GUIDELINES, AS OF THEIR EFFECTIVE DATE. AN FCC SUMMARY OF THE RULES AND THE RULES THEMSELVES APPEARS, AND ARE INCORPORATED INTO THESE GUIDELINES, AS APPENDICES 1A AND 1B (omitted here, see Appendix G). INFORMATION PROVIDERS MUST CONSULT THEIR OWN ATTORNEYS REGARDING THE APPLICATION OF THESE RULES TO THEIR PROGRAMS.

SCG Carrier Services

575 Scherers Court
Worthington, OH 43085
800-622-2200; 614-841-2421
This carrier's target market is mid- to large-sized IPs, service bureaus and established businesses. SCG Carrier Services does not offer premium billing services, so a third-party biller would have to be used. SCG does not charge any one-time set-up fees, however new customers are expected to commit to 25,000 minutes per month for the first six months. Transport fees are as follows:

SCG 900 Transport Pricing		
Minutes/ month*	900 Transport (cents per minute)	900 Short Rate (1st 30 seconds)
25,000-50,000	20.0	6.0
50,001-100,000	19.0	6.0
100,001-150,000	18.0	6.0
150,001-250,000	16.0	6.0
250,001-500,000	15.0	6.0
500,001-1,000,000	14.0	6.0
1,000,000-2,000,000	13.0	6.0
2,000,001+	12.0	5.5
*Aggregated across all SCG products, including 800 inbound, 500 inbound, outbound domestic and international		

Table F-2

INFO Services, Inc.
6707 Democracy Blvd., Suite 800
Bethesda, MD 20817
800-313-5655
This carrier serves primarily service bureaus and larger IPs, offering competitive rates for large-volume business. Both transport and premium billing services are offered.

Starlink Communications
1200 Fifth Avenue, Suite 701
Seattle, WA 98101
206-622-7100
This was the first alternative carrier to offer 900 services besides the big three (AT&T, MCI, Sprint). Like the other alternative carriers, its rates are competitive.

Federal TransTel
Two Chase Corporate Dr., Suite 170
Birmingham, AL 35244
800-933-6600
This is another new player in 900 transport. This company is also an alternative LEC billing company (Chapter 3).

Stentor (Canada)
Stentor is an alliance of the major telephone companies in Canada. The member companies provide local telephone service in their respective provinces, and Stentor is a cooperative association for coordinating long-distance services between the provinces, providing customers with national and international services. Long-distance 900 services will be provided by the member company in whose territory the service provider's equipment or service bureau is located.

Stentor — Phone Power
410 Laurier Ave. West, Room 200
Ottawa, Ontario, Canada K1R 7T3
800-567-7000 Fax: 800-461-2594

The following is a list of Stentor member companies. In general, ask for the "900 Specialists" at any given company:

AGT Limited
411 1st St., S.E.
Calgary, Alberta, T2G 4Y5
800-461-9990

BC Tel, Phone Power
2939 Bainbridge Ave.
Burnaby, BC, V5A 2S3
800-661-1088

SaskTel
Floor 4, 1825 Lorne St.
Regina, Saskatchewan, S4P
3Y2
800-667-3500

Manitoba Telephone System
191 Pioneer Ave.
Winnipeg, Manitoba, R3C 3V9
800-665-6394

Bell (Ontario)
483 Bay St., Floor 8, South
Tower
Toronto, Ontario, M5G 2E1
800-387-4441

Bell (Quebec)
3400 De Maisonneuve West,
Room 650
Montreal, Quebec, H3Z 3B8
800-361-8717

NBTel
1 Brunswick Square
P.O. Box 1430
Saint John, NB, E2L 4K2
800-567-7000

Maritime Tel & Tel
1505 Barrington St.
P.O. Box 880, Station Central
R.P.O.
Halifax, Nova Scotia, B3J 2W3
800-480-2144

Newfoundland Telephone
P.O. Box 2110
St. John's, NF, A1C 5H6
800-567-7000

Quebec Telephone (1)
6 Jules-A-Brillant, Dept. 700
Rimouski, Quebec, G5L 7E4
800-567-7000

NorthwesTel (2)
5201 50th Ave.
Yellowknife, NT, X1A 3S9
800-567-7000

Notes:
(1) 900 transport expected implementation: April 1996
(2) 900 transport not offered when this book went to press

Appendix G
NXX Assignments

Bell Communications Research, Inc. (Bellcore), acting in its capacity as administrator of the North American Numbering Plan (NANP), assigns 900 NXX (N is any number from 2 through 9; X is any number from 0 through 9) codes to the telephone companies, including RBOCs, local exchange carriers and interexchange carriers. The NXX is the group of three numbers immediately after the 900 prefix: 900-<u>NXX</u>-XXXX. In order to identify the carrier for proper routing, unique NXX codes are assigned, and at this time these NXXs are not transferable between carriers. According to Bellcore, there are currently no plans to limit the total number of codes assigned to each carrier.

Additional NXX codes can be assigned by request of the carrier, and the carrier's preference for a specific NXX code will be honored by Bellcore to the extent possible. According to Bellcore's *900 NXX Plan Code Assignments Guidelines,* "An NXX code is not permanently allocated to an LEC or IC (interexchange carrier), and no proprietary right is implied or intended with respect to the allocated NXXs."

The following NXX assignments are for long-distance carriers only. NXXs for RBOCs and LECs have been omitted because they would have no applicability to national 900 programs. A listing of Stentor NXXs is included for the Canadian telephone companies. This list is up-to-date as of this writing; however NXX assignments will change whenever carriers request new NXXs from Bellcore. For this reason, if knowing the latest NXX assignments is important, you should purchase Bellcore's *Service Access Codes (N00) NXX Assignments (500/800/900 List),* mentioned in Appendix C. Your service bureau will also have access to the latest NXX assignments for the IXCs it works with.

The obvious reason that NXX assignments are important is for spelling distinctive or "vanity" words that are recognizable, easy to remember, and related to the program content. People remember words more readily than meaningless numbers, and a good vanity number can be quite valuable, perhaps important enough to be the primary criteria for deciding which IXC to use.

A point to remember when planning your vanity number is that you do not have to limit the word to seven letters. For example, if your word consisted of 10 letters, the last three numbers dialed would not affect the call unless they were dialed after the call was connected, perhaps interfering with your interactive menu, a possibility so remote that it is safe to ignore it. Of course, an astute caller will recognize that she need not dial the last three numbers.

NXX Assignments (1-900-<u>NXX</u>-XXXX)

AT&T

200	342	490	730	896
210	344	500	737	903
220	350	520	738	909
225(1)	370	527	740	920
250	400	555(2)	773	932
260	407	590	786	933
268	410	600	820	976
288	420	650	840	986
300	436	660	850	
328	454	680	860	
339	480	720	884	

MCI

226	336	476	678	787
255	347	484	687	825
263	378	486	725	835
265	388	526	726	868
267	435	562	733(2)	945
285	438	622	745(3)	950
287	443	624	772	988
289	446	656	776	990
329	448	659	779	993

Sprint

230	346	468	642	800
246	386	535	646	847
262	463	568	700	929

Stentor (Canada)

273	565(2)	643	677	792
451	595	645	690	830
561	630	670	750	870

INFO Services, Inc.

234	321	456	741	963
258	369	654	872	999

SCG Carrier Services

382	414

Starlink Communications

286	360

Federal TransTel

444	537	666	674	938

Notes:
(1) Business-to-consumer use
(2) Business-to-business use
(3) For alternate billing with mostly adult programs

Glossary

ALTERNATIVE BILLING. A billing arrangement whereby an independent third party company performs billing and collection services otherwise performed by the telephone company as a part of its premium billing services. Also known as LEC, Telco or private party billing.

AUDIOTEXT (also Audiotex). This term broadly describes various telecommunications equipment and services that enable users to send or receive information by interacting with a voice processing system via a telephone connection, using audio input. Voice mail, interactive 800 or 900 programs, and telephone banking transactions are examples of applications that fall under this generic category.

AUTOMATIC NUMBER IDENTIFICATION (ANI). A means of identifying the telephone number of the party originating the telephone call to you or your program, through the use of analog or digital signals which are transmitted along with the call and equipment that can decipher those signals.

AUTOMATED ATTENDANT. A device, connected to a PBX, which performs simple voice processing functions limited to answering incoming calls and routing them in accordance with the touch-tone menu selections made by the caller.

AUTOMATIC CALL DISTRIBUTOR (ACD). A specialized phone system used for handling a high volume of incoming calls. An ACD will recognize and answer an incoming call, then refer to its programming for instructions on what to do with that call, and then, based on these instructions, it will send the call to a recording giving the caller further instructions or to a voice response unit (VRU). It can also route the call to a live operator as soon as that operator has completed his/her previous call, perhaps after the caller has heard the recorded message.

CENTRAL OFFICE. Telephone company facility where subscribers' lines are joined to switching equipment for connecting other subscribers to each other, locally and long distance. For example, when making a long distance call, your call first goes to your CO, where it connects to the long distance carrier's network (unless it had to get routed to another CO where the IXC's network is available), and then the call gets routed to a CO near the party you are calling, and then it finishes the trip over the local network connecting the CO with the other party.

CENTREX. A business telephone service offered by a local telephone company from a local central office. Centrex is basically single line telephone service with enhanced features added, allowing a small business with one phone line to have some of the features provided by expensive telephone systems. Those features can include intercom, call forwarding, call transfer, toll restrict, least cost routing and call hold (on single line phones), to name a few.

CLIENT OF RECORD. The person or company with the direct contractual relationship with the long distance carrier in providing pay-per-call services, either the information provider or the service bureau.

DIAL-A-PORN. For the purposes of this book, dial-a-porn is defined as containing "indecent" language, defined by the FCC as "the description or depiction of sexual or excretory activities or organs in a patently offensive manner as measured by contemporary standards for the telephone medium."

DIALED NUMBER IDENTIFICATION SERVICE (DNIS). DNIS is available on 800 and 900 lines, and is used to identify the numbers dialed (as opposed to caller's number). This would be important if you were a program sponsor with dozens of different 900 numbers tapping into the same program. DNIS allows you to keep track of which numbers are dialed so you can properly compensate your IPs who are promoting your program, or for keeping track of your advertising response using different 900 numbers with different ads.

DUAL TONE MULTI-FREQUENCY (DTMF). The technical term describing push button or touchtone dialing. When you touch a button on a telephone keypad, it makes a tone, which is actually a combination of two tones, one high frequency and one low frequency. Hence the name Dual Tone Multi-Frequency.

ENHANCED SERVICES. Services provided by the telephone company over its network facilities which may be provided without filing a tariff, usually involving some computer related feature such as formatting data or restructuring the information. Most Regional Bell Operating Companies (RBOCs) are prohibited from offering enhanced services at present.

GROUP ACCESS BRIDGING (GAB). Allows three or more callers to join in on a conference type phone call and to participate in the ongoing conversation. The 900 "party" lines are an example of this application.

INDECENT SERVICES. See DIAL-A-PORN.

INFORMATION PROVIDER (IP). A business or individual who delivers information or entertainment services to end users (callers) with the use of communications equipment and computer facilities. The call handling equipment is often not owned by the IP, and a separate service bureau is hired for this purpose.

INTERACTIVE. An audiotext capability that allows the caller to select options from a menu of programmed choices in order to control the flow of information. As the term implies, the caller truly interacts with the computer, following the program instructions and selecting the information he or she wishes to receive.

INTERACTIVE VOICE RESPONSE (IVR). The telephone keypad substitutes for the computer keyboard, allowing anyone with a touch-tone telephone to interact with a computer. Where a computer has a screen for showing the results, IVR uses a digitized synthesized voice to "read" the screen to the caller.

INTEREXCHANGE CARRIER (IXC). This term technically applies to carriers that provide telephone service between LATAs (see below). Long distance companies such as AT&T, Sprint, and MCI are also known as interexchange carriers.

LOCAL ACCESS TRANSPORT AREA (LATA). This is a geographic service area that generally conforms to standard metropolitan and statistical areas (SMSAs), and some 200 were created with the breakup of AT&T. The local telephone companies provide service within each LATA (Intra-LATA), while a long distance carrier (IXC) must be used for service between LATAs (Inter-LATA).

LOCAL EXCHANGE CARRIER (LEC). This is the local telephone company that provides service within each LATA. Also included in this category are independent LECs such as General Telephone (GTE). The LEC handles all billing and collections within its LATA, often including long distance charges (Inter-LATA), which are collected and forwarded to the appropriate interexchange carriers.

NORTH AMERICAN NUMBERING PLAN. The method of identifying telephone trunks and assigning service access codes (area codes) in the public network of North America, also known as World Numbering Zone 1.

NXX. In a seven digit local phone number, the first three digits identify the specific telephone company central office which serves that number. These digits are referred to as the NXX where N can be any number from 2 to 9 and X can be any number. For 800 and 900 numbers, the NXXs are assigned to telephone companies, primarily IXCs, as they are needed or requested.

ONLINE CALL DETAIL DATA (OCDD). Information summarizing inbound calling data, typically detailing call volumes originating from different telephone area codes or states. Useful for tracking response rates to regional advertising.

PAY-PER-CALL. The caller pays a pre-determined charge for accessing information services. 900 is not the only type of pay-per-call service available. For local, intra-LATA applications, a seven digit number is available with a 976 or 540 prefix. This service is usually quite a bit less expensive than long distance 900 services, and should be seriously considered for any local or regional pay-per-call applications that will not have the potential for expanding nationwide.

Pay-per-call services may also be offered over 800 or regular toll lines using credit card or other third party billing mechanisms. When the caller pays a premium above the regular transport charges for the information content of the program, regardless of how payment is made, it is considered a pay-per-call service.

PORT. For the purpose of this book, the interface between a voice processing system or program and a communications or transmission facility. For all practical purposes, the same thing as a telephone line.

POTS. Plain Old Telephone Service. The basic service supplying standard single line telephones, telephone lines and access to the public switched network. No enhanced services.

PRIVATE BRANCH EXCHANGE (PBX). PBX is a private telephone switching system (as opposed to public), usually located in an organization's premises, with an attendant console. It is connected to a group of lines from one or more central offices to provide services to a number of individual phones, such as in a hotel, business or government office.

PREMIUM BILLING SERVICES. Billing and collection services provided by the telephone companies to IPs or service bureaus, for their information programs. Premium billing usually involves both the LEC and the IXC for national 900 programs, with the LEC serving as the IXC's agent in collecting from the end customer in the monthly phone bill.

REGIONAL BELL OPERATING COMPANY (RBOC). These are the seven holding companies that were created by the breakup of AT&T (also known as Baby Bells):

1. NYNEX
2. Bell Atlantic
3. AMERITECH
4. Bell South
5. Southwestern Bell Corp.
6. U.S. West
7. Pacific Telesis

These companies own many of the various LECs. For example, NYNEX owns both New England Telephone and New York Telephone. However, there are numerous independent LECs that are not owned by any RBOC. For example, Southern New England Telecommunications Corp. (SNET) is an independent LEC serving most of Connecticut's residential customers, and has nothing to do with NYNEX.

SERVICE BUREAU. A company that provides voice processing / call handling / audiotext equipment and services and connection to telephone network facilities. For a fee, these companies allow an information provider (IP) to offer a pay-per-call program using the service bureau's equipment and facilities.

T-1 Also spelled T1. A digital transmission link with a capacity of 1.544 Mbps (1,544,000 bits per second). T-1 normally can handle 24 simultaneous voice conversations over two pairs of wires, like the ones serving your house, each one digitized at 64 Kbps. This is accomplished by using special encoding and decoding equipment at each end of the transmission path. T-1 is a standard for digital transmission in North America.

TARIFF. Documents filed by a regulated telephone company with a state public utility commission or the Federal Communications Commission. The tariff, a public document, describes and details services, equipment and pricing offered by the telephone company (a common carrier) to all potential customers. As a "common carrier," the telephone company must offer its services to the general public at the prices and conditions outlined in its tariffs.

TRUNK. A communication line between two switching systems. The term switching systems typically includes equipment in a central office (the telephone company) and PBXs. A tie trunk connects PBXs, while central office trunks connect a PBX to the switching system at the central office.

VARI-A-BILL. A 900 service of AT&T whereby the call price varies depending on the caller's selection of menu choices. This allows the IP to charge more fairly for information of varying value, such as live technical advice versus recorded instructions.

VOICE MAIL SYSTEM. A device that records, stores and retrieves voice messages. You can program the system (voice mail boxes) to forward messages, leave messages for inbound callers, add comments and deliver messages to you, etc. It is essentially a sophisticated answering machine for a large business with multiple phone lines (probably with a PBX), featuring a lot of bells and whistles.

VOICE PROCESSING. This is the general term encompassing the use of the telephone to communicate with a computer by way of the touch-tone keypad and synthesized voice response. Audiotex, speech recognition and IVR are subclassifications under voice processing.

VOICE RESPONSE UNIT (VRU). This is the building block of any voice processing system, essentially a voice computer. Instead of a computer keyboard for entering information (commands), a VRU uses remote touchtone telephones. Instead of a screen for showing the results, a VRU uses synthesized voice to "read" the information to the caller.

Index

M

N

O

Other Books of Interest
From Aegis Publishing Group:

Live personal consulting
with Robert Mastin:

If you want....

- ❒ an honest appraisal of your 900 program idea
- ❒ the latest intelligewnce on what's happening in the 900 arena
- ❒ to discuss the emerging opportunities
- ❒ some outstanding marketing advice

Call between 9 a.m. and 5 p.m. eastern time:

1-900-446-6075, extension 888

The charge is $2.95 per minute (the first 24 seconds free, in
case Bob is not available and you have to leave a message).
*Make sure you mention that you are calling on the 900
number.*

Get maximum value for your money by reading the
book first, and then prepare a list of questions and topics
before calling.